God

THEOLOGY
for
EVERY
PERSON

God

MALCOLM B. YARNELL III

B&H
PUBLISHING
BRENTWOOD, TENNESSEE

Published by B&H Publishing Group
Brentwood, Tennessee

Dewey Decimal Classification: 231
Subject Heading: GOD / DOCTRINAL THEOLOGY

Cover design by Brian Bobel. Author photo by his family.

1 2 3 4 5 6 • 27 26 25 24

This first volume is dedicated to the people of the churches of Jesus Christ who recognized my calling to teach the inspired Word of the triune God:

Lakeside Baptist Church of Granbury, Texas
Birchman Baptist Church of Fort Worth, Texas
Tabbs Creek Baptist Church of Oxford, North Carolina
Lakeview Baptist Church of Shreveport, Louisiana
Western Hills Baptist Church of Fort Worth, Texas
Barksdale Baptist Church of Bossier City, Louisiana
Summer Grove Baptist Church of Shreveport, Louisiana

Contents

◆

Preface ix

Chapter One: Welcome to the Grand Tour 1

Chapter Two: Why Study God? 15

Chapter Three: Does God Exist? 31

Chapter Four: When or Where Is God? 49

Chapter Five: Is God Trinity? 71

Chapter Six: What Is God Like? (Part 1) 95

Chapter Seven: What Is God Like? (Part 2) 109

Chapter Eight: How Do People Know about God? 127

Chapter Nine: What about Natural Theology? 145

Chapter Ten: How Can We Know God as Savior? 167

Chapter Eleven: Does Scripture Continue
      Special Revelation? 185

Chapter Twelve: What Is Scripture? 201

Chapter Thirteen: How Does the Church Serve
      the Word in the World? 223

Acknowledgments 249

Scripture Index 255

Preface

◆

IF YOU CAN READ OR hear these words, you are a theologian!
As a theologian, you are responsible both for your beliefs and
for your actions. (All responsible human actions come from
human beliefs.) The first theologian to argue that the Bible
should be in every person's language also argued theology is
not merely for professional scholars. I agree with Erasmus of
Rotterdam: Scripture is for everyone, so theology is for everyone. As for Scripture, he said, "Christ wishes his mysteries
published as open as possible." And as for our theology, which
derives from God's Word, "Let all the conversations of every
Christian be drawn from this source."[1]

Erasmus's argument was so powerful that it drove a young
Oxford scholar named William Tyndale to dedicate his life to
making the Bible accessible to every English-speaking person, male or female, rich or poor, laity or clergy. Tyndale literally surrendered his life so that we could have the Bible in
our language. William was strangled and burned at the stake
on October 6, 1536, for disobeying the church hierarchy and

---

1. These quotes derive from the *Paraclesis*, Erasmus of Rotterdam's preface to his groundbreaking Greek New Testament of 1516. John C. Olin, ed.,
Christian Humanism and the Reformation: Selected Writings of Erasmus, 3rd
ed. (New York: Fordham University Press, 1987), 101.

making the Bible accessible in English.[2] The English translations we have today are all based on Tyndale's work for the
most part. For instance, more than 95 percent of the King
James New Testament derives from his translation. My own
life has been devoted to continuing the theological work the
great English Reformer began.[3]

This three-volume series, Theology for Every Person, is
intended to help equip every Christian with their God-given
call to serve God as a theologian. In other words, it is for you as
a follower of Christ Jesus, whatever the other roles you fulfill
in life. I love the Christian academy, which has been built by
well-meaning and brilliant human beings, but the church was
established by the Lord Jesus Christ. Jesus called me to serve
him and serve his churches, in part through the academy, but
the priority always belongs to the churches. And his churches
are filled with the front-line theologians. Some may call these
Christians "lay theologians," but that terminology introduces
an extra-biblical and potentially damaging concept.

Division between laity and clergy is not taught in the
New Testament. All Christians are simultaneously "a people"
(Greek *laos*) (1 Pet. 2:9) and "those allotted" (Greek *cleros*)
(1 Pet. 5:3 NASB1995). The church is certainly served by bishops, elders, and pastors (1 Tim. 3:1–7; Titus 1:6–9), but its
ontological identity is one people united with God through
one Mediator (1 Tim. 2:5). This universal church, to which all
Christians belong, is called to serve God's Word to the world

---

2. David Daniell, *William Tyndale: A Biography* (New Haven, CT: Yale
University Press, 1994), 382.

3. On October 6, 1997—461 years to the day after his martyrdom—I
wrote the following words upon finishing the biography of William Tyndale
in the same city where he was once a student: "Lord, I may not have the
translation skills of W. T., but please let my life and death count for as much
in bringing people to you as did, does, & will W. T.'s life & death. In Jesus'
Name. Amen." Prayer recorded on page 384 in Yarnell Library copy of
Daniell's magisterial biography.

in the power of his Spirit for his glory. In other words, since every Christian is a theologian, and every Christian belongs to the church, the best term to describe a member of our audience is "church theologian." You, my friend, are the theologian for whom this book is written. Welcome to the journey to knowing God.

In Christ,
Malcolm B. Yarnell III
May 31, 2023
Benbrook, Texas

CHAPTER ONE

Welcome to the Grand Tour

◆

CHRISTIAN THEOLOGY TAKES YOU ON the grand tour of
ultimate truth. It is commonly said that "theology," which
is derived from the Greek terms for God (*Theos*) and Word
(*Logos*), simply means, "talk about God." Dogmatic theologians like Karl Barth define the task of "theology" more
abstractly as, "the criticism and correction of talk about God
according to the criterion of the Church's own principle."[1]

While respecting the precise efforts of such great minds
and freely drawing on their profound work, your tour guide
will nevertheless limit the academic as much as possible. He
will also reject the wearisome dogmatic attitude, even as he
affirms dogmatic truth. This author, his church, his seminary,
and his publisher hope to bring more of the people of God
into the universal church's ongoing theological conversation.
After all, as Erasmus pointed out, every Christian should read

---

1. Karl Barth, *Church Dogmatics*, Vol. I, Part 1, *The Doctrine of the Word
of God*, 2nd ed., ed. G. W. Bromiley and T. F. Torrance (Edinburgh: T&T
Clark, 1975), 6.

Scripture and share it with others. Thus, every Christian is a theologian.[2]

We use the metaphor of a tour because Christians intuitively understand they are starting a journey when they "take up" their cross "and follow" Jesus (Mark 8:34). And where does he lead his followers on this expedition? Ultimately, he promises the glorious vision of God on his heavenly throne (Matt. 5:8; Heb. 12:1–2; Rev. 21–22). So, with the theme of theology as a grand tour of ultimate truth culminating in the celestial vision, you are hereby invited to take part in following Christ into knowing God.

Our adventure together will bring joy amid light-hearted moments and enlightening discussions. However, the journey must be taken with utmost seriousness. Sometimes, the road will prove daunting as it surveys ultimate questions like the origin of life, the purpose of life, the problems of life, and the end of life. This series intends to help you follow the Lord with integrity, explaining God and his ways by interpreting his Word under the guidance of the Holy Spirit. My prayer is that, as you yourself grow closer to the Lord, you will invite others to adventure with us to glory.

Before You Can Start

Personal Transformation

As we begin this journey together, please note above all that crossing the starting line of theology requires a transforming faith. A young student, already recognized as a minister in his denomination, discovered in the middle of a semester of systematic theology that he had long been trying

---

2. Erasmus, "Paraclesis," in *Christian Humanism and the Reformation: Selected Writings of Erasmus*, 3rd ed., ed. John C. Olin (New York: Fordham University Press), 101–2.

to do theology without being born again. He was attempting to learn about God propositionally without truly knowing God personally. As he listened to these lectures, the Word of God worked upon his heart. One day, under the Spirit's conviction, he confessed the truth of God in Christ. Awestruck, a hundred students and I witnessed this young minister weep with joy as he confessed his new birth in Christ and truly began the journey of faith with us.[3]

The prerequisite of a personal transforming faith has been stressed by famous theologians throughout the history of the universal church. The greatest defender of Trinitarian orthodoxy, Athanasius of Alexandria, agreed. At the end of his most famous book, *On the Incarnation*, he emphasized our personal need for salvation and sanctification: "But for the searching and right understanding of the Scripture there is need of a good life and a pure soul, and for Christian virtue to guide the mind to grasp, so far as human nature can, the truth concerning God the Word."[4]

Another church father, Gregory of Nazianzus, began his famous five theological orations with the startling claim, "Theology is not for everyone." Gregory went on to clarify, "It is not for all people, but only for those who have been tested and have found a sound footing in study, and, more importantly, have undergone, or at the very least are undergoing, purification of body and soul."[5] The key qualification, accord-

---

3. Alex Sibley, "Student Born Again during Systematic Theology Lecture," *Southwestern News* (May 11, 2021; https://swbts.edu/news/from-the-profs-student-born-again-during-systematic-theology-lecture/).

4. St. Athanasius, *On the Incarnation: The Treatise De Incarnatione Verbi Dei*, intro. by C. S. Lewis (Crestwood, NY: St. Vladimir's Seminary Press, 1996), 96.

5. St. Gregory of Nazianzus, *On God and Christ: The Five Theological Orations and Two Letters to Cledonius*, transl. Frederick Williams and Lionel Wickham (Crestwood, NY: St. Vladimir's Seminary Press, 2002), 26–27.

ing to this leading Greek-speaking theologian, is dedication to the task of knowing God truly with all that you are.

Martin Luther learned the hard way that, yes, even an accomplished professor of theology can miss the point and remain lost in his sin. Luther was converted through learning to read Romans 1:17 properly.[6] He was given the grace of the Holy Spirit to understand Scripture only after he began teaching others how to interpret Scripture. He had sadly reached the point of hating the doctrine of divine righteousness.

But God led Friar Martin to see things differently. Struck in his heart, the great Reformer let go of his herculean but futile personal efforts to justify himself before God. Instead, he was justified by faith alone in Christ alone apart from personal works. "This immediately made me feel as though I had been born again, and as though I had entered through the open gates into paradise itself. From that moment, the whole face of Scripture appeared to me in a different light."[7]

Please Be Certain

In the light of the experiences of more than one theology student, indeed of one of the greatest theologians in history, may I challenge you as a fellow theologian to be certain about your own relationship with God? Your conscience bears witness of the bad news that you are a sinner deserving of death. But the good news is God does not want you to stay in that state. To save us from our sins, the eternal Son of God became a human being, Jesus Christ. He died on a cross. Then

---

6. "For I am not ashamed of the gospel, because it is the power of God for salvation to everyone who believes, first to the Jew, and also to the Greek. For in it the righteousness of God is revealed from faith to faith, just as it is written: *The righteous will live by faith*" (Rom. 1:16–17).

7. Alister E. McGrath, *Luther's Theology of the Cross: Martin Luther's Theological Breakthrough* (New York: Blackwell, 1985), 97.

he arose from the dead so that all who believe in him will be saved! If you do not believe in Christ and in the good news of his atoning death and justifying resurrection (Rom. 4:25), you cannot be declared righteous before the eternal court.

We will all one day have to stand before the throne of God and give an account for our evil deeds. I beg you to prepare even now for that day. Will you take a moment and pray? Will you confess your sinfulness and receive the righteousness of God through faith in Jesus (Rom. 10:9–10)? Will you even now receive the gift of a new life by Christ's gift of his Holy Spirit (John 3:8)? If you wish to be saved, in this very moment please pray to God. Repent of your sin and believe in Christ! (And please consult with a church about following Christ together.)

After you have made sure your salvation, you will find that in doing theology sometimes your previous ideas about God and his ways of working are confirmed. But at other times doing theology will challenge you to change and thereby grow. While we must concede there will be moments of effort, even pain, I promise you that seeking to know God will provide you with the strength and the joy you need for a fulfilling life journey. As John Bunyan, author of *Pilgrims Progress*, discovered,[8] reaching the final goal of this expedition in theology requires your readiness to receive truth through the gift of God's revelation of himself.

What will it be like on that day when God brings all things to their ultimate end? On that day the pure in heart will see God directly, and that sight will make sense of everything (Matt. 5:8). Every question will be answered in such a way that even our questions will be reframed by his gentle correction. God is always good, so the Lord also grants his people joyous glimpses of himself even now. Meaningful experiences in his

---

8. For a modern translation of this classic literary and theological text, see John Bunyan, *Pilgrim's Progress* (Abbotsford, WI: Aneko Press, 2014).

Word and by his Spirit equip us and sustain us as we fulfill his
command to witness of him in the world today. However, take
note that the Holy Spirit often works at unexpected times and
in various ways upon the disciples of Jesus. So please be careful
not to try to "put God in a box" (John 3:8).

Necessary Clarifications

We should consider a few points of clarification before
setting off on the journey of theology together. Four instructive clarifications will help you learn to engage in theology in
the right way. The first has to do with the origin of theology,
while the second and third have to do with the nature of reason and the grace of revelation. The final clarification has to
do with the heart attitude that is required of the Christ follower engaging in theology.

"Faith Seeking Understanding"

First, as is already evident, this is an exercise in Christian
theology. Although this book certainly may help those of
you who are examining the faith from the outside and need
an apologetic for the Christian faith, this work is primarily intended for those who already know God in Christ.
Orthodox Christians recognize that theology, or talk about
God, is "faith seeking understanding." The necessary presupposition of Christian theology is that the divine gift of faith
(Phil. 1:29) precedes the human response of reasoning about
that faith.

A fantastic theologian and prayer warrior, Anselm of
Canterbury, recognized that God created human beings in his
image so that we can relate to him with our minds as well as
our hearts. However, knowing God intellectually never means
grasping or comprehending God. "I do not try, Lord, to attain

your lofty heights, because my understanding is in no way equal to it. But I do desire to understand your truth a little, that truth that my heart believes and loves. For I do not seek to understand so that I may believe; but I believe so that I may understand."[9] For Anselm, theological reason proceeds from the faithful mind engaged in humble prayer to a great God. The priority of faith over reason carries with it three implications that follow directly from this first truth.

A Reasonable Faith

Second, the priority of faith does not mean faith remains in isolation. Faith still requires reason, but reason is properly grounded in God. Christian faith is reasonable because it derives from the One the apostle John named *Logos*. The divine Logos is pure and perfect reason. The Logos is the Eternal Son of God (John 1:1), who become human in Jesus Christ (John 1:14). Drawing on the apostle John, the great American evangelical theologian Carl Henry came to a large conclusion, "The Logos of God is the coordinating reality that holds together thought, life and experience."[10]

Reflecting upon Scripture, the earliest church fathers, and classical Greek philosophy, the Roman Catholic Pope Benedict XVI came to the same conclusion.[11] Faith is necessarily reasonable because Christian faith is in the One who is the ground of all human reason. Faith is reasonable, yet faith is not based on fallible human rationality but derives from

---

9. Anselm of Canterbury, *The Major Works*, ed. Brian Davies (New York: Oxford University Press, 1998), 87.

10. Carl F. H. Henry, *God, Revelation and Authority*, vol. 1, *God Who Speaks and Shows: Preliminary Considerations* (1976; reprint, Wheaton: Crossway, 1999), 95.

11. Joseph Cardinal Ratzinger, *The Nature and Mission of Theology: Essays to Orient Theology in Today's Debates*, transl. Adrian Walker (San Francisco: Ignatius Press, 1995), 13–29.

perfect rationality. The general illumination of reason is a divine grace for all humanity (John 1:9). In other words, faith is above reason, yet faith includes reason. Faith is never irrational; instead, it is perfectly rational.

A Trinitarian Grace

Our third point of clarification is this: Even as Scripture centers reason in the Son, who is the second person of the divine Trinity, so it centers grace in the Holy Spirit, who is the third person of the Trinity. The Holy Spirit is the One who executes the will of God among the creatures of God. The apostle James said that "every good and perfect gift is from above, coming down from the Father of lights" (James 1:17). But how does God the Father give his perfect gifts? Scripture demonstrates repeatedly that the Father works through his Son and his Spirit.

Augustine of Hippo described the biblical pattern of the inseparable operations of the Trinity in this way: "The Trinity which is equal in every respect likewise also works inseparably."[12] For instance, the apostle Paul brought the three persons together when considering the divine grace of personal salvation: "God sent the Spirit of his Son into our hearts, crying, '*Abba*, Father!'" (Gal. 4:6).

The Holy Spirit is the one who takes the truth about God in Christ and presents it clearly to our minds and hearts. He graciously convicts the world of its sin, of its impending judgment, and of the righteousness available through faith in Jesus Christ (John 16:7–11). The Holy Spirit may, therefore, be called the administrator of the divine will that has been expressed through the divine Word.

---

12. Saint Augustine, *The Trinity*, transl. Edmund Hill, ed. John E. Rotelle (Brooklyn: New City Press, 1991), 397.

As Basil of Caesarea said, "There is not one single gift which reaches creation without the Holy Spirit."[13] Our third point of clarification therefore ends on two notes: First, every divine act is Trinitarian, deriving from the Father through the Son in the Holy Spirit. Second, all knowledge of God, general or redemptive, comes by grace alone.

A Humble Follower of Christ

Our fourth and final point of clarification derives from the first three clarifications. First, we noted that God the Father's gift of faith precedes our understanding of that faith. Second, we noted that our ability to reason about anything, including the Christian faith, is a gift of God through the second person of the Trinity. Third, we noted that God works his grace through his Holy Spirit. (By the way, the Spirit works both through common grace to all people and redeeming grace to believers.) These three truths about faith and our understanding of that faith bring us to a fourth truth: The theologian must be a humble follower of Jesus.

Orthodox theology necessarily entails radical humility. Theological truth, which is centered on and controlled by the gospel of Jesus Christ, is something we can never initiate or handle in our own power. Paul therefore warns us against treating the gospel without proper respect, "*Do not say in your heart, 'Who will go up to heaven?'* that is, to bring Christ down or *'Who will go down into the abyss?'* that is, to bring Christ up from the dead" (Rom. 10:6b–7). Luther understood this too well. He had been taught a "theology of glory," but his conversion brought him to embrace a "theology of the cross." A theologian of glory thinks he has attained truth and lives

---

13. Basil, *On the Holy Spirit,* in *The Nicene and Post-Nicene Fathers,* ed. Philip Schaff and Henry Wace, vol. 8 (1895; reprint, Peabody, MA: Hendrickson, 1994), 35.

accordingly. He is proud of himself and develops sinful habits of thought and action. But a theologian of the cross humbly recognizes, "God can be found only in suffering and the cross."[14]

Dietrich Bonhoeffer, the famous German theologian martyred by Adolf Hitler, wrote similarly about the chasm between an inadequate "cheap grace" and the necessity of "costly grace." "Cheap grace is grace without discipleship, grace without the cross, grace without the living, incarnate Jesus Christ."[15] Great damage has been done to the testimony of the Christian faith by those who know only cheap grace. The direct opposite of cheap grace is costly grace. "It is costly because it calls to discipleship; it is grace because it calls us to follow *Jesus Christ*."[16] Christian theology must be done by humble disciples of the One who was crucified before he was glorified. We must humble ourselves before God to know God rightly.

Too many theologians operate with a Pelagian attitude of human self-confidence even while repeating an Augustinian doctrine of divine grace. (Pelagius argued a person can appropriate his own salvation, but Augustine stressed salvation is entirely a gift.[17]) Other theologians proclaim the love of God,

---

14. Martin Luther, *Heidelberg Disputation*, in *Luther's Works*, vol. 31, *Career of the Reformer I*, ed. Harold J. Grimm (Philadelphia: Muhlenberg Press, 1957), 53.

15. Dietrich Bonhoeffer, *Discipleship*, vol. 4, *Dietrich Bonhoeffer Works*, transl. Barbara Green and Reinhard Krauss, ed. Geffrey B. Kelly and John D. Godsey (Minneapolis: Fortress Press, 1996), 44.

16. Bonhoeffer, *Discipleship*, 45.

17. Pelagius taught that sin does not substantially alter the goodness of human nature, so salvation is entirely within the capability of individual free choice. Augustine believed all human nature was corrupted by Adam's Fall, so saving grace must transform the human being. We will rehearse their debate in more detail in volume two of this series. Cf. Otto W. Heick, *A History of Christian Thought*, vol. 1 (Philadelphia: Fortress Press, 1965), 196–206.

yet they use the gospel not to become justified from sin but to justify their personal continuance in it. Church history is filled with examples of the theological and moral wrecks caused by those who "went out from us, but they did not really belong to us" (1 John 2:19a NIV).[18]

The quickest way to join the ranks of "these people [who] create divisions and are worldly, not having the Spirit" (Jude 19), is to reject the humility of Christ. It is no accident that the greatest hymn to the gospel is contained in a Spirit-inspired call to humility. In that hymn, the apostle Paul commanded believers to "adopt the same attitude as that of Christ Jesus." As the eternal Son of God, he equally possesses the perfections of God. However, he humbled himself by "assuming the form of a servant." He even died on the cross for our sins. The incarnation and death of Jesus Christ are the perfect picture of the type of humility required of all Christ's followers (Phil. 2:1–11). I beg of you, my fellow disciple, let us be truly humble theologians like our Lord and Savior. If we engage in theology as an act of prayer, seeking for his guidance in humility, God will help us.

This Series of Books

Theology for Every Person

This series of books is intended for the typical disciple of Jesus Christ. Advanced readers, such as established ministers and academic theologians, will find them helpful for their own development. However, what you are reading is primarily written for those who are ministers-in-training and for those described as laypeople in some denominations. It is true that the author is an intellectual by vocation, but he is also

---

18. John Dickson, *Bullies and Saints: An Honest Look at the Good and Evil of Christian History* (Grand Rapids: Zondervan, 2021).

passionately committed to the priority of edifying the human spirit.

My calling has always been to build up the whole body of Christ, not just the clergy, although I very much love serving Christ and his church by serving their leaders. The New Testament gives no special category among the people of God for clergy, although most churches find it beneficial to develop a special leadership. Every Christian is granted the Word of God, is granted the Holy Spirit who illumines the Word, and is responsible for helping share the good news with others. This series will help you, whoever you are, to follow Jesus as Lord.

First of Three

While this first volume may be read on its own, it is also the first part of an integrated three-volume project that will introduce a summary of the whole of Christian theology to the Christian reader. This volume, simply entitled *God*, considers who God is, the way he shows himself, and the ways many Christians organize their thoughts about him. The second volume, *God's Word to the World*, will consider God in Christ and his works of creation, humanity, and the redemption of humanity. The third planned volume will be titled *God's Work in the World* and will consider God the Holy Spirit and the divine works of salvation, the church, and the end.

Your Bible

It will become apparent that these volumes constantly refer you to the Bible. You will want to keep a copy of God's Holy Word near you as you read these theological explanations, so that you may continually consult the inspired text "to see if these things [are] so" (Acts 17:11b). It will also become apparent that these volumes advocate the classical

Christian tradition expressed in the major creeds of worldwide Christianity. In the technical sense, therefore, they constitute an exercise in dogmatics.

An Open Approach

However, the books are not concerned with arguing and condemning, so they are not dogmatic in the modern negative sense. The odd exception to the peaceful style of these volumes may sometimes appear where the heart of the Christian faith is critically at stake, but the tone will even then seek to remain gentle.

The author is a committed free church theologian, an evangelical Baptist in particular, but the reader will find a constant appeal to the helpful contributions of other Christian traditions. As members of the universal church, we must humbly listen to other Christians throughout the ages, across the world, and from various traditions. There is so much good in the great truth of Christianity that it will soon become apparent it is detrimental to divide the spiritual communion of saints. The church is united in Christ by the Truth who attaches every believer to himself with bands of gentle love through the gift of the Spirit.

A Great Hope

My hope is that, as you and I humble ourselves before the limitless God, the Holy Spirit will lead us deeper into the truth of Jesus Christ. May we see God the Trinity ever more clearly as we embrace the faith of God ever more dearly, a faith which is conveyed by his Holy Word and interpreted by his Holy Spirit. With your personal faith hopefully settled and a few important points of clarification made, let us now begin the grand tour of ultimate truth. Of course, we must begin with God.

Study Questions

1. Describe when you were born again by faith in Jesus Christ.

2. Name three things you hope to learn in this grand tour of the Christian faith.

3. Which one of the four points of clarification in doing theology did you find most helpful? Why?

Suggested Resources

- John Bunyan, *The Pilgrim's Progress*

- Dietrich Bonhoeffer, *Discipleship* [also translated as *The Cost of Discipleship*]

- Roland H. Bainton, *Here I Stand: A Life of Martin Luther*

CHAPTER TWO

Why Study God?

◆

WHEN PEOPLE START DOING THEOLOGY, a question that often arises is, "Why should I study God?" My immediate answer typically points out how God's love is so perfect that we are just drawn to his truth. But to answer this question more completely, let's break it into two: First, why should I discover who God is? Second, why should I be concerned with what God does? The importance of understanding God and his actions will become clear as we survey who he is and what he is doing. But let's begin with the second question since the shape of God's activity provides the avenue for understanding the being of God. We know who God is through what God does.[1] God's actions will also provide the outline for the narrative of our grand tour.

---

1. Technically, the reality of God (or "divine ontology") precedes his activity (or "divine economy"). His eternal being determines his interactions with his creatures in time. However, we come to know his eternal ontology only through the divine economy he reveals in time.

Consider What God Does

We want theology, because knowing what God is doing brings us wondrous truth for our minds and blessed peace for our hearts. Three major acts in the divine economy show us the benefits of knowing him: First, let's study God so we can better understand our Creator. Second, let's study God because he loves us enough to reconcile us despite our failures. Third, let's study God because he will one day show himself to us in his glorious beauty, and that is worth more than everything else.

Knowing Our Creator

The first major theologian of the Western tradition, Augustine of Hippo, believed theology comes instinctively to human beings. Our natural inclination to know God arises from a fundamental need planted in the human heart at creation. Augustine discovered our overwhelming desire. He described this desire in a prayer at the beginning of his moving spiritual autobiography, *Confessions*. The thought of God stirs a person, he said, "so deeply that he cannot be content unless he praises you." Why do we have this deep desire? "Because you made us for yourself and our hearts find no peace until they rest in you."[2]

Augustine believed that God created us so that we might have an ongoing relationship with him. Our desperate need for the joy of that relationship inevitably draws every one of us to consider who God is and what he is doing. Humanity's ultimate purpose is to know God, to love God, to glorify God. We are created to relate to God through praising him. The goal of creation is worshipful communion with God. Human beings did not just spontaneously come into existence on our

---

2. Saint Augustine, *Confessions*, transl. R. S. Pine-Coffin (London: Penguin, 1961), 21.

own. We were created by an all-powerful God according to his design and for his purpose.

Experiencing God's Love

While Augustine answers our question with reference to creation, Moses and Jesus Christ answer by pointing to the greatest commandment of God. Moses delivered it to Israel as a summary of God's entire will for the people. After rehearsing the gift of the covenant and the Ten Commandments, Moses revealed "the command" above all commands (Deut. 6:1). This command was known among the Israelites by its first word, *Shema* [pronounced shuh-mah], which means, "Listen!" Recognizing its central claim on their hearts, the Israelites incorporated the *Shema* into their daily prayers:

> "Listen, Israel: The LORD our God, the LORD is one. Love the LORD your God with all your heart, with all your soul, and with all your strength." (Deut. 6:4–5)

This high and summative command, known by many as the Great Commandment, has both depth and simplicity. On the one hand, there is simplicity: The Lord is one, so his people must be devoted to him alone. On the other hand, there is depth: The devotion Israel should have for God is described as "love." This love must be conducted with one's whole heart, with one's whole soul, and with one's whole strength.

The simplicity and depth in the Great Commandment are also conveyed in the very term used for *love*. There were two major terms for love in the Hebrew Bible. The first, *Ahabah* [pronounced ah-ha-vah], describes the love that God initiates. *Ahabah* is God's electing love. The second Hebrew term, *Chesed* [pronounced khe-sed], concerns the continuing and faithful love of God. *Chesed* is God's covenantal love.

Because God is one, or simple, he does not have two radically different loves. Rather, his love is so great that it has multiple dimensions from our limited perspective. When you survey the biblical descriptions of God as merciful, gracious, and so on, it becomes clear how magnificent the love of God is.

In an interesting twist, the *Shema* commanded Israel to love God with *Ahabah*, electing love. This should cause you to pause and ask, If God is the One who initiates love, how can we as human beings love God with *Ahabah*? Because we are mere creatures and remain entirely dependent upon God for everything, we are never able to initiate something toward God. Instead, our love for God will always remain a responding love. As the apostle John wrote, "We love because he first loved us" (1 John 4:19). God grants us the ability to love, but this ability does not depend on our own power. Our hearts must receive the initiating love of God and reflect it back to him.

With the origin of love grounded in God, we must now consider a related question: What should characterize our human responsive love for God? The *Shema* says we must love God with every aspect of our lives and with the entirety of every aspect of ourselves. Moses wrote that each of us must love God in three ways, with the heart, with the soul, and with the strength. Moses also said loving God requires one's entire heart, one's entire soul, and one's entire strength. In other words, we must love God totally.

Jesus, the Messiah who fulfilled the prophecies of Moses, reminded his listeners about Moses's command to love God. He agreed that loving God is, among all the commandments of God, "the most important" (Mark 12:29). However, Jesus added a requirement that incorporated the mental focus of the Greek world in which Israel now lived.[3] Not only must you

---

3. Theology always brings human cultures into the theological conversation, because we must reach the inhabitants of those cultures with the eternal gospel.

love the Lord our God with all your heart, soul, and strength. Jesus also commands you to love God "with all your mind" too (Mark 12:30). Jesus clarified for us the prophecy given to Moses.

Jesus Christ commanded everyone to love God with everything we are and with everything we can do. We must love God with the affections of our imaginations; he must be the desire of our "heart." We must love God with the directing choices of our wills; he must be the delight of our "soul." We must love God with every aspect of our existence; he must be the origin and end of our "strength." Such all-engrossing love necessarily also includes loving God with your intellectual ability to abstract truth, with the gift of your "mind." You have a mind because you were also made in the image of the *Logos* (Mark 12:30).[4]

Loving God with your mind can never happen apart from loving God with every other aspect of your humanity. Jesus also made this clear. Of the major terms for the mind, Jesus uses one that indicates the movement not merely of the abstract intellect but of the whole human character. The Greek word, *dianoia*, considered the entire process of human contemplation of God. In other words, every aspect of your being must be focused on knowing, loving, and glorifying God. This includes exercising your intellect as well as your will and your emotions.[5]

---

4. On the human mind as made in the image of God, see the discussion about *Logos* in chapter 1 above.

5. Malcolm B. Yarnell III, "Systematic Theology," in *Theology, Church, and Ministry: A Handbook for Theological Education*, ed. David S. Dockery (Nashville: B&H, 2017), 258–59.

Seeing God's Glory

So, we do theology because, first, God originally created us and, second, because God lovingly commanded us to love him with all our mind. Third, moreover, we must engage in theology because our final goal includes the awesome privilege of experiencing God in his glory. In short, we should do theology by reason of his creating, his commanding, and his glory.

Augustine alluded to the third reason in his statement, "our hearts find no peace until they rest in you." An avid Bible reader, commentator, and preacher, the bishop of Hippo (a city in northern Africa), borrowed this idea of resting in God from the biblical canon. The fourth chapter of the letter to the Hebrews repeatedly commands the reader to "enter the rest" offered by God.

Herschel Hobbs, a leading Southern Baptist pastor theologian of the mid-twentieth century, noted the idea of "rest" in Hebrews looks back to God's sabbath rest at the conclusion of creation (Gen. 2:2; Heb. 4:4). To "enter the rest" also refers to Israel inhabiting the land that God promised to them. But most importantly, it refers to experiencing the final rest of God's glory. "This eschatological thought is an ultimate meaning."[6]

The New Testament scholar A. T. Robertson says our final rest will involve "not cessation of work, but rather of the weariness and pain in toil." More importantly, we will have entire

---

6. Herschel H. Hobbs, *How to Follow Jesus: The Challenge of Hebrews for Christian Life and Witness Today* (Nashville: Broadman, 1971), 45. A unique noun in Hebrews 4:9, *Sabbatismos*, indicates a forthcoming "Sabbath-rest," "the spiritual rest to be realized fully in the life to come." Moisés Silva, ed. *New International Dictionary of New Testament Theology and Exegesis*, vol. 4 (Grand Rapids: Zondervan, 2014), 223.

"harmony" with God.[7] To a great extent, the final rest can be experienced even now, as our rebellious wills are brought by spiritual conversion into harmony with God's will.[8]

We must study theology because God created us for it, because God loves us and commands us to love him in response, and because our hearts will find perfect rest only in him.

The Biblical Narrative

Biblical theologians have long recognized the narrative of Scripture is key to understanding what God is doing in the world. This narrative is focused on the Lord Jesus and proceeds from creation through reconciliation to the consummation. A negative example may help us to see the importance of clearly identifying this narrative of Scripture.

Beware of False Narratives

Irenaeus of Lyons, a great defender of biblical orthodoxy, identified the great problem with heresy. Heresy does not stick to the overarching thesis (*Hypothesis*) of Scripture. Heretics take the facts of Scripture and rearrange the details to create a false narrative. Heresy is like the destructive artist who disassembled the mosaic portrait of a king. This evil artisan then rearranged the stones to represent a dog or fox. Encouraging us only to pursue truthful interpretation of Scripture, Irenaeus by this metaphor reminds us that the biblical narrative centers

---

7. Archibald Thomas Robertson, *Word Pictures in the New Testament*, vol. 5 (Nashville: Broadman, 1932), 362.

8. Hobbs, *How to Follow Jesus*, 45–46.

on the king, Jesus Christ.[9] We should not impose a different narrative.

One of the greatest classical philosophers, Aristotle, investigated the arts and concluded a narrative is "a kind of imitation."[10] Similarly, correctly identifying theology's narrative requires us to examine the Word and imitate the narrative God has already disclosed. Irenaeus argued we must be careful to stick to the theme of Scripture, because heretics seek to deconstruct the truths of Scripture. They fashion a false narrative which uses the facts of Scripture but in a wrong way. The rearrangement of biblical truth is an ongoing problem in the church.

The Unity of the Narrative

Another problem is that some recently began denying the unity of biblical truth. Sadly, the indispensable idea that there exists a common biblical narrative has come under attack. Skeptical scholars trained in Enlightenment methods have imposed a series of competing narratives on Scripture. They view the Bible as merely a human compilation of documents written by fallible men who filled it with their human errors. Against this ultra-liberal division and destruction of Scripture, we note Scripture says it has been inspired by the Spirit of God (2 Tim. 3:16; 2 Pet. 1:20–21).

Relying on the inspiration of Scripture by God, orthodox Christians rightly say, "The Bible contains sixty-six books written by more than forty authors, but is ultimately one book

---

9. John J. O'Keefe and R. R. Reno, *Sanctified Vision: An Introduction to Early Christian Interpretation of the Bible* (Baltimore: Johns Hopkins University Press, 2005), 33–44.

10. Aristotle, *How to Tell a Story: An Ancient Guide to the Art of Storytelling for Writers and Readers*, transl. Philip Freeman (Princeton, NJ: Princeton University Press, 2022), 3.

written by one author, God the Holy Spirit."[11] The Spirit's gift of unity in the Bible means it conveys a singular narrative about God and his work in the world. Scripture contains many human stories, all of which are incorporated into the one divine story that makes sense of them all. God himself inspired the writers of Scripture to convey his message. And God's message contains our grand narrative.

The story of Scripture manifests a temporal progress. It connects the Old Testament with the New Testament. The story of Scripture proceeds from one profound event to another. It begins in Genesis, a book whose name literally means "beginning" and concludes in the book of Revelation. Reflecting the necessity of seeing a divine unity behind the progress of history, the apostolic author of Revelation was told to "write what you have seen, what is, and what will take place after this" (Rev. 1:19). So, the narrative of Scripture takes us from creation through our fall and the free offer of redemption to our final destiny.

Three Movements

Simply using the data about what we saw God doing in the previous section, we may summarize the narrative of Scripture as comprised of three divine movements: creation, reconciliation, and consummation: First, God is the One who created the heavens and the earth in the beginning (Gen. 1:1). Second, God is the One who is reconciling fallen creation with himself through the person and work of his Son Jesus Christ (Col. 1:20). Third, God is the One who will bring all things to their proper conclusion through the Spirit's bodily resurrection of the dead for his glory (1 Cor. 15:20–28). The thread holding

---

11. Matthew Y. Emerson, *The Story of Scripture: An Introduction to Biblical Theology*, Hobbs College Library (Nashville: B&H, 2017), 1.

together the narrative is the Trinity's purpose of building the kingdom of God in Jesus Christ: "For he must reign until he puts all his enemies under his feet" (1 Cor. 15:25).

The following chart summarizes the three primary movements of God emphasized in the Bible's narrative. In the parentheses after each movement, we note some particularly important moments in that movement. Recognizing how all the meaningful moments of Scripture are connected together in a historical series has the added benefit of helping us make sense of where we each fit in that story. It helps give meaning to our own lives.

Figure 1. The Three Primary Movements of God in the Biblical Narrative

The three key movements of creation and reconciliation and consummation hold many important moments. These moments occur, respectively, in (1) the creation, which was followed by the fall of humanity, but also by the Lord's promise of covenantal redemption; (2) the incarnation, death, resurrection, and ascension of the Lord Jesus Christ to enable human reconciliation through his gift of the Holy Spirit; and (3) the Second Coming of the Lord Jesus Christ to bring final judgment, which will result in either eternal blessing or eternal damnation for every person. Each movement furthers the kingdom of Jesus Christ. These three movements and their important moments summarize Scripture's presentation of the temporal progress of God's activity.[12]

The History of Humanity

The narrative of Scripture is concerned with human history because we are physical, located in time and space. But just as we are irreducibly physical, so we are also irreducibly spiritual. Ecclesiastes says of humanity, that God "put eternity in their hearts" (Eccles. 3:11). So we must keep in mind the heavenly dimension of theology. Human beings are embodied souls. We are not disembodied souls. But neither are we soul-less bodies. We are soulful bodies. We are simultaneously both physical and spiritual beings. We were created with bodies to rule the earth; we were created with spirits to relate to God in heaven. Both aspects make us human.

The first man was created a "living being" through the physical dust being formed and enlivened by God's Spirit (Gen. 2:7). Because of our sin, God withdrew his Spirit, resulting in human death (Gen. 6:3). (The origin of sin in human history is typically described as "the Fall" [Gen. 3].) Although

---

12. Other scholars add a few more "acts" to the "drama" of Scripture, but these typically describe some aspect of the three key moments. For instance, Bartholomew and Goheen identify six acts centered on the kingdom of Christ. The emphasis on the kingdom works well, but the Fall itself depends on creaturely agency and ought not be ascribed to God. Craig G. Bartholomew and Michael W. Goheen, *The Drama of Scripture: Finding Our Place in the Biblical Story*, 2nd ed. (Grand Rapids: Baker, 2014), 22–23. These six acts are:

Act 1: God Establishes His Kingdom: Creation
Act 2: Rebellion in the Kingdom: Fall
Act 3: The King Chooses Israel: Redemption Initiated
Act 4: The Coming of the King: Redemption Accomplished
Act 5: Spreading the News of the King: The Mission of the Church
Act 6: The Return of the King: Redemption Completed.

death stalks humanity, the Lord Jesus grants life through giving his Holy Spirit (John 1:33–34; 3:5–6; 14:16–17; 20:22).
In the end, every human being will one day be raised physi-
cally from death (1 Cor. 15:23–25). The regenerate will reign
with Christ, but the wicked will receive eternal condemnation
during the Final Judgment (Rev. 20:4–6, 12–15). Throughout
the whole story of a human being, from birth to death to eternity, both body and soul remain important.

Glimpses of Eternity

Scripture reveals the grand narrative of Scripture in the
form of the history of human bodies, but Scripture reveals
more than history alone. Scripture also reveals that which is
above the physical. Philosophers call this dimension of reality
the "metaphysical" and theologians call it "spiritual," "eternal,"
or "heavenly." Eternal heaven is the place where our spiritual
reality finds its center.

Scripture gives us glimpses of heaven, when the eternal
destinies of all God's creatures are decreed, observed, and
determined. For instance, God held a counsel to determine
the context of Job's life. Later, Christ saw Satan driven from
heaven. Finally, the Spirit showed the apostle John the very
throne of God, as the deliberations of God for the future of
the world are announced. John's vision also describes the glorious praise given to God, the Lamb, and the Spirit on the
throne by all creatures, whether angels or human beings (Job
1:6–12; 2:1–7; Luke 10:18; Rev. 4–5). The many narratives of
human history find their overarching narrative in the eternal
Trinity.

Consider Who God Is

Why study God? As we have already seen, one reason to engage the task of theology is because God acts through the grand narrative of human history. However, the divine economy is not the only reason for engaging in the study of God. God works ultimately to bring us to himself. God's economy intends to show us his reality. And when a person begins to see the reality of God, he or she is impelled to worship God. Therefore, above and beyond the work of God on our behalf, we should engage in theology simply for the glory of who God is.

When we later review the Triunity of God and the perfections of God, knowledge of his being will prompt adoration. I once found myself in tears as I wrote about the revelation of God as Trinity at the very end of Scripture. Take a moment to consider three things we know about God's character even now: his love, his holiness, and his righteousness. And as you consider who God is, know that studying to gain such knowledge brings its own eternal reward.

God Is Love

Our God is utterly lovely. The apostle John emphasizes, "God is love" (1 John 4:8, 16b). The Father and the Son and the Holy Spirit share a mutual love that directs all his actions. "God is in himself the fullness and perfection of Love in loving and being loved which out of sheer love overflows freely toward others."[13] Even apart from any command to do so, the fact that God is generous, selfless, boundless love should naturally prompt us to respond with love for him and for others.

---

13. Thomas F. Torrance, *The Christian Doctrine of God, One Being Three Persons* (Edinburgh: T&T Clark, 1996), 5.

God Is Holy

Our God is also utterly holy. The prophet Isaiah was granted a weighty vision of the throne of God. He heard the angels declare that God is not just holy, nor just holier than others, but that he is the holiest of all. God is the perfection of holy. He is "holy, holy, holy" (Isa. 6:3). His holiness drove the prophet to worship God in fear, to receive the gift of spiritual transformation, and to seek to obey God fully (Isa. 6:5–8). God's holiness should likewise drive us to revere God, to receive his grace, and to worship him with our lives.

God Is Righteous

Our God is also utterly righteous. The apostle Paul learned about the righteousness of God the hard way. He knew God was "just" and therefore always does right. The justice of God requires the punishment of sinners (Deut. 32:4, 39–42). Paul also discovered that all his efforts to establish his own righteousness failed. He learned that not only is God just, or "righteous," when punishing sinners. In addition, God is the Justifier, the One who will "declare righteous." God's righteousness on the one hand condemns the unrepentant sinner and, on the other hand, justifies the sinner who will simply trust in the promise of Jesus Christ (Rom. 3:26).

One of my theological teachers, the British Methodist Geoffrey Wainwright, understood well the importance of studying God with our minds simply because of who God is. He wrote an entire systematic theology to demonstrate this conviction. He said every aspect of "Christian worship, doctrine, and life" is "conjoined in a common 'upwards' and 'forwards' direction." "They intend God's praise."[14] He began

---

14. Wainwright thus entitled his systematic, *Doxology*, which literally means "the study of glory." Geoffrey Wainwright, *Doxology: The Praise of*

his theology with a description of who God is and God's creation of humanity in his image for communion. At every turn, Wainwright called the reader to recognize how doctrine and worship are integral to one another.[15]

Wainwright's closing hymn captured this deeply Christian conviction perfectly:

> Finish then Thy new creation,
>   Pure and spotless let us be;
> Let us see Thy great salvation,
>   Perfectly restored in Thee;
> Changed from glory to glory,
>   Till in heaven we take our place,
> Till we cast our crowns before Thee,
>   Lost in wonder, love, and praise.[16]

Why should we study God? Simply so that we might enjoy God's beauty and worship him forever as we are filled with "wonder, love, and praise." The study of God is its own reward, because he is the reward. The more you come to know God through your personal relationship with him, the more fulfilling your life will become. God not only makes sense of everything; knowing him is worth everything you could possibly give, and more.

God in Worship, Doctrine, and Life: A Systematic Theology (New York: Oxford University Press, 1980), 10.

15. The Latin phrase *lex orandi lex credendi* summarizes his conviction. Worship influences doctrine and doctrine influences worship. Wainwright, *Doxology*, 218.

16. Wainwright, *Doxology*, 462.

Study Questions

1. What do these three Hebrew terms mean? *Shema* and *Ahabah* and *Chesed*

2. In your own words, describe the overarching story of the Bible.

3. Provide three of your own reasons why you think we should study God.

Suggested Resources

- Augustine, *Confessions*

- A. T. Robertson, *Word Pictures in the New Testament*

- Matthew Emerson, *The Story of Scripture*

CHAPTER THREE

Does God Exist?

◆

I TYPICALLY REFRAIN FROM STRONG argument, including arguing about God's existence. My reluctance, besides avoiding a contentious attitude, comes from a positive conviction that only the Spirit-filled preaching of the good news of Jesus Christ brings a person to saving faith. The arguments for the existence of God do not rely on the special facts of the gospel but on generally revealed truths for their force, so they cannot bring salvation on their own. But out of respect for people who find the following arguments helpful in clearing away unbelief, I include this chapter.[1]

We will approach the question of God's existence through three related questions: First, how does Scripture look at the existence of God? Second, how do reasonable people look at

---

1. A medieval theologian was pressed by his brothers to argue for the divine being. Despite his similar reluctance, many found his famous rational argument in *Proslogion* beneficial. His argument proved very helpful to many people, but it did not convince some of his fellow believers, like the monk Guanilo. Anselm of Canterbury, *The Major Works*, ed. Brian Davies (New York: Oxford University Press, 1998), 5, 111–22.

the existence of God? Third, why must we believe in the existence of God?

How Does Scripture Look at the Existence of God?

Genesis 1:1 may be the most well-known verse in the Bible, only rivaled perhaps by John 3:16. It is significant that the Bible begins with the presupposition that God exists. Moses started with this foundational claim, "In the beginning God created the heavens and the earth." That simple and short verse sets the basis for everything which follows in Scripture and theology. Genesis 1:1 teaches us the following foundational truths: God pre-exists everything else. God created everything else. And God's creatures are divided between heaven and earth. The text does not try to prove God's existence; it only affirms God's existence.

Likewise, Hebrews 11:6 teaches that, rather than depending upon proofs from reason or experience, God's existence must be accepted as a matter of faith. "Now without faith it is impossible to please God, since the one who draws near to him must believe that he exists and that he rewards those who seek him." Ultimately, the truth of God's existence must be received not as a matter of logical demonstration but as a matter of heartfelt faith. Faith is a gift of God which comes through God's revelation of himself. With that qualification, we note that Scripture provides numerous calls to trust in the existence of God.

The Hebrew name of God points to his existence. *Hayah 'aser hayah* is the longer name God provided to Moses when the prophet asked God to identify himself (Exod. 3:14). The phrase is typically translated, "I am who I am." It can also be translated, "I am because I am," or "I will be who I will be," or even "I will be because I will be." God then revealed a shorter name for himself, *Hayah*, "I am." These two Hebrew names indicate God's existence. They are also the names which lie behind the special covenant name of God, *Yahweh* (Exod. 3:15). Yahweh has typically been translated by allusion, out of respect for the exalted nature of his name, as "the LORD." In other words, the name of God says, "God is." Whether we encounter him in our past, our present, or our future, the eternal God simply exists.

Scripture demands from us a simple but basic faith in the existence of God. However, Scripture also indicates we should offer people the reasons we have for believing in God. The apostle Peter commanded, "In your hearts regard Christ the Lord as holy, ready at any time to give a defense to anyone who asks you for a reason for the hope that is in you" (1 Pet. 3:15). So, although we receive saving knowledge about the existence of God by the grace of faith, we must also be prepared to explain our faith. Faith in Christ includes trust in the existence of God.

Following Peter's command, we should be ready to defend two things in any conversation: First, we should be ready to defend our general belief in God. General belief in the fact that God exists is known as "theism." Second, we should also be ready to defend our hope in Jesus Christ to anyone and at any time. In other words, Scripture commands us to learn about the reasons for faith in God generally and about saving faith in Jesus Christ specifically.

When asked to give reasons for how I can believe in the existence of God, I often start with Psalm 14. The psalm begins, "The fool says in his heart, 'There's no God.' They are corrupt; they do vile deeds. There is no one who does good" (cf. Ps. 53). The language chosen by the psalmist is strong. A person who does not believe in God is *nabal*, "senseless" or "foolish." In other words, the person who denies the very existence of God is not rational in the first place. He or she does not treat the data coming from their mind and senses in a reasonable way. A truly reasonable person must accept the existence of God. The opposite of being reasonable is being foolish. This brings us to the second question.

How Do Reasonable People Look at the Existence of God?

According to the apostle Paul, the foolishness of disbelief is present in many people. "For his invisible attributes, that is, his eternal power and divine nature, have been clearly seen since the creation of the world, being understood through what he has made. As a result, people are without excuse" (Rom. 1:20). In other words, people have plenty of proofs for God's existence in the world around them. The problem is not with the atheist's sensory perception. The problem is with what a person willingly does with the proofs provided by God to their inner minds and outward senses. Paul continues, "For though they knew God, they did not glorify him as God or show gratitude. Instead, their thinking became worthless, and their senseless hearts were darkened. Claiming to be wise, they became fools" (Rom. 1:21–22).

There are so many proofs for the existence of God, both in the world around us and in our own selves. Before we begin looking at various proofs for God's existence, please remember that these proofs only demonstrate "theism," the existence of a God. Rational proofs cannot, do not, and will not save a person on their own. Mere mental affirmation of divine existence is not all that is required for saving faith. It takes hearing the good news about Jesus Christ for a person to be brought into a right relationship with God. However, the Christian who presents an unbeliever with proofs for the existence of God can help remove false mental presumptions in preparation to receive saving faith.

Thomas Aquinas, the leading Roman Catholic theologian of the High Middle Ages, wrote, "The existence of God can be proved in five ways."[2] Later, an influential German philosopher, Immanuel Kant, reduced the various rational proofs for the existence of God to three. He then collapsed all three into one argument for divine existence before dismissing it and proposing his own alternative proof.[3] I have divided the many arguments for the existence of God into seven. Some proofs may not appeal as much as others to different people, but their cumulative effect is impressive. I classify the various arguments for God's existence this way:

The Proof from Cause

Drawing from the ancient Greek philosopher Aristotle, Thomas Aquinas believed the argument from causation should come first. In his estimation, it is the most obvious approach to argue for the existence of God. Thomas observed that "whatever is in motion must be put in motion by another." All subsequent effects point toward the existence of their causes. And something started the entire process of causation. Before there was anything else, there had to be a first cause. A first mover is necessary for every other motion to exist. This prime mover or first cause "everyone understands to be God."[4]

A Baptist student of the Presbyterian theologian, Charles Hodge, agreed. In his class notes, he wrote, "Nothing can be produced and yet be without cause."[5] Stated positively we can

---

2. Thomas Aquinas, *Summa Theologica*, transl. Fathers of the English Dominican Province, 5 vols. (1911; reprint, Westminster, MD: Christian Classics, 1981), vol. 1, 13.

3. Roger Scruton, *Kant: A Very Short Introduction* (New York: Oxford University Press, 2001), 66.

4. Aquinas, *Summa Theologica*, vol. 1, 13.

5. James Petigru Boyce, *Abstract of Systematic Theology* (1887; reprint, Hanford, CA: Den Dulk Christian Foundation, [n.d.]), 23.

say everything is caused by something—every effect has a cause. These many causes and effects in creation point to an original self-referential cause which started the whole universe. The universal phenomenon of movement points to a prime mover. Some modern scientists approach this idea, even if reluctantly, with theories of a Big Bang at the beginning of the universe.[6]

The Proof from Design

Aquinas gave this proof in its classic form too. The evidence of design in the universe points to a great designer. Everything in the world has a purpose to fulfill, from inanimate matter to animate matter, from the unintelligent to the intelligent, whether it be small or great. Somebody is taking care of us and that somebody "we call God."[7] In Acts 14:17, Paul similarly told unbelievers that the provision of their food and water in nature is the sign of a divine provider.[8]

William Paley famously argued from the example of a watch. If you were to find a watch laying in a field, would you think it appeared there naturally? No, a rational person would conclude an intelligent being must have left it there. And an intelligent being must have first intentionally constructed then assembled its parts in proper order. "The inference, we think, is inevitable; that the watch must have had a maker."[9] In the same way, the wonders of the human body indicate

---

6. Tawa J. Anderson, *Why Believe: Christian Apologetics for a Skeptical Age* (Nashville: B&H Academic, 2021), 84–86.

7. Aquinas, *Summa Theologica*, vol. 1, 14.

8. "Although he did not leave himself without a witness, since he did what is good by giving you rain from heaven and fruitful seasons and filling you with food and your hearts with joy."

9. William Paley, *Natural Theology or Evidence of the Existence and Attributes of the Deity, Collected from the Appearances of Nature*, ed. Matthew D. Eddy and David Knight (New York: Oxford University Press, 2008), 8.

evidence of design. Paley's basic conclusion was, "There cannot be design without a designer."[10]

William Tolar spoke of how easy it would be for the earth to become inhospitable for life. If the earth were to come a little closer to the sun, it would burn up. If it were to move a little further out, it would veer into space, becoming a ball of ice. If it were not tilted exactly right, if it were not spinning exactly right, if it were not following an elliptical orbit, and so on goes Professor Tolar's list. According to his calculations, the chances are multiple trillions to one that someone had to design the earth exactly as it is for human life to be possible. This evidence of careful design points to God.[11]

The Proof from Perfection

The proof from perfection is also known as "the ontological argument" for the existence of God. It is a difficult argument for people who are more practical in orientation. However, it can be grasped with a little effort. Jesus said, "your heavenly Father is perfect" (Matt. 5:48). Building on this truth, some argue that we know God is perfect with intuitive perception. Anselm said the idea of a perfect being would not be possible did that perfect being not exist. The human mind is like a boat on water which rises to a certain level. We can picture that level of water only because it has risen that far.

Anselm, who expressed this argument in its classic form, affirmed God is perfect. God is, literally, "something-than-which-nothing-greater-can-be-thought." He continued, "Even the Fool, then, is forced to agree that something-than-which-nothing-greater-can-be-thought exists in the mind, since he

---

10. Paley, *Natural Theology*, 12.

11. William B. Tolar, "Religious Faith in a Scientific Age or The Creation: Chance or Choice?" (Fort Worth, TX: Author's Personal Manuscript, 1990), 4–7.

understands this when he hears it, and whatever is understood is in the mind." Anselm then drove the point home, noting how God's perfections draw our human minds toward him. "And surely that-than-which-nothing-greater-can-be-thought cannot exist in the mind alone. For if it exists solely in the mind, it can be thought to exist in reality also, which is greater."[12]

Our minds grasp, even if dimly, the abstract idea of the perfect God. And the concrete reality of God's perfection is of course greater than our mind's abstract picture of him. Even the atheist must first posit God in his mind before he can later deny God. The atheist's mind knows of a perfect being, but recognizing his own human imperfection, or being disappointed that God did not do something he wanted, the atheist denies God. The atheist does not operate exclusively from reason but from his will. The atheist may not want a perfect God to hold him to his perfect standard. The atheist, therefore, denies the very God whom he could not conceive existed were God not greater than the atheist's thoughts of God. Anselm repeats with the psalmist that the fool says in his heart that there is no God.[13]

The Proof from Worship

In the previous chapter we introduced Augustine's sense of his natural need to know God. His fuller statement is worth hearing, because he speaks not only about our desire for God but our misuse of that desire. We were created to worship God, but our sin inhibits us.

> Man is one of your creatures, Lord, and his instinct is to praise you. He bears about him the mark of death, the sign of his own sin,

---

12. Anselm of Canterbury, *The Major Works*, 87.
13. Anselm of Canterbury, *The Major Works*, 88.

to remind him that you thwart the proud. But still, since he is a part of your creation, he wishes to praise you. The thought of you stirs him so deeply that he cannot be content unless he praises you, because you made us for yourself and our hearts find no peace until they rest in you.[14]

Paul agrees that we have a created inclination to worship God. He also comments on how we misuse worship by engaging in idolatry. In Romans 1:25, speaking of those who knew of God but denied him anyway, Paul wrote, "They exchanged the truth of God for a lie, and worshiped and served what has been created instead of the Creator, who is praised forever. Amen." The need to worship God is everywhere, and the misuse of it is too. In every culture throughout human history, there are religious mechanisms by which man tries to reach a god, the ultimate truth, the Good, or the ground of being. These are, of course, substitute and vague names for the concrete personal being we call God.

The need for worship which human cultures everywhere report "is so stupendous and has been made in such a widespread manner," says the Quaker Christian philosopher Elton Trueblood, "that no philosophy can afford to neglect it."[15] Careful evaluation of the universal human drive to engage in worship will lead a truly rational person, one who is not misled by a defective will, to recognize the truth that God exists.

---

14. Augustine, *Confessions*, 21.

15. David Elton Trueblood, *Philosophy of Religion* (San Francisco: Harper and Row, 1957), 145.

The Proof from Conscience

Paul argued that every person will be held accountable to God. "So, when Gentiles, who do not by nature have the law, do what the law demands, they are a law to themselves even though they do not have the law. They show that the work of the law is written on their hearts. Their consciences confirm this. Their competing thoughts either accuse or even excuse them" (Rom. 2:14–15).

After establishing the universality of conscience, the apostle argued that the conscience points to each person's responsibility before the divine court. "Their competing thoughts either accuse or even excuse them on the day when God judges what people have kept secret" (Rom. 2:15b–16a). By convicting a person's conscience, God provides a sure sign of personal accountability. The approaching judgment invariably serves as irrefutable evidence of God's existence.

Cicero, the great classical Roman legal theorist, traced the existence of law, including the law within individuals, the laws within nations, and the laws within nature back to a great Lawgiver. The universal existence of law points to a single foundation of law according to which the entire universe operates. This foundational law would not exist unless someone established that law in the beginning.[16] The philosophical tradition which evaluates natural law and the laws of nations derives from the logic of the innate human conscience.

Nearly two millennia later, Kant said he did not trust pure reason to prove the existence of God. However, he did recognize the existence of a moral law. According to this otherwise skeptical scholar, the human need to do right even in the face of certain death points to something beyond death. The compulsion to moral duty indicates a divine Judge will

---

16. Cicero traces the origin of laws through humanity, the gods, nature, and God. Cicero, *The Republic and The Laws*, transl. Niall Rudd (Oxford University Press, 1998), 104–7.

hold us accountable, either rewarding us or punishing us for our actions in this life. "For morality not only shows that we have need of God, but it also teaches us that he is already present in the nature of things and that the order of things leads to him."[17] Kant went on to argue that the universal evidence of human moral duty indicates the attributes of God include that he is "omniscient, omnipotent, eternal, and not in time."[18]

The Proof from History

Speaking once to the academy of Athens, Paul argued that God left evidence of himself in the universe. Paul noted how human nations rose and fall. He argued that national histories were directed by God's guiding hand. "From one man he has made every nationality to live over the whole earth and has determined their appointed times and the boundaries of where they live. He did this so that they might seek God, and perhaps they might reach out and find him, though he is not far from each one of us" (Acts 17:26–27). Human beings are drawn to seek this God they do not know personally. Paul then cited a pagan philosopher to prove this point and concluded, "For in him we live, and move, and have our being" (Acts 17:28).

In an anti-historical age, the proof for the existence of God from history is perhaps the most difficult argument to make. But if you are a believer, think about this chain of events: Why did you become a Christian? You became a Christian when somebody shared Scripture and a word of personal testimony with you. Why did they become a Christian? They became a Christian in the same way. And where did this witness for Christ originate? Your faith goes

---

17. Kant, *Lectures on Philosophical Theology*, transl. Allen W. Wood and Gertrude M. Clark (Ithaca, NY: Cornell University Press, 1978), 110–11.

18. Kant, *Lectures on Philosophical Theology*, 111.

back through history—through the Enlightenment, through the Reformation, through the Middle Ages, and through the persecuted early church—back to the apostles' transformative encounter with the risen Lord Jesus Christ. The church of Jesus is the continuing historic witness to the existence of God in Christ and to his amazing resurrection from the dead.

I once had a skeptic ask me, "How do you know God exists? How do you know this Jesus exists? Have you ever met him? Can you show me him right now?" Then he held up his pen and said, "I can touch this. I can feel this. This is all I believe in." I responded, "Tell me. Do you believe there is a nation on the other side of the world called China?" Of course, he did. "How do you know this China exists? Have you ever been there?" He had not. "Can you show it to me right now?" He could not. I continued, "Do you believe in George Washington?" Yes, he did. "How do you know he was real? Have you ever met him? Can you show me him? Can you touch him? Can you feel him?" Despite the utter lack of any direct evidence, this skeptic believed in both China and Washington. Why? Because of the witness of history.

Placing to the side the many disputes over the scientific evaluation of fossils and layers of soil,[19] we find tangible evidence from written history. Consider the rise of the universities in the West,[20] the development of benevolent ministries and hospitals by the Christian churches,[21] the movement of civilization toward recognizing universal human dignity and

---

19. John Newport identified seven different approaches to interpreting the scientific evidence of creation. Newport, *Life's Ultimate Questions: A Contemporary Philosophy of Religion* (Dallas: Word, 1989), 139–55.

20. Charles Homer Haskin, *The Rise of Universities* (Ithaca, NY: Cornell University Press, 1957).

21. Rodney Stark, *The Rise of Christianity: How the Obscure, Marginal Jesus Movement Became the Dominant Religious Force in the Western World in a Few Centuries* (San Francisco: Harper Collins, 1996).

human rights,[22] and the origins of modern science.[23] Each of these historical developments, alongside many others, point to the good influence of faith in God.

These historic truths remain positive indicators, despite the involvement of some believers in such evil institutions as the crusades, the inquisition, and race-based chattel slavery. We must also remember that the crusading spirit has been replaced by the advocacy of universal religious liberty,[24] that the abolition of slavery came through Christian proclamation and activism,[25] and of the incontrovertible evidence of wide-spread sustained Christian opposition to abortion. History demonstrates that belief in God has been beneficial for advancing human dignity and human flourishing, even while it also demonstrates the problem of human sinfulness.

The Proof from Probability

The author of Hebrews says that the person who believes in God possesses an assured hope (Heb. 11:1–2). The testimony of the seventeenth-century Catholic philosopher Blaise Pascal is helpful here. Pascal pointed to the problem of unbelief from a mathematical perspective. He called the unbeliever to consider the odds he was taking with his life. "Yes, but

---

22. Larry Siedentop, *Inventing the Individual: The Origins of Western Liberalism* (New York: Allen Lane, 2014); Tom Holland, *Dominion: How the Christian Revolution Remade the World* (New York: Basic Books, 2019).

23. Herbert Butterfield, *The Origins of Modern Science 1300–1800*, revised ed. (1957; reprint, New York: Simon & Schuster, 1965).

24. Jason G. Duesing, Thomas White, and Malcolm B. Yarnell III, eds., *First Freedom: The Beginning and End of Religious Liberty*, 2nd ed. (Nashville: B&H Academic, 2016).

25. William Wilberforce, *A Practical View of the Prevailing Religious System of Professed Christians in the Higher and Middle Classes, Contrasted with Real Christianity* (Philadelphia: John Ormrod, 1798); John Pollock, *Wilberforce* (Belleville, MI: Lion Publishing, 1977).

you must wager. There is no choice, you are already committed. Which will you choose then? Let us see: since a choice
must be made, let us see which offers you the least interest."
Pascal described the importance of what was at stake. "You
have two things to lose: the true and the good; and two things
to stake, your reason and your will, your knowledge and your
happiness; and your nature has two things to avoid: error and
wretchedness."[26]

Pascal asked the unbeliever to consider the eternal disposition of one's own soul. Eternal happiness involves a critical
wager. Making a choice in the matter of God's existence constitutes not an affront to reason but a rational requirement. A
choice must be made. "Since you must necessarily choose, your
reason is no more affronted by choosing one rather than the
other."[27] Then comes the critical wager about one's well-being.
"But your happiness? Let us weigh up the gain and the loss
involved in calling heads that God exists. Let us assess the two
cases: if you win you win everything; if you lose you lose nothing." The decision, therefore, is rather easy: "Do not hesitate
then; wager that he does exist."[28] The person who wants life
will be wise and opt for God's existence.

Why Must We Believe in the Existence of God?

The psalmist tells us the foolish person denies God's
existence in his heart. The opposite of foolishness is wisdom.
We must believe in the existence of God if we are to be wise.
The wise person believes in God's existence in his heart. The

---

26. Blaise Pascal, *Pensées*, transl. A. J. Krailshamer (New York: Penguin,
1966), 150.

27. Pascal, *Pensées*, 150.

28. Pascal, *Pensées*, 150–51.

person who denies God's existence is foolish and brings the fearful certainty of "dread" into his or her life (Ps. 14:5).

A Heart Issue

The psalmist used the Hebrew term for "heart" (*leb*) to designate the location of faith in God's existence (Ps. 14:1). This wholistic term indicates how faith in God is not just a matter of the intellect. True faith in God occupies the will and the emotions as well as the mind. A person must not hold divine existence at an abstract distance. A person must believe that God is real, and that he is supremely powerful, and that he wants to bless. One must believe not in an abstract God dispassionately but in the one personal God passionately.[29]

We must move beyond merely affirming the existence of God and come to know him in the incarnate Lord Jesus Christ. Such a saving knowledge will fill your heart with worship and love. Pascal reminded his interlocutor, "If my words please you and seem cogent, you must know that they come from a man who went down upon his knees before and after to pray."[30] The person who holds to God's existence from a merely abstract perspective does not have true faith. We must proceed to faith in Christ, to prayer and true worship.

A true saving faith in the holy God will become evident in a changed heart engaged in holy worship and in holy actions. The problem with the fool, the person who does not believe in God, is that he or she does "vile deeds," not "good" ones (Ps. 14:1b–c). In other words, the visible outward test of true

---

29. Emil Brunner said the problem of mere theism is that it does not know God is the personal Lord incarnate in Jesus Christ. "The God of Aristotle is neither a 'Lord-God' nor a Creator, neither the One who freely elects, nor the One who stoops down to man." Brunner, *The Christian Doctrine of God*, vol. 1, *Dogmatics*, transl. Olive Wyon (Philadelphia: Westminster Press, 1950), 152.

30. Pascal, *Pensées*, 153.

faith is found in human action, while the inner test of true faith is found in worship from the heart.

Beware Practical Atheism

The really bad news, according to the psalmist, is that everyone has been a practical atheist in life. "All have turned away; all alike have become corrupt. There is no one who does good, not even one" (Ps. 14:3). But thankfully, God is not merely powerful and holy, ready to bring judgment upon sinners. God is also patient, merciful, and loving. The Lord is concerned for "the oppressed" and will become "his refuge" (Ps. 14:6).

Believing that God exists is necessary, but theism is not enough. Knowing that God is going to bring judgment is not enough either. We must also know how God is love if we are to avoid sinking into despair. In the next several chapters, as we look at God's perfect attributes, I hope you will come to know him better and truly worship him.

Study Questions

1. Which of the above seven proofs for God's existence do you find most compelling?

2. Is "theism" the same as saving faith? Why or why not?

3. Do you have personal experience with God? Describe your personal conversion on a piece of paper, then tell an unbeliever about your powerful personal proof for God.

Suggested Resources

- William Paley, *Natural Theology*

- Tom Holland, *Dominion: How the Christian Revolution Remade the World*

- Tawa J. Anderson, *Why Believe: Christian Apologetics for a Skeptical Age*

CHAPTER FOUR

When or Where Is God?

◆

THIS MAY BE THE MOST difficult chapter a contemporary student of God's Word will read. There are three reasons for this difficulty: First, peering into divine eternity from the perspective of creaturely time exceeds our natural experiences and limited capabilities. The only way we can even understand eternity, the place where, or the time whence God abides, is through God's gift of revelation to us. (The terms *where* and *whence* apply the creaturely dimensions of space and time to the eternal Creator, but only by distant comparison.)

The second difficulty contemporary readers face when thinking about God in eternity concerns the fact that, since the advent of Enlightenment skepticism, Western Christians have been taught to doubt all claims about reality. Eternity and its related concepts are dismissed out of hand as mere speculation. Most of us now lack anything beyond the most basic vocabulary in theology and philosophy, including the concept of eternity.

A third contemporary problem is that people have been indoctrinated, typically without their awareness or approval, into the lower philosophies of secularism and naturalism, and into theological liberalism. To overcome this modernistic indoctrination, which privileges the physical world at the expense of spiritual reality, we must question the conceptions we were taught. Gaining a proper perspective on the physical is required to fully embrace spiritual truth.

Despite such challenges, divine revelation manifestly teaches that God is infinite. We must therefore believe in and work to understand his eternality and omnipresence. God gave us his Word and his Spirit to help us see what we could otherwise not see due to our natural limits and fallen minds.

The revelation of divine eternity occurs in three general stages: First, God put a natural desire for eternity into each human heart, even though heaven exceeds our capacity to comprehend it (Eccles. 3:11). Second, God sent his Son, Jesus Christ, into the world precisely to make known his eternal will and his perfect ways to sinners, so that we can be saved through faith in him (John 3:16). Third, at the Final Judgment, every person shall be granted incontrovertible truth of the eternity of God and of our eternal responsibility (Rev. 20:11–15).

While the infinity of God includes both his eternity and his immensity, we shall focus on eternity. At this stage in systematic theology, the best way to begin getting a handle on the meaning of eternity is not so much by looking past the end point of history in eschatology, but by examining its beginning point in creation, and learning to look beyond it to God.[1] By rehearsing important biblical texts which treat the concepts of "eternity," "time," and "beginning," we can form a proper view of divine eternity and our relation to it.

---

1. *Eschatology*, the doctrine of the last, will be covered in the third volume of this series.

Eternity

Some definitions will prove helpful. There are several relatively simple ideas which require our attention when thinking about the infinity, particularly the eternity, of God. These ideas can be divided into two major groups, those terms which are more exalted or ethereal in character, and those terms which are more earthy or physical. On the one hand, we consider exalted terms like *infinity*, *eternity*, and *immensity*. On the other hand, we ponder various earthy terms like *time*, *history*, and *biography*. Some terms, like *heaven* and *beginning*, have both exalted and earthy meanings.

Infinity

John Gill said God's *infinity* means, "He is unbounded and unlimited, unmeasurable or immense, unsearchable and not to be comprehended."[2] Scripture teaches God is beyond our ability to contain him, even in our minds, through texts like the following: "Our Lord is great, vast in power; his understanding is infinite" (Ps. 147:5). "'Do I not fill the heavens and the earth?'—the Lord's declaration" (Jer. 23:24). And "Jesus Christ is the same yesterday, today, and forever" (Heb. 13:8; cf. Heb. 7:3).

There are two major aspects to the profound truth that God is infinite, one relating to time, the other to space. Regarding his location, we must learn to say God is "not bounded by space, and therefore is everywhere." Regarding his relationship to history, God is "not bounded by time, so he is eternal."[3] We must affirm God's immensity, his omnipresence vis-à-vis space. We must also affirm his eternity vis-à-vis time.

---

2. John Gill, *A Body of Doctrinal Divinity; Or a System of Evangelical Truths, Deduced from the Sacred Scriptures*, new ed. (London, 1839), 41.

3. Gill, *A Body of Doctrinal Divinity*, 41.

Eternity

For a simple definition of *eternity* [Hebrew *'olam*], Augustine's claim that eternity is "outside time," where God abides, is valuable.[4] Eternity contains time but is not limited or even defined by time. Rather, the eternal God defines time. Eternity describes the "when" or "where" of the divine life.

Heaven

Creaturely life in God's eternal presence is indicated by the term *heaven*. Heaven [Hebrew *samayim*] has a natural meaning of "sky" or "expanse," but it also has a supernatural meaning. Its supernatural sense signifies God's "holy dwelling." God observes his creatures and acts upon them from heaven (Deut. 26:15).

Although we refer to heaven in temporal and spatial ways, we must recognize the accommodation to our creaturely understanding. That Christ was with God "before the world existed" or "before the world's foundation" (John 17:5, 24) does not mean he came to exist in a time "before" time.[5] Rather, "before" and "above," when used of God, are truthful metaphors. These metaphors draw upon our limited reality to point toward his unlimited reality.

Why does God speak to us in this way? God chose to reveal his infinite self with finite terms because those are the only terms we understand. We exist in time and space, so God

---

4. Augustine, *Confessions*, transl. R. S. Pine-Coffin (New York: Penguin, 1961), 253. The classical view has been challenged in recent years by philosophers who believe a timeless God cannot relate to creatures in time. On the debate in general, see Gregory E. Ganssle, "Introduction," in *God and Time: Four Views*, ed. idem (Downers Grove, IL: InterVarsity Press, 2004), 9–27. The classic position rehearsed by Paul Helm remains the best explanation. Helm, "Divine Timeless Eternity," in *God and Time*, 28–60.

5. This is an idea identified with the heresy of Arianism.

"condescends" from eternity with temporal and spatial language to teach us about himself. Although he "accommodates" his revelation of himself to our limited capacity, we must never assume that God is therefore limited like us.

The language of time and space helps us see the eternal God through "accommodation" and "condescension." Such terms must never be used in a carnal or rude way. God condescends to us, but we dare not be condescending toward God.[6] We must not, for instance, import the idea of succession into eternity. God is not defined by time or space.[7] Rather, God creates and defines time and space. Temporal and spatial categories define our creaturely existence, not the Creator's existence. Time and space may not be used to limit God's unlimited nature.[8]

Theology Proper

Two terms dealing with theology proper—*ontology* and *metaphysics*—are philosophical and theological concepts related to eternity. *Ontology* may be defined simply as the study of being. Ontology is important because we understand who we are through who God is, and vice versa. *Theology*

---

6. The language of "before" must be taken as a limited comparison. Remember that God is sometimes referred to with spatial and temporal terms, and even bodily terms. For instance, we read of the "finger of God" (cf. Deut. 9:10; Luke 11:20), but God is not bound by matter, so this phrase properly refers to God's power. Limited terms are used of God "in accommodation and condescension to our weak minds, which are not capable of perceiving duration but as successive." Gill, *A Body of Doctrinal Divinity*, 49.

7. The language of "eternity past," "eternity present," or "eternity future" may be used in a limited sense, but they can tend toward limiting God with the succession of time.

8. "[W]e can conceive nothing before time but eternity." Gill, *A Body of Doctrinal Divinity*, 47. "The Eternity of God, or his being from everlasting to everlasting, is without succession, or any distinctions of time succeeding one another." Gill, *A Body of Doctrinal Divinity*, 48.

proper, also known as "divine ontology," helps us to identify the One we worship. Properly identifying the being of God, as much as possible given our limits, is extremely important. Worshiping the wrong god is an act of idolatry, which the one true God deems worthy of judgment (Exod. 20:1). *Metaphysics* may be defined simply as the study of that ultimate reality which transcends the physical world.[9]

Time

The author of the biblical book of Ecclesiastes made a clear distinction between "eternity" and "heaven," on the one hand, and "time" (Hebrew *'et*), on the other. For instance, Ecclesiastes 3:11 states, "He has made everything appropriate in its time. He has also put eternity in their hearts, but no one can discover the work God has done from beginning to end." This raises the question of what time really is. Defining the limits of time on the one hand will prove helpful in gaining a better understanding of eternity on the other.

Time

First, we must continually remember that time is distinguished from eternity. The author of Ecclesiastes taught that the external world relates mediately through our bodies while eternity relates directly to the heart. Second, the work of God is "from beginning to end," indicating time possesses a linear character. Third, the work of God upon time is always

---

9. Yandall Woodfin defines ontology and metaphysics synonymously as the effort "to discover what reality is in its totality as compared or contrasted to a mere function, appearance, linguistic symbol, or partial manifestation." Woodfin, *With All Your Mind: A Christian Philosophy* (Nashville: Abingdon Press, 1980), 83.

"appropriate." Time is subject to God's providential guidance. The biblical definition of time takes on a fourth characteristic in Ecclesiastes 3:1, which states, "There is an occasion for everything, and a time for every activity under heaven." The "occasions" of time are related via divine providence to the "activities" of various created things.

In conclusion, we may say that time, which is unlike eternity, concerns the orderly progress of the activities of created things between their beginning and their end, and that their progress develops appropriately according to the guidance of God. Nature is manifestly governed by divinely given laws concerning time. Modern science arose from the human effort to understand the processes of nature which have been determined by divine law.

Ecclesiastes provides yet more detail about the progress of time. The laws respecting creaturely time include, in the case of all animals and humans, the crisis events of birth and death (Eccles. 3:2a). Arranged between the beginning point of birth and the end point of death are the various occasions or events in a creature's life before God (Eccles. 3:2b–8).

According to the witness of the whole canon, time begins with creation (Gen. 1:1–3), is redeemed through the person and work of the promised Messiah and through the promised Spirit (Rom. 8:11, 18–23), and reaches its consummation with the final judgment (Rev. 20:11–15). In the eschaton, the new Jerusalem descends to unite heaven with a purified and restored earth (Rev. 21:2). The eternal God will then dwell with humanity (Rev. 21:3).

History

History is a human discipline which examines "the processes of things in time."[10] General history considers the progress of creatures in relation to one another in time. The narrower disciplines of "natural history" and "human history" attempt to tell the various stories of God's creatures in their progress with one another. The discipline of "religious history" tells the chronological story of human creatures according to how religion "shaped the mentality" of various peoples.[11]

Christian history tells the story of God's creatures in relation to God, who himself transcends chronology, and in relation to his Christ, who brought eternity into history for the sake of human redemption. Because of the incarnation, the death, and the resurrection of Jesus Christ, Christianity remains "an historical religion."[12] In the first great history of the world written from a Christian perspective, Augustine of Hippo related all history to Scripture and to the eternal God.[13]

Biography

Biography, the history of a human person, considers the natural journey of a particular creature through time. Human beings are bodily creatures (Gen. 2:7) who, made in the image of God (Gen. 1:26–27), began their existence at a definite

---

10. Herbert Butterfield, *The Origins of History*, ed. Adam Watson (New York: Basic Books, 1981), 14.

11. Butterfield, *The Origins of History*, 15.

12. "Christianity is an historical religion in a particularly technical sense that the term possesses—it presents us with religious doctrines which are at the same time historical events or historical interpretations. In particular it confronts us with the questions of the Incarnation, the Crucifixion and the Resurrection." Butterfield, *Christianity and History* (New York: Charles Scribner's Sons, 1950), 3.

13. Saint Augustine, *The City of God*, transl. Marcus Dods (New York: Modern Library, 1993).

time (Gen. 1:31). The Bible is concerned to relay the history of both individual persons and human community.

The biographies of Adam and Eve are particularly important, because as the first human beings they shaped the history of the entire human community. Their fall resulted in the coming of personal death upon humanity (Gen. 2:15–17; 3:6–7; Rom. 5:12). We were separated from God until Christ overcame sin and death through his death and resurrection. Personal faith in Christ is required for personal salvation (Mark 1:15).

Whether we examine history from a general perspective or a biographical perspective, it is important to subsume time under eternity. Addressing metaphysical matters in his speech before the Academy of Athens, which met at the Areopagus, the apostle Paul encouraged the leading philosophers of his day to locate the world under divine sovereignty. Using a spatial metaphor, Paul located human history within divine eternity. "For in him we live and move and have our being" (Acts 17:28a). One might say that God has created within his infinite self the relevant laws of finite space and finite time for his finite creatures to exist.[14] God grants his creatures the lives they possess (Acts 17:25). By his providence, he also sets the spatial boundaries of their existence (Acts 17:26).

Time exists under eternity by divine grace. Time is not eternal; it has a beginning; and that beginning points to God.

---

14. Jürgen Moltmann connects *creatio ex nihilo* (that God does not create out of preexisting matter) with this doctrine. Moltmann, *God in Creation: A New Theology of Creation and the Spirit*, transl. Margaret Kohl (Minneapolis: Fortress Press, 1993), 86–90. Moltmann's efforts hereby to limit God should be rejected.

Access to Eternity?

Access Affirmed

The journey of grace from lostness to salvation through personal encounter with the eternal God has been described in various spiritual autobiographies. Augustine of Hippo's *Confessions*, written in the late fourth century, is the most well-known one. He relates eternity to time from both a personal perspective and a universal perspective.[15] Written in the form of a prayer, Augustine tells us how he came to know God and himself. "Suffused as they are with a dramatic sense of God's interventions in Augustine's life," this great African theologian's reflections refer constantly to Scripture, especially the Psalms.[16]

More than a millennium later, Martin Luther's descriptions of his conversion and life,[17] and John Bunyan's personal and allegorical descriptions of the Christian's walk with God,[18] indicate the common belief that human beings could access the eternal God by faith continued into the early modern period.

Anne Dutton's *A Brief Account of the Gracious Dealings of God* provides proof of the ongoing belief in the possibility of a dynamic personal encounter with an infinite God. This eighteenth-century English Baptist theologian described her access to the revelation of God with passion: "Oh, Eternity!

---

15. Books 1–10 of Augustine's *Confessions* convey his personal journey; books 11–13 consider the human community's encounter with eternity.

16. Peter Brown, *Augustine of Hippo, A Biography* (Los Angeles: University of California Press, 1967), 174.

17. Roland Bainton, *Here I Stand: A Life of Martin Luther* (New York: Abingdon-Cokesbury Press, 1950).

18. John Bunyan, *Grace Abounding to the Chief of Sinners* (London: Oliphant Anderson & Ferrier, [n.d.]); idem, *The Pilgrim's Progress: From This World to That Which Is to Come* (Uhrichsville, OH: Barbour, 1985).

Eternity was ever before mine Eyes! And the worth of my own Soul, as an immortal Spirit, capable of the highest Glory in the eternal enjoyment of God, or of the utmost Misery in an everlasting Separation from him; was strongly impress'd upon my Mind."[19] Anne's salvation then came through faith in the work of the transcendent God's only begotten Son. God revealed this salvation by means of his Word and his Spirit. "O, I was born first from Beneath! And then born from above."[20] God also used the witness of the church.

Access Denied

However, Europe's universities, once tied closely to the church, soon spread doubts about human access to God. In Britain, David Hume advocated philosophical skepticism, but it was the work of Immanuel Kant which made theological conversation almost prohibitive. Kant described his *Critique of Pure Reason*, published in 1781, as a "Copernican Revolution" in human thought.[21] Kant deemed human access to ultimate reality entirely speculative. He argued that space and time were mere forms of human intuition imposed upon the evidence. Our experiences of the world, he said, are shaped by measurable "phenomena," but their reality belongs to inaccessible "noumena." Reasonable judgments are "valid only for

---

19. Anne Dutton, "A Brief Account of the Gracious Dealings of God with a Poor, Sinful, Unworthy Creature, in Three Parts (1750)," in *Selected Spiritual Writings of Anne Dutton: Eighteenth-Century, British-Baptist, Woman Theologian*, vol. 3, *The Autobiography*, ed. JoAnn Ford Watson (Macon, GA: Mercer University Press, 2006), 8.

20 Taken from a hymn by Mason. Dutton, "A Brief Account of the Gracious Dealings of God," 21.

21. Kant said Hume woke him from his "dogmatic slumbers." Nigel Warburton, *Philosophy: The Classics*, 4th ed. (New York: Routledge, 2014), 126–27.

objects of possible experience," which does not include the underlying reality of things.[22]

Kant was not an avowed atheist, but he inhibited human access to metaphysical reality, especially to God. "Without looking upon myself as a remarkably combative person," he wrote, "I shall not decline to detect the fallacy and destroy the pretensions of every attempt at speculative theology."[23]

Kant's revolt against theology proper concluded in his demand that modern persons leave behind their "self-incurred immaturity" to embrace "Enlightenment." He derided believers as lazy and cowardly: "Dare to be wise! Have courage to use your own understanding!"[24] Kant was especially critical toward Christian clergy. He challenged them to exercise their "freedom" and criticize the "mistaken aspects" of the church's doctrine and "to offer a better arrangement of religious and ecclesiastical affairs."[25] He said they should change the church's faith to ensure "man's upward progress" and secure "the sacred rights of mankind."[26]

Kant's revolutionary denial of human access to eternal truth, followed by his clarion call to reconfigure church dogma, encouraged the modern movements of secularism and theological liberalism. Secularism entirely supplanted eternal truth with earthly reality. Theological liberalism challenged the historical confidence of Christians through the modern critical method of Bible study. Liberalism did not stop with history. Liberal theologians also sowed doubt about settled doctrines, especially theology proper. The temporal "Jesus of history" was

22. Immanuel Kant, *The Critique of Pure Reason* (1781), transl. J. M. D. Meiklejohn, in *Great Books of the Western World*, vol. 41, *Kant*, ed. Robert Maynard Hutchins (Chicago: Encyclopaedia Britannica, 1952), 33.

23. Kant, *The Critique of Pure Reason*, 192.

24. Immanuel Kant, *An Answer to the Question: What Is Enlightenment?* transl. H. B. Nisbet (New York: Penguin, 2009), 1.

25. Kant, *What Is Enlightenment?*, 5.

26. Kant, *What Is Enlightenment?*, 7–8.

diminished, and the eternal "Christ of faith" was denied. The assault on Christian certainty about God was intense.

The Beginning and the Absolute Beginning

The classical Christian view of eternity and time was severely challenged by the Enlightenment. However, a plain reading of Scripture requires the traditional view. Beyond the biblical texts from Ecclesiastes and Acts rehearsed above, several others describe the relation of time to eternity. For instance, in Scripture, the word *beginning* (Hebrew *resit*; Greek *arche*) can refer either to a quantity or a quality. The quantitative meaning is used "with reference to time." But the qualitative sense refers to "eternity."[27] The context of the biblical passage determines whether time or eternity is intended.

In the Bible, history is regarded in a linear way. History is not chaotic or circular, as in other religious worldviews. Rather, the Christian canon portrays history with a beginning and an end, and significant events develop between those two points. Because God is identified as the one who creates, guides, and concludes, history indicates a relentless progress from creation to final consummation.[28]

---

27. William Sanford LaSor, "Beginning," in *The International Standard Bible Encyclopedia*, revised ed., ed. Geoffrey W. Bromiley, 4 vols. (Grand Rapids: Eerdmans, 1979), 451.

28. For more on the different conceptions of history and its biblical sense, see Malcolm B. Yarnell III, "History," in *Holman Illustrated Bible Dictionary*, revised ed., ed. Chad Brand et al. (Nashville: Holman Reference, 1998), 767–78. We shall take up the fuller meaning of the second terminus of history, its "end," at various points in these volumes. The final endpoint of history shall be considered in depth in the third volume, when we treat *eschatology*, which means the study of "the end" or "the last."

The Beginning

The quantitative meaning of "beginning," when applied to creation, refers to the original temporal starting point. An important example of the quantitative meaning of "beginning" can be found in Genesis 1:1, "In the beginning God created the heavens and the earth." William Sanford LaSor says the sentence structure indicates "beginning" here means "the first stage of a historical process or sequence."[29] Keil and Delitzsch agree but note the unique context. "*Reshith* in itself is a relative notion, indicating the commencement of a series of things or events; but here the context gives it the meaning of the very first beginning, the commencement of the world, when time itself began."[30] The creative activity of God starts history as his Spirit forms creation out of nothing (Gen. 1:2) and his Word utters their progress (Gen. 1:3, 6, 9).[31] "Beginning" in Genesis 1 obviously has a natural and limited, if unique, meaning.[32]

Sadly, the Enlightenment encouraged theologians to suppress any consideration other than the quantitative meaning. Even evangelical theologians have been reluctant

---

29. LaSor, "Beginning," 451.

30. C. F. Keil and F. Delitzsch, *Commentary on the Old Testament*, vol. 1, *The Pentateuch*, transl. James Martin (Grand Rapids: Eerdmans, 1985), 46–47.

31. Yarnell, *Who Is the Holy Spirit? Biblical Insights into His Divine Person* (Nashville: B&H Academic, 2019), 5–14.

32. In the history of Christian thought, *beginning* has been used in various quantitative ways. For instance, modern Christians typically use the term to describe a temporal event or a personal change. These uses focus upon creaturely meaning rather than absolute meaning, although they sometimes indicate a human encounter with God. Peter James Flamming found that modern Christians "use the word beginning" at three "levels."

The Temporal Level: "first as a simple notation about time."

The Transitional Level: "to suggest a significant transition in life."

The Redemptive Level: "beginning again at the deepest personal level."

Peter James Flamming, *God and Creation*, Layman's Library of Christian Doctrine (Nashville: Broadman Press, 1985), 21–26.

to refer to the qualitative meaning of absolute eternity. Howard Marshall, a generally orthodox writer, exemplified this concession. First, Marshall downplayed ontology while admitting the apostle John's reference in 1 John 1:1 indicated "the absolute beginning." Marshall treated God's absolute nature elusively[33] and relativized its importance by focusing on his work instead.[34]

The difficulty with modern exegesis is twofold. First, modern interpretation has been handicapped by a widespread reluctance to refer to the eternal God. Modern theologians speak of Jesus's work but refer only indirectly to divine being. Second, scholarship from previous eras is typically dismissed or discounted. Scholars today should reverse this trend and appropriate exegesis from the early church, the medieval period, and the Reformation.[35] Earlier theologians readily recognized the qualitative nature of "beginning" alongside its quantitative meanings.

The Absolute Beginning

Several passages in Scripture use the word *beginning* to point beyond our timebound existence. These uses take the reader to the origin of time and then wave beyond it toward eternity. In these cases, beginning takes on a qualitative meaning. They refer to the absolute beginning of every creaturely thing, God their Creator.

---

33. I. Howard Marshall, *The Epistles of John*, New International Commentary on the New Testament (Grand Rapids: Eerdmans, 1978), 101.

34. "Eternal life is found only in Jesus. He incorporates the life of God, which was with God at the beginning, and it is in him that God has revealed his life; the content of the Christian message is Jesus, the Word of life." Marshall, *The Epistles of John*, 106.

35. There has been some clumsiness in the treatment of theology proper since the Reformation.

Three Johannine uses of "beginning" in the New Testament are particularly relevant. First, at the beginning of his Gospel, John echoes Genesis 1:1 but exceeds the quantitative use of the term by Moses. John states, "In the beginning was the Word, and the Word was with God, and the Word was God" (John 1:1).

In the second passage, the apostle John likewise uses "beginning" in an absolute or eternal sense in his first epistle. There he wrote, "What was from the beginning, what we have heard, what we have seen with our eyes, what we have observed and have touched with our hands, concerning the word of life" (1 John 1:1).

"Beginning" in John 1:1 and 1 John 1:1 must be taken qualitatively as references to divine eternity. *Arche* in John 1:1 "refers to the existence of the Word prior to creation," hence "before time" or "in eternity."[36] When reading such allusive texts, we must be careful not to bind God in time in the rush to comprehend it. As the author of Hebrews reminds us, Melchizedek, the eternal Christ, has "neither beginning of days nor end of life" (Heb. 7:3).

In a third significant Johannine passage, at the conclusion of his Apocalypse, John used the term with an unmistakably absolute and personal divine meaning. The eternal Lord says repeatedly, "I am . . . the beginning and the end" (Rev. 21:6; 22:13; cf. Rev. 1:8, 17). The first statement at the end of time is made by the eternal Father, while the second is made by his eternal Son.

In all these texts, God is "the beginning," in the sense that every creaturely thing looks to the Creator as its absolute source. God the Trinity is eternal, creating and comprehending "the beginning and the end" of time (cf. Heb. 9:14). God the Trinity is eternal, so time is entirely relative from his perspective. The apostle Peter thus concludes, "With the Lord

---

36. LaSor, "Beginning," 451.

one day is like a thousand years, and a thousand years like one day" (2 Pet. 3:8).

Knowing the Eternal God

Christian history demonstrates that the classical assumption that we may access knowledge about the eternal God through his grace of revelation is preferable to the undue skepticism of Modernity. The enlightening responses of Gregory of Nazianzus, Augustine of Hippo, Thomas Aquinas, Martin Luther, John Calvin, and Dietrich Bonhoeffer together demonstrate the darkness of some recent philosophies.

Gregory of Nazianzus

Gregory led the ecumenical Council of Constantinople (381), which crafted the Nicene Creed still used in worship by orthodox Christians of all denominations around the world. In his famous theological orations, Gregory said human beings affirm God's nature, but we cannot define his nature due to God's utter otherness. "Yes, far more than these things does their transcendent cause, the incomprehensible and boundless nature pass understanding. I mean understanding what that nature is, not understanding that it exists."[37]

Gregory argued that we must respect both the truth of the transcendent God and remember our limited capacity. We must therefore learn to speak of God's eternal nature in two ways. Theology proper works "both by negation of what the thing is

---

37. Gregory of Nazianzus, *On God and Christ: The Five Theological Orations and Two Letters to Cledonius*, transl. Frederick Williams and Lionel Wickham (Crestwood, NY: St. Vladimir's Seminary Press, 2002), 40. Cf. Nazianzus, *On God and Christ*, 49–52.

not and also by positive assertion of what it is."[38] We must speak of God with rational certainty when he reveals himself, but we must resort to reverent worship where he does not.

Augustine of Hippo

Augustine approximated Gregory's theology. He conveyed three great truths about interpreting biblical references to the absolute God. First, the Johannine language of "beginning" points beyond the quantitative sign to an absolute reality by treating literal descriptions of God as true metaphors. The limits of human capability to know the eternal God require limited analogies to reveal the Creator. God reveals himself truly, but his glory exceeds our limits. The heavens and the earth reveal God: "The very fact that they are there proclaims that they were created." But creation remains below God, "for they are subject to change and variation."[39]

Second, since Genesis 1 is part of the biblical canon, Augustine read the words of Moses along with the words of the apostles. Genesis 1:3, which says that God spoke, necessarily echoes John 1:1, which says God's Word is God.[40] Creation is a work of the Word of God, who is "co-eternal" with God.[41] "The Beginning" indicates the truth of the personal divine Word, who is "for us" and "speaks to us."[42]

Third, Augustine differentiated divine eternity from creaturely time. "There was no time before heaven and earth were

---

38. Nazianzus, *On God and Christ*, 43. These two ways have become known as "positive theology" and "negative theology."

39. Augustine, *Confessions*, 256.

40. Contemporary biblical scholars are beginning to recover this orthodox hermeneutic. Richard B. Hays, *Reading Backwards: Figural Christology and the Fourfold Gospel Witness* (Waco, TX: Baylor University Press, 2016).

41. Augustine, *Confessions*, 259.

42. Augustine, *Confessions*, 259–60.

created."[43] The otherness of eternity can be discerned from divine immutability, the unchanging nature of God. Time is not co-eternal with God, "because you never change."[44] Augustine refused to elevate time to the same status as the co-eternal Word. There is no succession in eternity, for God is eternal. God and his Word transcend time.

Thomas Aquinas

The medieval theologians followed the trail blazed by Gregory and Augustine. Thomas Aquinas grounded divine eternity in divine immutability, and divine immutability in biblical revelation. On the one hand, because God is immutable, he is also eternal. Psalm 101, among other texts, requires this connection.[45] On the other hand, humans are mutable, so we may not impose our temporal understandings on God.[46] Aquinas said we must receive knowledge of the eternal God by faith since our minds can never entirely comprehend the eternal God. We must speak of God by way of negation or "remotion."[47]

---

43. Augustine, *Confessions*, 263.

44. Augustine, *Confessions*, 263.

45. "To this truth divine authority offers witness. The Psalmist says: 'But Thou, O Lord, endurest forever'; and he goes on to say: 'But Thou art always the selfsame: and Thy years shall not fail' (Ps. 101:13, 28)." Thomas Aquinas, *Summa Contra Gentiles*, vol. 1, *Book One: God*, transl. Anton C. Pegis (Notre Dame, IN: University of Notre Dame, 1975), 99.

46. "Since, however, we have shown that God is absolutely immutable, He is eternal, lacking all beginning or end." *Summa Contra Gentiles*, 98.

47. "For, by its immensity, the divine substance surpasses every form that our intellect reaches; thus, we are unable to apprehend it by knowing what it is. Yet we are able to have some knowledge of it by knowing what it is not." Aquinas, *Summa Contra Gentiles*, 96–97.

The Reformers

Although they critically evaluated the whole theological tradition, the Reformers retained these ontological truths. Luther said John's statements teach that, "in the very beginning—antedating the creation of the universe, of the heavens, or of any other creature—the Word existed, that this Word was with God, that God was this Word, and that this Word had existed from all eternity." Although Luther reluctantly employed analogy, he came to the same theological conclusion, warning that God "is far too lofty for our reason."[48] John Calvin deepened Luther's reticence but likewise affirmed the tradition's conclusions.[49]

Dietrich Bonhoeffer

As we saw above, liberal theologians denigrated human access to eternity and diminished the absolute meaning of "beginning" during the Enlightenment. However, orthodox theologians still recall the traditional interpretation. For instance, Dietrich Bonhoeffer affirmed the limits of human knowledge about the absolute beginning,[50] the grace of a divine

---

48. "Nothing but faith can comprehend this. Whoever refuses to accept it in faith, to believe it before he understands it, but insists on exploring it with his reason and his five senses, let him persist in this if he will. But our mind will never master this doctrine; it is far too lofty for our reason." Martin Luther, *Luther's Works*, vol. 22, *Sermons on the Gospel of St. John,* ed. Jaroslav Pelikan (St. Louis, MO: Concordia Publishing, 1957), 8.

49. John Calvin, *Calvin's Commentaries*, vol. 22, *Commentaries on the Catholic Epistles*, transl. John Owen (reprint, Grand Rapids: Baker Book House, 1996), 156–60.

50. "That the Bible should speak of the beginning provokes the world, provokes us. For we cannot speak of the beginning. Where the beginning begins, there our thinking stops; there it comes to an end." Dietrich Bonhoeffer, *Creation and Fall: A Theological Exposition of Genesis 1-3*, transl.

revelation which overcomes those limits,[51] and the existence of absolute eternity beyond creation's temporal beginning.[52]

Bonhoeffer didn't stop there. He also said that the absolute God who created us has the freedom to resurrect us.[53] God gave us temporal bodily life in the beginning, and God will renew our bodily reality by grace at the end. Of our hope in the resurrection, we have more to learn.

Releasing Our Beloved to the Eternal God

Death reminds human beings that eternity is beyond our grasp, but the Christian has a hope in life beyond death. Recently, my brothers and I laid our mother's body to rest as she went to be with Jesus. There is no more intense moment than during a funeral for the truth about eternity to remind us of its relationship to our everyday lives.

My brothers and I found great comfort in many biblical passages. However, one of the most meaningful came in

Douglas Stephen Bax, vol. 3, *Dietrich Bonhoeffer Works* (Minneapolis: Fortress Press, 1997), 25.

51. "The one who was in the beginning, the very God, Christ, the Holy Spirit. No one can speak of the beginning but the one who was in the beginning." Bonhoeffer, *Creation and Fall*, 29. "God alone tells us that God is in the beginning; God testifies of God by no other means than through this word. . . . God wills to be found." Bonhoeffer, *Creation and Fall*, 30.

52. "From this it follows that the beginning is not to be thought of in temporal terms. We can always go back behind a temporal beginning. But the beginning is distinguished by something utterly unique—unique not in the sense of a number . . . but in a qualitative sense, . . . that it is completely free." Bonhoeffer, *Creation and Fall*, 32.

53. "The world exists in the midst of nothing, which means in the beginning. This means nothing else than that it exists wholly by God's freedom. What has been created belongs to the Creator. It means also, however, that the God of creation, of the utter beginning, is the God of the resurrection." Bonhoeffer, *Creation and Fall*, 34.

Psalm 90, which was given the hopeful title, *Domine refugium* ("Lord, our refuge"), in Christian tradition.[54] As we let our mother go, we remembered, "Lord, you have been our refuge in every generation" (Ps. 90:1).

Because our God is eternal, one generation may let go of another in Christ. "Before the mountains were born, before you gave birth to the earth and the world, from eternity to eternity, you are God" (Ps. 90:2). Such an eternal God offers each generation hope that not only our parents but our children will see his glory (Ps. 90:16). In his person, Jesus Christ unites divine eternity with our human time. And in his work, he has opened the door to an eternal hope beyond our wildest imaginations to conceive.

Study Questions

1. How would you define *time*?

2. How would you define *eternity*?

3. What is your personal experience with the eternal God?

Suggested Resources

- Peter Brown, *Augustine of Hippo, A Biography*

- Anne Dutton, *A Brief Account of the Gracious Dealings of God*

- Herbert Butterfield, *Christianity and History*

---

54. Thomas Cranmer, ed., *The Book of Common Prayer* (New York: Oxford University Press, 1969), 390.

CHAPTER FIVE

Is God Trinity?

◆

THE TRINITY IS DEEMED "THE central dogma of Christian theology."[1] That is a high claim for a typically reserved academic dictionary. Most evangelicals agree that the doctrine is true, yet the Trinity received little attention in the pulpit during the last few centuries.[2] As a result, when American beliefs are surveyed, we find widespread confusion over its meaning. A majority affirm the Trinity in theory, but their understanding is perplexed. In large numbers, they describe the Son as a created person and the Holy Spirit as a force rather than a person.[3] Both opinions are, sadly, heretical.

---

1. F. L. Cross and E. A. Livingstone, eds., *The Oxford Dictionary of the Christian Church*, 2nd ed. (New York: Oxford University Press, 1974), 1394.

2. Malcolm B. Yarnell III, "Preaching," in *The Trinity in the Canon: A Biblical, Theological, Historical, and Practical Proposal*, ed. Brandon D. Smith (Nashville: B&H Academic, 2023), 369–400.

3. Aaron Earls, "Theology: Truth or Opinion?" Lifeway Research (September 28, 2020; https://research.lifeway.com/2020/09/08/americans-hold-complex-conflicting-religious-beliefs-according-to-latest-state-of-theology-study/).

In this chapter we will explore the doctrine of the eternal oneness and threeness of God, that God is one being and three Persons. We will first examine Scripture, then explore how the doctrine developed in church history. Finally, we propose a short ten-point system for teaching the Trinity in your church today.

The Trinity in the Bible

The Old Testament Witness

The Hebrew Bible emphasizes the unity or oneness of God. The basic confession in Hebrew worship is known as the Shema.[4] The Shema emphasizes the believer's sole devotion to the only God: "Listen, Israel: The Lᴏʀᴅ our God, the Lᴏʀᴅ is one. Love the Lᴏʀᴅ your God with all your heart, with all your soul, and with all your strength" (Deut. 6:4–5). According to Jesus, the unique devotion to God demanded by the Shema constitutes "the most important" commandment (Mark 12:28–30). God alone requires our singular love.

While the unique nature of God is in the greatest commandment, the Hebrew text includes markers of divine plurality. Several indications of God's threeness are found in the first chapter of the Bible. For instance, the first three verses indicate a threefold economy in God's action: "In the beginning," God created everything (Gen. 1:1); the Spirit of God hovered over creation (Gen. 1:2); and God created through his word (Gen. 1:3). In addition, the common name for God (*Elohim*) is a plural term used in a singular way (Gen. 1:1–5).[5] Finally, God refers to himself in the first chapter with a plural

---

4. The first Hebrew word of the confession, *Shema*, means "Listen!"

5. "More probable is the view that *'elohim* comes from *'eloah* as a unique development of the Hebrew Scriptures and represents chiefly the plurality of the persons in the Trinity of the godhead." Jack B. Scott, "אלה," ed. R. Laird

verb and a plural pronoun when creating the man and the woman (Gen. 1:26), as well as at other times (Gen. 3:22; 11:7; 18:2–3; Isa. 6:8).

Some scholars believe certain Old Testament texts which unite the Lord with his messenger, "the angel of the Lord" (Gen. 16:7–14; Exod. 3:2–4), indicate a preincarnate appearance of Christ.[6] The Old Testament also treats "the Word" (Ps. 147:15–18), "the Spirit" (Ps. 104:30), and "Wisdom" (Prov. 8:22–31) as persons with agency who share in the divine perfections of eternity and power with Elohim. Drawing on this Old Testament pattern, the New Testament apostles commonly used "the Word" as another name for the Son of God and "the Spirit" as another name for the Holy Spirit. The early church fathers stood on solid ground, therefore, when asserting "Wisdom" refers to the Son of God. After all, Proverbs 8:25 indicates Wisdom was eternally begotten of the Father.[7]

The New Testament Witness to the One Who Is Three

Where references to the Trinity remain implicit in the Old Testament, they become explicit in the New Testament. Due to the numerous references to the Trinity, over a thousand according to one scholar,[8] we limit our review to a few significant passages. As we walk through these texts, consider the unity of God, the differentiation of the three persons,

---

Harris, Gleason L. Archer Jr., and Bruce K. Waltke, *Theological Wordbook of the Old Testament* (Chicago: Moody Press, 1999), 41.

6. Others argue the appearances are a theophany rather than a Christophany. René A. López, "Identifying the 'Angel of the Lord' in the Book of Judges: A Model for Reconsidering the Referent in Other Old Testament Loci," *Bulletin for Biblical Research* 20 (2010): 1–18.

7. Maurice Dowling, "Proverbs 8:22–31 in the Christology of the Early Fathers," *Irish Biblical Studies* 24 (2002): 116–17.

8. Samuel Clarke reviewed 1,251 texts. Clarke, *The Scripture-Doctrine of the Trinity, in Three Parts* (London, 1712).

and the relations between the three. Note also how God as Trinity acts toward his creation. These acts are known as the triune "economy." God's divine acts issue forth from his being. Scholars refer to the Trinitarian being with terms like *ontology*, *nature*, or *essence*. Finally, mark how the three Persons are worshipped as the one God.

According to Jesus, baptism is the new believer's initial act of public worship and follows a set form. After new "disciples" are made, the church must "baptize them in the name of the Father and of the Son and of the Holy Spirit" (Matt. 28:19). "The name" is another way to speak of the one true God we worship (Matt. 6:9). In baptism we worship the one name, yet we worship three names, "Father" and "Son" and "Holy Spirit." The conjunction "and" marks both an unrelenting equality and an unceasing distinction between the Three. Since worshipping one God in three Persons constitutes our first act of worship, God's eternal Trinitarian identity grounds the entire Christian faith.

Second Corinthians 13:14 (NASB1995) conveys a second yet ongoing act of Trinitarian worship, the Benediction: "The grace of the Lord Jesus Christ, and the love of God, and the fellowship of the Holy Spirit, be with all of you." Where the Great Commission teaches ontological equality and unity between the three Persons, the Benediction teaches economic equality and unity between the three Persons. The Benediction ascribes the divine acts of "grace," "love," and "fellowship" to distinct persons, but the same acts are ascribed to each of the three Persons throughout the Pauline writings. Again, the conjunction "and" marks both an unrelenting equality and an unceasing distinction between the Three. The work of the one God is indivisible between the three Persons. The Benediction is likewise a prayer, indicating the Trinitarian identity is the object of biblically led worship.

Many New Testament texts address the three Persons together, while others focus on the relations between two

Persons. The interpretive method of "relational exegesis" or "personal exegesis"[9] asks the question, "Which divine Person is speaking to or acting upon another divine Person?" This method allows us to discover truths about each Person in their relation to one another. For instance, some passages provide information about the relationship between the Father and the Son, others disclose the relationship between the Father and the Spirit, while still others relate the Son to the Spirit.

The New Testament Witness to the Son's Eternal Generation

In John 1:18, we learn about the unique relation between the Father and the Son. The Greek phrase *monogenes theos* may be strictly translated "the only begotten God" or, loosely, "the one and only Son, who is himself God." Accenting the intimate relation, John adds that the Son is "in the lap" or "bosom" of the Father. Due to their divine unity, the Son may reveal the Father. The Father is seen by no other than his Son; so the Son alone "interprets" the Father to us. Orthodox teachers thus describe the relation between the first two Persons of the Trinity as *eternal generation.*

John 3:16 tells us God "gave" his only begotten Son to the world to bring eternal life to all who believe. This indicates the Son's generation is prior to the incarnation, that generation is eternal. Hebrews 1:5–6 reiterates the Son's eternal relation to the Father is "generated" or "begotten." The Son was "begotten" (Greek *gegenneka*) from the Father in eternity; the "firstborn" (Greek *prototokos*) was then "brought into the world." When Proverbs 8:25 speaks of "Wisdom" as being "given birth" (Hebrew *taba*ʿ) before creation, we understand

---

9. Scholars use the Greek term *prosopon*, "person," or "prosopological exegesis" rather than "personal exegesis."

this refers to the eternal generation of God the Son from God the Father.

Scripture speaks of the perfect God in his relations, so one may not imagine the language of "generation" in a rude or carnal sense. The Son's being begotten should be taken in a holy and exalted way. The ontological relation between God the Father and God the Son is one of eternal generation. The life of the Son is "eternal" (1 John 1:2), and the Father is "eternal" because he has an eternal Son (Isa. 9:6). The being of the Son comes from the Father, for the Father gives himself entirely to the Son. The generation of the Son indicates the divine nature is entirely, perfectly, and eternally the possession of the Son just as the divine attributes remain entirely, perfectly, and eternally the possession of the Father.

Jesus thus asserts, "Everything the Father has is mine" (John 16:15). And John can write both that "the Word was with God," indicating the eternal distinction between the Father and the Son, and that "the Word was God," indicating the perfect identity of the Son with the Father (John 1:1). Paul can thus proclaim both that the Father has "all his fullness dwell" in the Son (Col. 1:19) and that the Son need not grasp after "equality with God" (Phil. 2:6).[10] Peter can thus profess of Christ, "You are the . . . Son of the living God" (Matt. 16:16). Thomas can thus wholeheartedly shout of the resurrected Jesus standing before him, "My Lord and my God!" (John 20:28). Universally recognizing this profound truth, at the end of time, "every knee will bow" and "every tongue will confess that Jesus Christ is Lord" (Phil. 2:10–11).

The New Testament teaches Christ is the eternally begotten Son of God the Father. His generation entails possession of all the divine attributes by the Son as by the Father. One

---

10. The Son does not relinquish his deity in the incarnation. The eternal Son "empties" himself in the sense of "humbling" himself as an act of grace toward humanity (Phil. 2:7–8).

may never say the Son is less than the Father in wisdom, power, or authority, in righteousness, holiness, or love, or in any other divine perfection. The orthodox theologian must exalt the Son just as he or she must exalt the Father, for he or she is baptized in the one name and worships the one God. The teacher who would diminish the Son in any way, including his authority (Matt. 28:18), must be avoided. All creation must worship Christ as one with the Father (Rev. 5:14).

The New Testament Witness to the Spirit's Eternal Procession

The Holy Spirit is also related eternally to the Father and to the Son, and his relation also entails full equality with the Father and the Son. The worship due the Spirit is the same as the worship due the Father and the Son. The Spirit is essentially God yet personally distinct from the Father and the Son. We call the eternal relation of the Spirit "procession" in emulation of Scripture. John 15:26 says "the Counselor," the Holy Spirit, "proceeds from [Greek *ekporeuetai*] the Father." Where the Son's eternal relation to the Father is called "generation," the Spirit's relation is "procession."

Some surmise the Spirit proceeds not only from the Father but also from the Son. The Bible does not explicitly use "proceeding" for the Spirit's relation to the Son, but indications abound of a similar relation. Just like the Father "sent" the Son (John 20:21) and "will send" the Spirit (John 14:26), the Son "sends" the Spirit (John 15:26). Indeed, the Son "breathed" the Holy Spirit upon the disciples so that the Spirit would come to them (John 20:22). On the basis of such evidence, Western Christians added the term *Filioque* (Latin "and the Son") to the Nicene Creed. We can thereby say the Holy Spirit eternally "proceeds from the Father and the Son."

The eternal relations of the Holy Spirit to God the Father and to God the Son prompt us to insist the Holy Spirit is God in essence. The Holy Spirit is not merely the power of God, although he definitively acts with divine power. The Spirit possesses the divine perfections with the Father and the Son. "The Spirit is the one who gives life" (John 6:63), "convicts the world" (John 16:8), and freely "takes from" and distributes knowledge which belongs only to the Father and the Son (John 16:14–15). The Spirit brought life originally (Gen. 2:7) and sovereignly generates new life (John 3:5–8). He is the "spirit of judgment" and "spirit of burning" (Isa. 4:4). The Spirit acts with divine authority, is ascribed divine perfections, and thus must be worshipped as God.

Worship of the Holy Spirit is revealed in various ways. For instance, to sin against "the Holy Spirit" (Acts 5:3) is to sin against "God" (Acts 5:4). Moreover, the Father and the Son and the sevenfold Spirit, united as the "one" God "on the throne," never bow before the throne, although all creatures must (Rev. 5:6; 13–14). Negatively, blaspheming the Spirit is so heinous that it is unforgiveable (Mark 3:28–29). Positively, receiving baptism in the name of the Spirit (Matt. 28:19) and blessing with the Spirit (2 Cor. 13:13) indicate worship of the Spirit with the Father and the Son. We know, we are saved by, and we worship one God, who is Father and Son and Holy Spirit.

The New Testament's Diverse Triadic Patterns

The New Testament reveals triadic patterns about God. Leo Garrett surveyed nine such passages, while Rodrick Durst conducted a thorough and prayerful reading of the New Testament, examining how the "triadic orders" form a "trinitarian matrix."[11] Durst concluded, "There are seventy-five different times that New Testament passages talk about all three Persons of the Trinity, and every one of those six different orderings has at least seven passages that use that specific order." These "diverse" patterns indicate God is both "consistent" and "flexible" in how he works as Trinity.[12]

The prepositions used of the three Persons reveal similar triadic patterns. In their relations, the Father is typically referred to as "of whom," indicating origin; while the Son is spoken of as "through whom," indicating instrumentality; and the Spirit is "in whom," indicating locality. However, the same prepositions are applied to the other Persons. The New Testament also applies "of" (*ech* or *apo*) to the Son (John 1:16) and the Spirit (John 3:6); "through" (*dia*) to the Father (1 Cor. 1:9) and the Spirit (1 Cor. 12:8); and "in" (*en*) to the Son (Rom. 8:2) and the Father (Eph. 3:9). The Three remain, therefore, equally related even as a typical order is revealed in the seminal act of Trinitarian worship in baptism reinforced by the eternal relations of origin.

The Trinity in Christian History

The early church's major doctrinal controversies and dogmatic conclusions swirled around Christianity's two central teachings, that God is Trinity and that the gospel of Jesus Christ saves. The classical creeds of the Christian churches reflect these two emphases. The Apostles' Creed, the Nicene Creed, and the Athanasian Creed simultaneously emphasize

---

11. James Leo Garrett Jr., *Systematic Theology: Biblical, Historical, and Evangelical*, vol. 1, 2nd ed. (North Richland Hills, TX: Bibal Press), 314; Rodrick K. Durst, *Reordering the Trinity: Six Movements of God in the New Testament* (Grand Rapids: Kregel, 2016), 16–21.

12. Durst, *Reordering the Trinity*, 334.

the doctrine of the Trinity and the gospel.[13] The creeds were developed from Scripture and are useful for worship, for teaching the faith, and for refuting the recurring problem of anti-Trinitarian heresy.

The Development of the Creeds

The classical creeds received their Trinitarian structure from the baptismal worship required by Christ. The earliest churches would teach new believers the faith, then require its restatement before receiving baptism. Cyril of Jerusalem's famous *Catechetical Lectures* provide an example of Trinitarian teaching during the forty days which led up to a new believer receiving baptism and first communion at Easter.[14] As Christian teachers explained each Person of the Trinity mentioned in the baptismal act, they worked to provide a helpful account of who each Person is and what he does.

For instance, the Apostles' Creed is comprised of three articles. Each article begins respectively with affirmation of a divine person: "I believe in God the Father," "I believe in Jesus Christ," and "I believe in the Holy Spirit." After each personal affirmation comes a longer depiction of who that divine Person is and what he does. The threefold order follows the Great Commission. The longest article focuses on the second divine Person, accentuating his taking of human nature and the gospel we preach.

---

13. Please consult the appendices of Yarnell, *God the Trinity*, which contains contemporary translations of these three major creeds. A fourth major creed, the Chalcedonian Formula, which teaches Jesus Christ is one person with two natures, will be discussed in the second volume of this series.

14. *The Works of Saint Cyril of Jerusalem*, transl. Leo P. McCauley and Anthony A. Stephenson, 2 vols. (Washington, DC: Catholic University of America Press, 1968–1970), 1:91–249, 2:4–140

The details of each article in these representative ecumenical creeds[15] were carefully reasoned to ensure that what the apostles taught was preserved by the churches. The earliest forms of the classical creeds derive from scriptural passages recalling the apostolic church's worship of God. Matthew 28:19 and 2 Corinthians 13:13 provided their Trinitarian structure, while 1 Corinthians 8:6, Philippians 2:5–11, and 1 Timothy 3:16 provided their Christological outline. As the church exposited the New Testament writings, which along with the Old Testament became the church's canonical "rule of faith," they read it according to the Trinitarian and Christological "rule of faith" they learned from the apostles.[16]

In fulfillment of 1 Corinthians 11:19, which prophesied the rise of heresies, orthodox teachers learned to describe God properly while responding to false teachers. First, the earliest churches refuted mythical Gnosticism by teaching that God the Father, not a subsequent aeon, is "Creator." Second, when the churches faced questions about the Son, they returned to Scripture to discern his identity. They proclaimed in biblical terms and contemporary speech that the Son is one with God yet distinct from the Father. The Nicene Creed thus established the Lord Jesus Christ is "the Son of God, the only-begotten, begotten of the Father before all ages; Light of Light; true God of true God; begotten, not made; of one essence with the Father." Third, in response to the Pneumatomachians, the doctrine of the Spirit was clarified at

---

15. *Ecumenical* means the creed is universally accepted among true Christian churches.

16. On the twofold yet intertwined meaning of the canon or "rule" of faith as both Scripture and the summary of apostolic teaching as Trinity and gospel, please see chapters 8 and 11 in David S. Dockery and Malcolm B. Yarnell III, *Special Revelation and Scripture* (Nashville: B&H Academic, 2024).

the Council of Constantinople in 381. Those "Spirit-fighters" were successfully contradicted.[17]

Anti-Trinitarian Heresies

The greatest heresy confronting the early church came from the Alexandrian presbyter Arius. Arius reacted against an earlier Trinitarian heresy, Modalism, which taught the three Persons were really one person. He rightly rejected Modalism's loss of personal distinctions but wrongly diminished the Son. The Arians taught that the Son had less eternity, less authority, and a lesser nature than the Father. Although they said the Son could be worshipped, their ontological "Subordinationism" proved theologically unstable. Alexander, the bishop of Alexandria, helped lead the first ecumenical council, which met in Nicea in 325, to condemn Arianism. The Nicene phrase, "of one essence with the Father," was a direct, necessary, and helpful rejection of the Arian claim the Son possessed a different nature.[18]

Three major heresies regarding the Trinity arose in the history of the church. The first major heresy, Modalism or Sabellianism, maintained the divine unity by erasing the eternal distinctions between the three Persons. Modalism can be found today in aberrant groups like Oneness Pentecostalism.

The second major heresy, Subordinationism or Arianism, reduced the deity of the Son and of the Holy Spirit to preserve the uniqueness of the Father. Subordinationism can be

---

17. J. N. D. Kelly, *Early Christian Doctrines*, Revised ed. (San Francisco: HarperCollins, 1960), 83–88, 226–37, 255–63.

18. Rowan Williams, *Arius: Heresy and Tradition*, Revised ed. (Grand Rapids: Eerdmans, 2001), 95–116; Robert C. Gregg and Dennis E. Groh, *Early Arianism: A View of Salvation* (Philadelphia; Fortress Press, 1981), 1–30.

found today in non-Christian groups like Unitarianism and Jehovah's Witnesses.

The third major heresy, Tritheism, pushes the difference between the Father and the Son and the Holy Spirit to the point of compromising the divine unity. Contemporary teachers of social Trinitarianism have been accused of tending toward Tritheism.

Characteristic of each major heresy is an emphasis on one aspect of Scripture's teaching about God to the detriment of other aspects. Human illustrations and human ideologies too easily replace the subtle biblical portraits of God, so they must be used with care and reticence. Even though we find illustrations and ideas helpful in proclamation, we must be careful not to emphasize any one truth to the exclusion of other revealed truths about the Trinitarian God.

Contemporary Developments

We noted above that the Trinity has been widely circumvented in recent centuries. For instance, Baptist churches long held a healthy doctrine of the Trinity through widespread use of the *New Hampshire Confession of Faith* (1833, revised 1853). That confession's article on the Trinity includes clear affirmations of divine unity, divine threeness, personal equality, indivisible operations, proper operations, and the divine worship due the Trinity.[19] The second article of that confession states,

---

19. Absent from this article of the *New Hampshire Confession*, however, is a description of the eternal relations of origin. This omission can be found in other American free church denominations too. Consult, for instance, "Article II—Godhead," in the leading faith statement of American Dispensationalism. "Board of Incorporate Members' Update on the DTS Doctrinal Statement," *Dallas Theological Seminary* (May 2022; https://www.dts.edu/2022-dts-doctrinal-statement-strengthening/).

> We believe that there is one, and only one
> living and true God, an infinite intelli-
> gent Spirit, whose name is JEHOVAH, the
> Maker and Supreme Ruler of heaven and
> earth; inexpressibly glorious in holiness; and
> worthy of all possible honor, confidence, and
> love; that in the unity of the Godhead there
> are three persons, the Father, the Son, and the
> Holy Ghost; equal in every divine perfection
> and executing distinct but harmonious offices
> in the great work of redemption.[20]

Despite this thicker description, a thin conception of the Trinity was chosen for the influential *Abstract of Principles* (1858) of The Southern Baptist Theological Seminary. The theologians of Southern Seminary were led by James Boyce, slaveowner and student of the Presbyterian fundamental- ist, Charles Hodge.[21] Their abstract did not clearly affirm Trinitarian ontology but focused on the Trinitarian economy: "God is revealed to us as Father, Son and Holy Spirit each with distinct personal attributes, but without division of nature, essence or being."[22]

---

20. In the 1853 edition, "that in the unity of the Godhead there are three persons, the Father, . . . ," replaced the 1833 phrase that God is "revealed under the personal and relative distinctions of, the Father, . . ." William L. Lumpkin, *Baptist Confessions of Faith*, Revised ed. (Valley Forge, PA: 1969), 362. This revision indicates the publisher was aware of the potential Modalism of the previous statement.

21. For a fuller treatment of Baptists and Trinitarian theology, see Malcolm B. Yarnell III, "Baptists, Classic Trinitarianism, and the Christian Tradition," in *Baptists and the Christian Tradition: Towards an Evangelical Baptist Catholicity*, ed. Matthew Y. Emerson, Christopher W. Morgan, and R. Lucas Stamps (Nashville: B&H Academic, 2020), 55–79.

22. James Petigru Boyce, *Abstract of Systematic Theology* (1887; reprint, Hanford, CA: Den Dulk Christian Foundation, [n.d]), Appendix B.

In 1925, when the Southern Baptist Convention adopted
its first convention-wide confession of faith, the *New
Hampshire Confession* favored by The Southwestern Baptist
Theological Seminary provided the structure. But the chair of
the committee, Edgar Young Mullins of Southern Seminary,
inserted the *Abstract of Principles'* weaker Trinitarianism. *The
Baptist Faith and Message* allowed for Modalist interpretations until the article was later revised. The revision of 2000
inserted the term "triune," clarifying God was eternally triune,
not merely triune in the economy of revelation.[23] However,
"the Trinity remains one of the most underdeveloped doctrines in the new Baptist Faith & Message."[24]

Contemporary evangelical theologians have begun to
address the doctrine of the Trinity more frequently. Fine
short studies have been published by evangelical scholars like
Rodrick Durst, Michael Reeves, and Scott Swain.[25] However,
inordinate use of the Trinity in debates over human gender
roles prompted the steadfast evangelical theologian Millard
Erickson to warn against "tampering with the Trinity."[26] In

23. The 1925 Baptist Faith and Message stated, "The eternal God
reveals Himself to us as Father, Son, and Holy Spirit . . ." Lumpkin,
Baptist Confessions of Faith, 393; Benjamin S. Cole, "Significance of
1 Word Noted in SBC's Updated Statement of Beliefs," Baptist Press
(November 3, 2003; https://www.baptistpress.com/resource-library/news/
significance-of-1-word-noted-in-sbcs-updated-statement-of-beliefs/).

24. James Leo Garrett Jr., "Theology Professor Examines Background to
Statement Changes" (2000), in *The Collected Writings of James Leo Garrett Jr.,
1950–2015*, ed. Wyman Lewis Richardson, vol. 2 (Eugene, OR: Wipf and
Stock, 2018), 64.

25. Michael Reeves, *Delighting in the Trinity: An Introduction to the
Christian Faith* (Downers Grove, IL: IVP Academic, 2012); Scott R.
Swain, *The Trinity: An Introduction* (Wheaton, IL: Crossway, 2020); idem,
The Trinity and the Bible: On Theological Interpretation (Bellingham, WA:
Lexham Academic, 2021).

26. Millard J. Erickson, *Who's Tampering with the Trinity? An Assessment
of the Subordination Debate* (Grand Rapids: Kregel, 2009).

2016, evangelicals who promote the novel doctrine of Eternal Functional Subordination reversed their denial of eternal generation and nominally reaffirmed Nicene orthodoxy. Despite these helpful reverses, they still retained the subordination of the Son's authority. On a positive note, however, a growing evangelical consensus has reaffirmed the classical ascription of equality of authority to the three Persons, refused to divide the divine nature and will, and recalled the biblical and creedal terminology of the relations of origin.[27]

The Trinity in Theology

Ten truths about the Trinity are held by orthodox Christian teachers. The first six deal with Trinitarian ontology[28] while the remainder describe the Trinitarian economy.

One God

We must affirm the unity or oneness of God. Applying the language of "nature," "substance," or "essence" to God's unity has proven helpful. God is eternally one, so we speak of the three Persons as possessing the same nature or essence (Latin *substantia*, Greek *ousia*). Classical Christian language regarding the divine essence finds parallels in the biblical terms

---

27. Keith S. Whitfield, ed., *Trinitarian Theology: Theological Models and Doctrinal Application* (Nashville: B&H Academic, 2019). The sixteenth-century Evangelical Anabaptist theologian, Pilgram Marpeck, ascribed equality of "authority" to all three Persons of the Trinity in his *Verantwortung*. Translation in Malcolm B. Yarnell III, *The Formation of Christian Doctrine* (Nashville: B&H Academic, 2007), 84. Cf. Michael F. Bird and Scott Harrower, eds., *Trinity without Hierarchy: Reclaiming Nicene Orthodoxy in Evangelical Theology* (Grand Rapids: Kregel, 2019).

28. "Trinitarian ontology" refers to the internal being of God, while "Trinitarian economy" refers to the external acts of God upon his creation.

theios (Acts 17:29), *theiotes* (Rom. 1:20), and *theotes* (Col. 2:9). "Nature" is also connoted in biblical terms like *morphe* (Phil. 2:6) and *pleroma* (Col. 1:19). Tertullian of Carthage, therefore, stood on good ground when he became the first to say the "Unity" of the "Trinity" is in God's one "substance."[29] There are not three gods or three lords with three natures and three wills, but one Lord God with one nature and one will.

Three Persons

We must simultaneously affirm the threeness of God. We may speak of three "persons" (Latin *personae*, Greek *hypostaseis*), because Hebrews 1:3 uses *hypostasis* ("nature" or "person") to describe that aspect of the Father of which the Son has "the exact expression." The long history of Trinitarian theological conversation, however, warns against imposing a worldly definition of "person." A human person is one who faces another in relationship; a divine person eternally faces the other divine persons. To avoid loosening the concept of the divine "person" from the divine "substance," while still not confusing the concepts, the medieval theologian Thomas Aquinas defined the divine persons as "subsisting relations."[30] We might say the divine persons are the eternal realities who relate to one another yet fully share the divine nature without confusion, separation, addition, or division.

29. Tertullian, *Against Praxeas*, in *Latin Christianity: Its Founder, Tertullian*, Ante-Nicene Fathers, vol. 3, ed. Alexander Roberts, James Donaldson, and A. Cleveland Coxe (1885; reprint, Peabody, MA: Hendrickson, 1994), 598.

30. Thomas Aquinas, *Summa Theologica*, vol. 1, transl. Fathers of the English Dominican Province (1911; reprint, Westminster, MD: Christian Classics, 1948), 155–60.

Equality

The equality of the divine Persons is made clear in the baptismal formula commanded by Christ (Matt. 28:19) and in the Benediction inspired by the Holy Spirit (2 Cor. 13:13). In both passages, the Greek conjunction *kai* ("and") indicates an equality of relationship and not a hierarchy. The Son of God, therefore, calls God "his own Father, making himself equal to God" (John 5:18), speaks of sharing divine glory with the Father "before the world existed" (John 17:5), and claims, "Everything the Father has is mine" (John 16:15). Likewise, Jesus said the Spirit freely "takes from what is mine" (John 16:15b). while Paul said the Spirit knows everything about God (1 Cor. 2:10–11). Indeed, "the Lord is the Spirit" (2 Cor. 3:17). These and like passages teach a radical equality between the three Persons. The Athanasian Creed thus affirms, "What the Father is, so is the Son, and so is the Holy Spirit."

Eternal Relations of Origin

Who is the Father, and how does he relate to the Son and the Holy Spirit? The fourth-century Cappadocian Fathers— Basil of Caesarea, Gregory of Nazianzus, and Gregory of Nyssa—examined Scripture to discern how the three divine Persons relate to one another.[31] Expositing the relevant biblical passages, they learned the Father is the eternal source of the Godhead, that the Son is begotten of the Father eternally, and that the Spirit proceeds eternally. That the Son is generate

---

31. The five "theological orations" of Gregory of Nazianzus should be required reading for every student training for Christian ministry. They are masterpieces of theological interpretation of Scripture and clearly retell the biblical revelation of God. The clearest modern translation is in Gregory of Nazianzus, *On God and Christ: The Five Theological Orations and Two Letters to Cledonius,* transl. Frederick Williams and Lionel Wickham (Yonkers, NY: St. Vladimir's Seminary Press, 2002).

and the Holy Spirit proceeds entails full participation in the deity of the Father. Via the eternal relations of origin, we learn the fullness of the Godhead's perfection is in each of the Three without any diminishing.

Order

Does the equality of the three Persons erase their ordered distinctions? The simple answer is no, but we must also separate the biblical portrayal of order in the Godhead (Greek *taxis*) from human orders. Limited and sinful human minds are prone to fashion mythological hierarchies of natures, powers, and authorities. Attempts to establish extrabiblical pyramids abound in every human era, from the medieval "divine right of kings" and "great chain of being" to modern racism and paternalism. Some have misused the Bible to buttress such ideas.[32] Arius fashioned a natural patriarchy between the Father and the Son, thereby fostering the heresy of "Subordinationism." Against Arian impiety, Athanasius of Alexandria taught Christians to garner theology not for philosophy, society, or politics but from careful biblical exegesis.[33] The Father as the font of the Trinity entails no difference in nature, dignity, or authority between the three Persons.

---

32. John Neville Figgis, *The Divine Right of Kings*, 2nd ed. (Cambridge: Cambridge University Press, 1914); E. M. W. Tillyard, *The Elizabethan World Picture* (New York: Penguin, 1943), 33–90; T. B. Maston, *The Conscience of a Christian* (Waco: Word, 1971), 113–19.

33. Athanasius should also be required reading for every minister. Athanasius, *On the Incarnation: The Treatise* De Incarnatione Verbi Dei, introduced by C. S. Lewis, transl. C.S.M.V. (Crestwood, NY: St. Vladimir's Seminary Press, 1996). On the Arian interplay of theology and politics, see George Huntston Williams, "Christology and Church-State Relations in the Fourth Century," [two parts] *Church History* 20.3 (1951): 3–33, and 20.4 (1951): 3–26.

Perichoresis

John of Damascus said the Three "have their being in each other." His Greek term, *perichoresis*, which can be translated as "mutual indwelling," comprehends the interpersonal relations of the one God.[34] The term summarizes the statements of Jesus that "I am in the Father and the Father is in me" (John 14:10–11). Similarly, although Jesus left the disciples, he could still say, "I am coming to you" (v. 19). The relationship between the Son and the Spirit is so intertwined that the Son comes to his disciples via the Spirit who resides "with" and "in" his disciples (John 14:17c–18). Because the Three are "in" one another, the personal identities are never compromised even while the substantial identity of the One is maintained. The Persons "dwell in one another, in no wise confused but cleaving together."[35]

Ontology then Economy

The ontology of God as Three and One informs our perception of God's actions upon his creatures. By evaluating Karl Rahner's axiom, "The 'economic' Trinity is the 'immanent' Trinity and the 'immanent' Trinity is the 'economic' Trinity," scholars have realized we can reliably discern truths regarding God's internal reality through his external actions.[36] But

---

34. John of Damascus, *Exposition of the Christian Faith*, transl. D. F. Salmond, in *Hilary of Poitiers, John of Damascus,* Nicene and Post-Nicene Fathers, 2nd Series, vol. 9 (1899; reprint, Peabody, MA: Hendrickson, 1994), 11.

35. "But the three subsistences have one and the same movement. For each one of them is related as closely to the other as to itself." Moreover, there is "but one simple essence, surpassing and preceding perfection, existing in three perfect subsistences." John of Damascus, *Exposition of the Christian Faith*, 10.

36. Karl Rahner, *The Trinity*, transl. Joseph Donceel (New York: Crossroad Herder, 2004), 22. For a summary of the critical debate and my

we must be careful not to say that creaturely changes determine God's immutable being. On the one hand, God's eternal reality as Trinity shapes God's temporal actions upon his creatures. The Father both begets the Son eternally and sends the Son into the world. On the other hand, creation does not determine the reality of God in eternity. God is "pure act," so his actions do not change him in any way. For example, God did not become Trinity through the incarnation; rather, the coming of the Son in flesh revealed God's eternal Trinity.

Inseparable Operations

Because God is united in being, we must affirm he is also united in acting. Augustine of Hippo concluded, after careful theological exegesis of the biblical text, that "the trinity which is equal in every respect likewise works inseparably."[37] The Father may send the Son, and the Father and the Son may send the Holy Spirit, but the one God forever acts as one. The Word expresses the will of the Father, just as the Spirit inspires and illumines the Word, but the Father and the Word and the Spirit together reveal one God. The Son dies upon the cross, and the Spirit raises him from the dead, but one God saves humanity. We may never separate the work of the One in his acts of revelation, creation, salvation, or consummation.

Proper Operations

If it is an error to separate the action of God from any of the divine Persons, so it is an error to confuse the proper working of each Person. A Roman teacher named Praxeas

---

proposed revision of the axiom, see Malcolm B. Yarnell III, *God the Trinity: Biblical Portraits* (Nashville: B&H Academic, 2016), 164–76.

37. Augustine, *The Trinity*, transl. Edmund Hill, ed. John E. Rotelle (Brooklyn, NY: New City Press, 1991), 397.

emphasized the divine unity to the extent that he said God
the Father suffered as the Son. Tertullian thus condemned
Praxeas for having "crucified the Father."[38] Praxeas both contradicted the biblical text and brought change into the immutable Godhead with his bizarre teaching. So, even as we affirm
the inseparability of God's work, we must carefully distinguish the work of each Person. This is especially evident in
the case of the Son, who is "the one mediator between God
and humanity" by virtue of his unique incarnation as a human
being, even as he remains united in his deity with the "one
God" (1 Tim. 2:5).

The Central Dogma of the Christian Faith

Finally, all Christians would be wise to follow the lead
of the *Oxford Dictionary of the Christian Church* in avowing
the Trinity as "the central dogma of the Christian Faith." The
doctrinal and practical implications of this great claim are
thoroughgoing. Christianity's central dogma teaches that we
are created by the Trinity, redeemed by the Trinity, and judged
in the end by the Trinity. Because God is the Trinity, we are
required to worship God as One and Three.

Just as the one God spoke as Trinity in the first chapters
of the Bible, so the three Persons of the one Trinity speak in
the final chapters of Holy Scripture. Speaking as Three yet
One, God invites us freely and promises eternal life to those
who repent and believe. But the Trinity also warns us about
the eternal condemnation awaiting the wicked.[39] The critical
question for every human being is whether he or she will hear

---

38. Michael Walsh, ed., *Dictionary of Christian Biography* (Collegeville,
MN: Liturgical Press, 2001), 986.

39. Each of the divine Persons speaks three times at the end of Scripture:
the Father (Rev. 21:5a, 6), the Lamb (Rev. 22:7, 12–16, 20), and the Spirit
(Rev. 22:17a, 17b, 17c).

and believe the Trinity's revelation of himself, receive the free gift of salvation, and worship God as Trinity.

Study Questions

1. What biblical passages teach the doctrine of the Trinity in the context of Christian worship? How does this worship context impact our understanding of the Trinity's significance?

2. List and describe the three major Trinitarian heresies.

3. Describe the eternal relations between the Father and the Son and the Holy Spirit.

Suggested Resources

- Gregory of Nazianzus, *Five Theological Orations*

- Scott R. Swain, *The Trinity: An Introduction*

- F. L. Cross, *The Oxford Dictionary of the Christian Church*

CHAPTER SIX

What Is God Like? (Part 1)

◆

WHEN YOU HEAR SOMEONE SAY "Lord," "God," or "Creator,"
what enters your mind? When you read Scripture's descriptions of God as holy, loving, or righteous, what images arise?
And when you hear that God is mysterious, incomprehensible, or infinite, do you find yourself reaching the limit of your
abilities? Such questions prompt us to consider what God is
like.

We must use the comparative "like" when speaking of the
identity of God, because truly his infinite "ways" and "thoughts"
exceed our own (Isa. 55:8–9). We remain utterly dependent
upon God's gracious self-revelation in his Word to know anything about him (Isa. 55:10–11). God's revelation of himself is
true, so we must trust all that his Word says. But we can never
grasp him perfectly, for God is ultimately incomprehensible.
God comprehends us, but we cannot comprehend God; for
we exist in God rather than vice versa (Acts 17:28). Therefore,
when we talk about God's "essence," "names," and "attributes,"

this requires us to exercise a certain mental reserve, a humble chasteness against carnal hastiness.[1]

We will explore the doctrine of humanity in the second volume of this series, but the created reflection of God in man requires our momentary attention (Gen. 1:26–27). Beginning in the Fall, our temptation has been to presume more for the human self than God gives (Gen. 3:5). Creating idols for ourselves from what we know about God is part of fallen human nature; it prompts each of us to sin (Rom. 1:21–25; 5:12). Because the human mind is "a perpetual factory of idols,"[2] we must consistently return to listen to the Word of God with the church while praying for the Holy Spirit's guidance to perceive God correctly. We are made in the image of God; God ought not be remade in the image of fallen human ideologies.[3]

In this chapter, in our effort to better understand the character of God, we will first summarize the names of God in Scripture before contemplating his attributes. Theological conversation about the "divine attributes" rehearses the characteristics or perfections of God which he reveals about himself. The authoritative source for our sufficient knowledge of God's attributes remains Scripture alone. But Scripture shows

---

1. "Concerning the nature and operations of God, we can know only what he has vouchsafed to reveal to us, and with every conception, either of his being or his acts, there must always attend an element of incomprehensibility, which is inseparable from infinitude." A. A. Hodge, *Outlines of Theology*, revised ed. (1879; reprint, London: Banner of Truth, 1972), 135–36. In classroom lectures, I instruct students to approach discussions about the divine being by keeping five truths in mind: human finitude, God's ultimacy, God's mystery, the gift of revelation, and Trinitarian participation.

2. John Calvin, *Institutes of the Christian Religion*, ed. John T. McNeill, transl. Ford Lewis Battles, 2 vols. (Philadelphia: Westminster Press, 1960), 1:108.

3. One key to proper theological interpretation of Scripture is to retain the priority of God to humanity. Scripture teaches us to see God, and from him we can properly understand humanity, not vice versa.

that humans can know some truths about God from his creation and in their consciences (Rom. 1:19–20; 2:15–16).

Theologians have offered various schemes for discussing the divine attributes. Garrett reviewed seven such patterns.[4] We will use two major categories, first discussing those divine perfections which reveal his unique transcendent person. We call these attributes "transcendent" or "metaphysical" to indicate their loftiness. Our second category delineates truths about the Lord which are more "immanent" or "relative" to us. God shares true knowledge about himself with humanity by grace, but his essence or nature remains beyond our capacity to comprehend.

Before we begin rehearsing God's names and attributes, please remember that any theological system remains a human approach to describing God. No doctrinal system may define, redefine, or compose God. For instance, recognizing both God's love and God's wrath entails no contradiction, partition, or progression in God, although they may seem so to some human beings. We can see the larger reality of God and must speak of him as he reveals himself, but our perceptions of him may never restrict him. If we faithfully represent what we can know about God through his Word, a particular system of classification should remain a matter of Christian freedom.

The Names of God

Names in Scripture are important. "A person's name stands for the person. It suggests the reality of the person, and

---

4. James Leo Garrett Jr., *Systematic Theology: Biblical, Historical, and Evangelical*, vol. 1, 2nd ed. (North Richland Hills, TX: Bibal Press, 2000), 232–36.

it conjures up awareness of the person."[5] In Scripture, when "the Name" is used in the singular for God, it "becomes synonymous with God."[6] Our sovereign God's "name is holy" (Isa. 57:15). His name also indicates his power and authority (Matt. 28:19). The Lord is jealous for the right use of his name (Exod. 20:7), so we must always be reverent when speaking of him. His most common names are "God" and "Lord," but other titles abound too.

God

The ancient name for a deity in the Semitic languages provided the Hebrews with the root for their term, *'el*. *'El* indicated power and *Elah*, reverence. The Old Testament used *'El* to form compound divine names like *'El-'Elyon*, "God most high," *'El-Shaddai*, "Almighty God," and *'El-'Olam*, "Eternal God."[7]

'Elohim was the plural noun commonly used to describe the preeminent God. Although grammatically a plural noun, it appears with the singular verb to indicate the one God.[8] The Greek term *theos* typically translated the Hebrew *'Elohim* and became the most common term for "God" in the New Testament.

Theos indicates the Father personally yet extends to the Son and the Spirit. *Theos* is never used of false gods but remains exclusive to the one transcendent God. The *Theos* of

---

5. John Goldingay, *Biblical Theology: The God of the Christian Scriptures* (Downers Grove, IL: IVP Academic, 2016), 58.

6. Louis Berkhof, *Systematic Theology*, 4th ed., 2 vols. (Grand Rapids: Eerdmans, 1941), 2:47.

7. C. J. H. Wright, "Names of God," in *International Standard Bible Encyclopedia*, Revised ed., ed. Geoffrey W. Bromiley, 4 vols. (Grand Rapids: Eerdmans, 1982) 2:506.

8. Rarely, *'elohim* could refer to multiple gods.

the New Testament is the same God as the *'Elohim* of the Old Testament.[9]

Lord

The Hebrew covenant name for the one true God was *Yhwh*. Derived from the Hebrew verb *hayah*, the name means simply, "I am." Theologically, this name "expresses self-existence and unchangeableness."[10] The Jews did not pronounce the word, "Yahweh," out of deep reverence for his covenant name. *'Adonai*, "Lord," served as a nominal substitute. *'Adonai* exclusively indicated the one true God.

The Greek version of the Hebrew Bible, the Septuagint, translated both *Yhwh* and *'Adonai* with *kurios*, "Lord."[11] According to the New Testament, to say that Jesus is *kurios* is the inspired saving confession. It indicates both the deity of Jesus Christ and one's personal submission to him (Rom. 10:9–10; 1 Cor. 12:3).

The combination name "Lord Jesus Christ" was commonly used by various apostles but especially Paul.

Divine Titles

He has other names than "God," "Lord," and their compounds. These other names or titles typically relate God to his

---

9. Moisés Silva, *New International Dictionary of New Testament Theology and Exegesis*, 2nd ed., 4 vols. (Grand Rapids: Zondervan, 2014), 2:437–441.

10. Hodge, *Outlines of Theology*, 134. *'Elohim* was not used to make compounds. William L. Holladay, *A Concise Hebrew and Aramaic Lexicon of the Old Testament* (Grand Rapids: Eerdmans, 1988), 15.

11. Silva, *New International Dictionary of New Testament Theology and Exegesis*, 2:769. Modern English translations often use Yahweh as "Lord" and Adonai as "Lord." Cf. "Introduction," *Holy Bible: The Old and New Testaments, Holman Christian Standard Bible* (Nashville: Holman, 2012), viii.

creation. The Old and New Testaments also call God, "Father, Shepherd, Redeemer or Savior, Judge, King, and Lord."[12]

In addition to these names, Christian tradition entitled him, "Creator." Philosophers imply him when they refer to such titles as "the Good" or "the Prime Mover." We now turn to the divine attributes.[13]

The Transcendent or Metaphysical Attributes of God

Several divine attributes which indicate his exalted nature press beyond our limited capacity to easily grasp. These transcendent or metaphysical attributes point toward the incomprehensible reality of God. These attributes include God's mystery, infinity, simplicity, and aseity. These four have a negative character in that they tell us what we cannot say about God. Theologians describe these attributes as "incommunicable," because God does not share them with us. We know about them, but we don't possess or exercise them ourselves.

Four other metaphysical attributes—blessedness, sufficiency, spirituality, and personality—are deemed positive because they describe what we can say about God. We have a slightly better ability to comprehend these four positive transcendent attributes. God can and does share such attributes with us by grace, so we can understand them better. Those attributes which God shares with us are known as "communicable" attributes.

---

12. Garrett, *Systematic Theology*, 1:221.

13. In the following discussion of divine attributes, for the sake of brevity we typically cite a text from the Old Testament and a text from the New Testament. Many more relevant texts, however, can be found in both testaments.

Negative Metaphysical Attributes

Mystery

It is beneficial to mention first among the transcendent attributes of God the truth of his eternal mystery. There necessarily remains a creaturely limit to our knowledge of the limitless Creator. Scripture says that we as human creatures are by nature incapable of seeing him (Exod. 33:20; 1 Tim. 6:15–16).

Anselm of Canterbury thus prayed, "Truly, O Lord, this is the unapproachable light in which thou dwellest; for truly there is nothing else which can penetrate this light, that it may see thee there."[14] We cannot see God in his being, but we can receive truth about him through the grace of revelation. God's "incomprehensibility" to us derives from his transcendent mystery. Overcoming the incomprehensibility of God to us is entirely subject to his gracious revelation.

Infinity

Second, by divine infinity we mean God is not contained in time and space. We discussed the biblical basis for God's "eternity" in chapter 4. Alongside affirming God's eternity in relation to time, we must also affirm God's "immensity" in relation to space.

The prophet Jeremiah spoke of God's immensity in this way: "'Do I not fill the heavens and the earth?'—the LORD's declaration" (Jer. 23:24). Paul similarly circumscribed creaturely reality with divine reality by instructing the Athenian academy that "In Him we live and move and exist" (Acts 17:28 NASB1995).

---

14. Anselm, *Proslogium*, in *St. Anselm: Basic Writings*, 2nd ed., transl. S. N. Deane (Peru, IL: Open Court, 1962), 68. Cf. Anselm, *Proslogium*, 60–61, 70.

Simplicity

Third, God also possesses simplicity. Nothing about God is either divisible or contradictory. God is not composed of parts. Scripture teaches divine simplicity not only from his unity (Deut. 6:4) and absoluteness (Job 38:1–7) but from his simple rather than duplicitous acts. The apostle James thus speaks of God as giving "simply."[15]

Augustine responded to the biblical witness, "Therefore one and the same thing is being said, whether you say God is eternal or immortal or incorruptible or unchangeable; and again whether you say he is living or understanding, which is the same as wise, the same thing is being said" (John 8:58).[16]

We may recall the parable of the blindfolded men describing their encounter with an object: one said it was a tree, another a snake, another a hill, but they each happened upon an elephant. God's simplicity requires us, moreover, to speak of his "immutability" or unchanging nature.

Aseity

The fourth negative metaphysical attribute concerns God's aseity. God is not dependent upon any being, because he is the source of his own reality. God is *a se*; the Greek phrase means "of himself." Aseity expresses the independence of the Creator with regard to his creatures. God's longer self-description,

---

15. Greek *aplos*; James 1:5. Evangelicals have given substantial attention to the doctrine of divine simplicity in the last few years. Cf. Jordan P. Barrett, *Divine Simplicity: A Biblical and Trinitarian Account* (Philadelphia: Fortress Press, 2017); James E. Dolezal, *God without Parts: Divine Simplicity and the Metaphysics of God's Absoluteness* (Eugene, OR: Pickwick, 2011); Steven J. Duby, *Divine Simplicity: A Dogmatic Account* (New York: T&T Clark, 2018); Paul R. Hinlicky, *Christ the Crisis of Metaphysics* (Grand Rapids: Baker, 2016).

16. Cf. Augustine, *The Trinity*, transl. Edmund Hill, ed. John E. Rotelle (Brooklyn: New City Press, 1991), 400.

Hayah 'aser hayah ("I am who I am"), in Exodus 3:14 grounds this doctrine.

God is the one who is because he is, and he will be because he will be. God, the only one whose existence is his essence, creates all other beings. He is of himself by nature; all else derives from him by creation. According to divine aseity, any creature's claim to participate by nature in divine reality should raise an eyebrow. Aseity thus underlay Jesus's claim, "I assure you: Before Abraham was, I am."[17]

Positive Metaphysical Attributes

The above transcendent attributes of mystery, infinity, simplicity, and aseity may be ascribed to God. They are necessarily cast in a negative form. Other divine attributes, however, find comparative analogies in human beings because God shares that aspect of his nature with us by grace. Although the positive transcendent attributes of blessedness, sufficiency, spirituality, and personhood derive from the incomprehensible perfection of God, they find some measure of comparison in blessed human beings.

Blessedness

We list divine blessedness or goodness first among the positive metaphysical attributes of God. Both the Catholic theologian Thomas Aquinas and the Baptist theologian John Gill did the same.[18] In the Old Testament, God is the one

---

17. The profound truth that the transcendent, metaphysical God makes himself available to us by grace is emotionally overwhelming to me. I cannot but weep thinking of his grace.

18. Thomas Aquinas, *Summa Theologica*, vol. 1, transl. Fathers of the English Dominican Province (1911; reprint, Westminster, MD: Christian Classics, 1948), 28–30. Gill treated the attributes of love, grace, mercy, and

"who blesses" (Num. 23:20; Ps. 109:28). Jesus reminded a man seeking eternal blessing that "God alone is good." He did this as a way of pointing to his own unique relation to God (Mark 10:17–18). Jesus also informed Caiaphas that he was indeed "the Son of the Blessed One," God (Mark 14:61–62; cf. 1 Tim. 1:11; 6:15).

Jesus affirmed the possibility of human participation in blessedness through obedience to the Law (Mark 10:19). The only way we receive God's eternal blessedness is by God's grace (Mark 10:26–27) through believing in Christ, the only one who obeyed the Law fully (Mark 16:15–16). Only because we have received divine blessings, may we as human beings bless God and bless others (Gen. 14:18–20; Heb. 7:1).

A Pattern for Communicable Attributes

A review of the biblical doctrine of blessedness (Hebrew *berekoth* or *baruk*; Greek *eulogeo*)[19] demonstrates a pattern behind God's sharing of certain attributes with his creatures. The pattern of God's gracious communication of his perfections, such as his attribute of blessedness, is fourfold:

1. God may and does share his communicable attributes with his creatures by his freely chosen acts of grace.
2. These communicable divine attributes like blessedness originate with and remain dependent upon God. Blessedness is not relinquished by God but shared.
3. God's sharing of his blessedness enables his creatures to reflect blessedness back

---

long-suffering first but affirmed they "all proceed" from God's goodness. John Gill, *A Body of Doctrinal Divinity; Or a System of Evangelical Truths, Deduced from the Sacred Scriptures*, new ed. (London, 1839), 91.

19. Cf. *makarios, agathos.*

to the Creator. Blessed humanity, if you will, acts as a mirror to reflect the light of God's blessedness back to him.

4. The divine gift of blessedness may also be reflected derivatively upon other creatures.[20] God hereby remains not only the source but the standard of the perfection of blessedness.

This pattern whereby God graces his creatures with some of his perfections is also found in other communicable attributes, such as sufficiency, love, justice, and holiness.

Sufficiency

Second among the positive communicable attributes of God, we must avow God's perfect sufficiency. In 2 Corinthians 3:5–6, the apostle Paul grounds sufficiency in the divine being. God also grants sufficiency by grace. These meanings are seen in Paul's manifold use of the primary Greek terms for "sufficiency."

Paul first notes that men are not "sufficient" (the Greek adjective *ikanoi*) in themselves. Instead, our "sufficiency" (the Greek noun *ikanotes*) is "from God." Moreover, God makes us "sufficient" (the Greek verb *ikanosen*) to serve him. God communicates his sufficiency to his redeemed creatures by his "Spirit."

According to Paul's description of Scripture in 2 Timothy 3:15–17, God also gives sufficiency to his prophets and apostles along with their writings through the Spirit's inspiration.

---

20. "Boëthius says (*De Hebdom.*) that all things but God are good by participation. Therefore they are not good essentially." Aquinas, *Summa Theologica*, 1:29. Cf. Anthony C. Thiselton, *Thiselton Companion to Christian Theology* (Grand Rapids: Eerdmans, 2016), 153.

Human words are thereby made both "able" (Greek *duna-mena*) and "profitable" (Greek *ophelmos*).[21]

In summary, God is sufficient in himself. Moreover, his sufficiency can also become a communicable attribute. For instance, God graces the redeemed with his sufficiency. Moreover, he also grants sufficiency to Scripture. The sufficiency of Scripture as the Word of God is an important truth which we must explore further in chapter 12.

Spiritual

Third among the positive attributes of God is the fact that God is spiritual. In the Old Testament, references to God as Spirit are linked with his power (Gen. 1:2), his holiness (Ps. 51:11), and his omnipresence (Ps. 139:7). In the New Testament, Jesus leads the woman at the well to stop confining God to a place: "God is spirit, and those who worship him must worship in Spirit and in truth" (John 4:24).

Today, people who have been influenced by modern naturalism often use "spiritual" in a dismissive way to mean that which is less than tangible. However, according to Stephen Charnock, the divine Spirit is "the most excellent substance," "as infinitely above the beings of creatures as above the conceptions of creatures."[22] God's spiritual nature indicates, moreover, that he is Creator, One, invisible, infinite, independent, immutable, omnipresent, and perfect.[23]

---

21. Malcolm B. Yarnell III and David S. Dockery, "Introduction," in *The Authority and Sufficiency of Scripture*, ed. Adam W. Greenway and David S. Dockery (Fort Worth: Seminary Hill Press, 2022), 8–9.

22. Stephen Charnock, *Discourses upon the Existence and Attributes of God*, 2 vols. (1853; reprint, Grand Rapids: Baker, 1979), 1:183.

23. Charnock, *Discourses*, 1:183–88.

Personal

The last positive metaphysical attribute concerns God's personal character. God's relational personhood was revealed when he made humanity in his image, called them to rule the earth for God (Gen. 1:26–27), and blessed humanity linguistically with life (Gen. 1:28–29). The Trinity's intrapersonal nature is on display when God speaks of the Son and the Spirit descends upon the Son (Matt. 3:16–17), when the Son prays to the Father (Matt. 26:39; John 17), and when the Son commands baptism in the one threefold holy name (Matt. 28:19).

According to Martin Buber, persons encounter one another with their "whole being" rather than as mere things.[24] According to John Zizioulas, one person defines another by "being in communion."[25] God is by reason of his Triunity complete in his own personhood. By grace, the Trinity shares personhood with his image-bearers. God created us as persons for relationship with himself.

Transcendence and Immanence

Theologians typically distinguish divine transcendence from divine immanence. Divine transcendence refers to the radical otherness of God. Transcendence emphasizes God's difference from humanity. Divine immanence refers to the closeness of God to his creation. Immanence emphasizes the close relationship between human beings and God. The Lord God is both transcendent and immanent.

In this chapter, we have considered the transcendent or metaphysical attributes of God. In the next chapter, we will

---

24. Martin Buber, *I and Thou*, transl. Walter Kaufmann (New York: Scribner's, 1970), 53–54.

25. John D. Zizioulas, *Being as Communion: Studies in Personhood and Church* (Crestwood, NY: St. Vladimir's Seminary Press, 1997).

turn our attention to those attributes which are more immanent and therefore more relative to humanity.

Study Questions

1. List three names or titles which Scripture ascribes to God
and discuss with someone the proper attitude human beings
should have toward his Name.

2. What is the difference between the "incommunicable" attributes of God and his "communicable" attributes?

3. What is the difference between God's "transcendent" or
"metaphysical" attributes and his more "immanent" or "relative" attributes?

Suggested Resources

- Anselm of Canterbury, *Proslogium*

- Stephen Charnock, *Discourses upon the Existence and
  Attributes of God*

- Donald Bloesch, *God the Almighty*

CHAPTER SEVEN

What Is God Like? (Part 2)

◆

JOHN OF DAMASCUS, "THE OUTSTANDING theologian of the eighth century and one of the most influential in both the east and the west,"[1] settled Greek patristic theology as a system. His *Exposition of the Orthodox Faith* provided several lists of divine attributes. He typically began with the negative metaphysical attributes, as we did in the last chapter.

John's most comprehensive catalog grouped the divine attributes into seven categories.[2] The exact categories we use to consider the attributes of God will vary by theologian. As

---

1. Ken Parry, "John of Damascus (c. 665–749)," in *The Dictionary of Historical Theology*, ed. Trevor A. Hart (Grand Rapids: Eerdmans, 2000), 288.

2. We may describe these as negative attributes, positive attributes, absolute attributes, sovereign or ordering attributes, relative or communicable attributes, knowledge attributes, and uniting attributes. John of Damascus, *Exposition of the Orthodox Faith*, transl. S. D. F. Salmond, in *Hilary of Poitiers, John of Damascus*, ed. Philip Schaff and Henry Wace, Nicene and Post-Nicene Fathers, Second Series, vol. 9 (1899; reprint, Peabody, MA: Hendrickson, 1994), 6. For other lists of the attributes, see John of Damascus, *Exposition of the Orthodox Faith*, 1–2, 13.

noted previously, choosing an exact scheme of attributes constitutes a matter of freedom as long as God is represented well.

In the previous chapter, we classified the first set of attributes as transcendent or metaphysical. We argued that these attributes point us beyond ourselves toward the incomprehensible otherness of God.

In this chapter, we will classify the remaining divine attributes as "immanent" or "relative." We more easily understand these remaining attributes through our experiences with God. These relative attributes let us know what God is like through his direct, sovereign, and gracious encounter with us.[3]

Leo Garrett arranged most of the characteristics of God around two primary attributes, the Old Testament emphasis upon divine holiness and the New Testament emphasis upon divine love. Garrett identified a third major attribute, righteousness, as the "bridge" between God's love and God's holiness. Garrett's paradigm has the helpful benefit of both collecting the various attributes together in a simple scheme and centering the revelation of God's perfect and awesome character upon the saving mystery of Christ's cross.[4]

Following my mentor's lead, we shall discuss the relative attributes of God, the attributes with which God engages us, under the categories of holiness, love, and righteousness. We will also discuss the divine attribute of freedom.

---

3. Heinrich Heppe said, "the attributes of God are the divine nature itself in its relation to the world." Heppe, *Reformed Dogmatics*, ed. Ernst Bizer, transl. G. T. Thomson (London: Allen & Unwin, 1950), 57.

4. Garrett, *Systematic Theology*, 1:239. I write these words on Good Friday and am struck again by how horrible yet beautiful is the cross of Christ.

Divine Holiness and Ten Related Attributes

Divine Holiness

When most people hear the word *holiness* today, they focus upon ethical purity. However, the Hebrew idea of the "holy" (*qadosh*) first concerned that which was separate, consecrated, or set apart. Rudolf Otto argued for the recovery of this first meaning under the rubric *mysterium tremendum.* According to Otto, holiness invokes in the human being a sense of dread, overwhelming power, and fascination with the living One who is "wholly other."[5] For instance, during their first encounter God informed Moses that divine holiness required from Moses both personal reverence toward God and separation from the mundane—"Do not come closer" (Exod. 3:5).

While God's awe-inspiring holiness separates him from creation, he nevertheless demands from and grants holiness to his people. Israel was set aside as a "holy nation" (Exod. 19:6). The holy God calls his people unto holiness (Lev. 11:44–45). Therefore, Israel must keep "holy" the time of the sabbath (Exod. 20:8, 11), as well as the place where they worship (Exod. 26:33–34). The prophet Isaiah was himself set apart through an encounter with the thrice "holy" God (Isa. 6:3). Isaiah repeatedly called Israel to honor "the Holy One of Israel" (Isa. 1:4).[6] Alas, the nation failed to heed the call to holiness. Therefore, a "stump" was set apart to carry "the holy seed," who is Christ (Isa. 6:13; cf. Rom. 9:7–8; Gal. 3:16).

The New Testament locates holiness in the Triune God who graciously consecrates his people unto moral purity. Jesus Christ was explicitly identified as "the Holy One of God,"[7]

---

5. Rudolf Otto, *The Idea of the Holy: An Inquiry into the Non-Rational Factor in the Idea of the Divine and Its Relation to the Rational,* 2nd ed., transl. John W. Harvey (New York: Oxford University Press, 1950), 12–41.

6. Also mentioned twenty-six other times.

7. *Ho hagios tou theou:* John 6:69.

indicating divine holiness was also the possession of the Son of God (Mark 1:24). Christ commands his disciples to sanctify (*hagiastheto*, "make holy" or "honor as holy") the Father's name (Matt. 6:9). Moreover, because God is holy, the New Testament church must also "be holy in all your conduct" (1 Pet. 1:15–16). In other words, the transcendent otherness of God requires the moral otherness of the people of God (Eph. 5:3). Here is why the New Testament applies the term *saints* (*hagioi*) to all Christians and not just one group of Christians (Acts 9:13, 23; Phil. 4:21).

Eternity

Garrett included eternity as the first attribute related to holiness likely due to its emphasis upon his transcendence.[8] God is "from eternity to eternity" (Ps. 90:2). He is "the one who is, who was, and who is to come" (Rev. 1:8). As eternal, God is above and beyond creation such that all times are present before him. Chapter 4, it will be remembered, considered this important attribute of God in great depth.

Immutability

Second, God's immutability derives from his eternality. He says of himself, "I, the Lord, have not changed" (Mal. 3:6). He is "the Father of lights, who does not change like shifting shadows" (James 1:17). Divine immutability ought not be construed as static lifelessness but as dynamic constancy, for the Lord is "the living God" (Matt. 16:16).[9]

---

8. Garrett, *Systematic Theology*, 1:247–49.
9. Donald G. Bloesch, *God the Almighty: Power, Wisdom, Holiness, Love* (Downers Grove, IL: InterVarsity Press, 1995), 92–93.

Wisdom

Third, God created the earth with his wisdom (Prov. 3:19–20). The Proverbs personify "wisdom" as a teacher and mediator (Prov. 8:1–21). Christ himself is "the wisdom of God" (1 Cor. 1:24). In addition, "Wisdom is not only an attribute of God but also a gift of God."[10]

Omniscience, Omnipotence, and Omnipresence

Related to God's transcendent holiness are the three "omni" attributes: omniscience, omnipotence, and omnipresence.

God is omniscient, possessing universal knowledge. He has no need for anyone to instruct him (Isa. 40:12–14), because "he knows all things" (1 John 3:20).

God is omnipotent, possessing universal power and authority. The book of Revelation repeatedly calls God the Father *Pantokrator*, "the Almighty" or "the All-Powerful" (Rev. 1:8; 4:8; 11:17). Jesus Christ also possesses universal power and authority eternally (Matt. 28:18), and the Holy Spirit likewise wields the eternal power of God in freedom (1 Sam. 16; John 3:8).[11]

God is omnipresent. He possesses universal presence. God's attendance to all places at all times derives from his immensity, discussed above. His omnipresence points toward his immanence, his special presence to his creatures made in his image. It is impossible to avoid God (Ps. 139:5–10).

Jealousy, Anger, and Wrath

Next, God's perfections of jealousy, anger, and wrath both frighten and dismay human beings. Scripture clearly

10. Bloesch, *God the Almighty*, 122.
11. Malcolm B. Yarnell III, *Who Is the Holy Spirit? Biblical Insights into His Divine Person* (Nashville: B&H Academic, 2019), 29.

and repeatedly describes God in such terms, so we must fully accept them. However, we must also be careful not to cast human perversions back upon the perfections of God.

Paul said, "God's wrath is revealed from heaven against all godlessness and unrighteousness of people who by their unrighteousness suppress the truth" (Rom. 1:18). Moses located the motivation behind God's anger at sin in God's love for humanity: "For I, the Lord your God, am a jealous God" (Exod. 20:5).

Martin Luther referred to divine wrath as God's "alien work."[12] After warning against imposing human examples of wrath upon God and noting wrath must confront wickedness, Emil Brunner wrote, "His wrath is simply the result of the infinitely serious love of God."[13] Sinful humanity's only hope of escape is faith, "For Christ has reconciled wrath."[14]

Glory

Finally, among the attributes related to holiness, the glory of the holy God refers to God's self-manifestation. The Hebrew root for "glory" (*kabod*) indicated a "weight" or "difficulty." The Greek term *doxa*, from which we garner such terms as *orthodoxy* and *doxology*, meant "opinion" or "reputation." The glory of God is revealed clearly in the life, death, and resurrection of Jesus Christ (John 1:14; 9:32; 12:28). He participates in divine glory eternally (John 17:5). "The glory of God is the majestic manifestation and recognition of God as holy and worthy of worship and praise."[15]

---

12. Paul Althaus, *The Theology of Martin Luther*, transl. Robert C. Schulz (Philadelphia: Fortress Press, 1966), 169–78.

13. Emil Brunner, *The Christian Doctrine of God*, transl. Olive Wyon (Philadelphia: Westminster Press, 1950), 161, 170.

14. Althaus, *The Theology of Martin Luther*, 171.

15. Garrett, *Systematic Theology*, 1:264.

The Bridge Attribute of Divine Righteousness

Divine Righteousness in Scripture

We must pay careful attention to the ways Scripture uses the primary Hebrew and Greek terms for the noun "righteousness" (Hebrew *tsedaqah*; Greek *dikaiosyne*), the adjective "righteous" (Greek *dikaios*), and the verb "justify" or "declare righteous" (Greek *dikaioun)*. In the Old Testament, God's righteousness is universal. God always judges everyone with righteousness (Gen. 18:25).

His righteousness is manifested in the three covenantal movements of mandating, punishing, and redeeming: The Lord commands his people from his righteousness (Ps. 119:137–138). He punishes with righteousness (Dan. 9:14). However, and this we must be quick to remember, God also redeems due to his righteousness (Isa. 45:21–22).

The New Testament teaches that God is "righteous" or "just" by nature. God the Father is "righteous" and demands humanity to be right and to do right (1 John 3:7). Jesus Christ is "the Righteous One" (1 John 2:1) who came as a human being "to fulfill all righteousness" (Matt. 3:15).

The phrase "the righteousness of God" (*dikaiosyne theou*) carries a great deal of theological weight, both in Scripture and in Christian history. The perfect righteousness of God was displayed in the propitiatory sacrifice of Christ. His righteousness is granted to those who have faith (Rom. 3:21–26). God's righteousness is revealed in the gospel of Jesus Christ so that people can be declared righteous (Rom. 1:16–17). Believers must continue to seek both the rule and righteousness of God as a matter of priority (Matt. 6:33).

Divine Righteousness in Christian History

With shocking emotional vulnerability, a Bible professor once confessed, "I had hated that phrase 'the righteousness of God.'" Martin Luther's detestation of this significant phrase derived from his exclusive focus upon what Medieval scholars called God's "formal or active righteousness." God's formal righteousness is that "by which God is righteous, and punished sinners."[16] In other words, Luther the Bible professor knew only about the mandatory and punitive meanings of divine righteousness.

However, "at last, God being merciful, as I meditated day and night" on the uses of the phrase in Paul's letter to the Romans, Luther said he came to a deeper understanding. He learned that "the righteousness of God" may and must also be taken in a "passive" way. The righteousness of God is also that righteousness "by which the merciful God justifies us by faith."[17]

In this way, through great human anxiety and prayerful recourse to the Word of God, Luther was granted a "theological breakthrough." Luther later wrote, "This immediately made me feel as though I had been born again, and as though I had entered through open gates into paradise itself."

The discovery of God's redemptive righteousness, which comes to those who believe in Christ, allowed Luther to see "the whole face of Scripture . . . in a different light." His justification before God by grace through faith in Jesus Christ now caused "the righteousness of God" to become "the sweetest of words" and "the very gate of paradise."[18] The theologian who launched the world-changing Protestant Reformation had discovered righteousness could be his by faith alone.

---

16. Alister E. McGrath, *Luther's Theology of the Cross: Martin Luther's Theological Breakthrough* (New York: Basil Blackwell, 1985), 96.

17. McGrath, *Luther's Theology of the Cross*, 96–97.

18. McGrath, *Luther's Theology of the Cross*, 97.

A shift toward a proper theology of the divine attribute of righteousness transformed one Bible teacher in sixteenth-century Germany, and the impact of his discovery has profoundly affected millions of believers. Martin Luther's discovery is a reminder of the power of the gospel to save people who reach the end of their own efforts and trust in Christ alone. It is also a reminder that the proper construal of the perfections of God, including divine righteousness, carries great personal and historical implications.

Divine Love and Seven Related Attributes

Divine Love

When speaking of divine love, we must think both of God's essential nature of self-giving and his economic activity of electing and keeping his covenants.

Two Hebrew terms, *'ahabah* and *chesed*, convey the Old Testament idea of divine love. *'Ahabah*, whose root indicated the starting of a fire, meant that God elected to establish a covenant with Israel for no other reason than his own love (Deut. 7:7–8). God's "Election-Love," by which he established the covenant, continues in God's "Covenant-Love."[19]

In contrast, *chesed*, whose root indicates an ardent desire, has been translated, "faithfulness" (Mic. 6:8). Both partners in a covenant ought to be faithful, as prophetically figured in the husband–wife relation and the father–son relation (Hosea 3:1–3; 2 Chron. 7:14–15). God's covenant love is steadfast and eternal. God remained faithful even when Israel did not (Jer. 3:20). Garrett concluded God's covenant-making love

---

19. Norman Snaith, *The Distinctive Ideas of the Old Testament* (London: Epworth Press, 1984), 95; Garrett, *Systematic Theology*, 1:275.

(*'ahabah*) and covenant-keeping love (*chesed*) "clearly limited Yahweh's love to the people of the covenant."[20]

Various meanings have been attached to the English word, *love*. C. S. Lewis found five definitions; the latter four were ascending types of human love: "likings and loves for the sub-human," "affection," "friendship," "eros," and "charity."[21] The Greek language possesses various terms for "love," including *philia* ("friendship love"), *eros* ("possessive love"), and *agape* ("selfless love"). The Septuagint typically used the Greek *agape* to translate the Hebrew noun *'ahabah*, and *agapao* to translate the verb *'ahab*.[22] The New Testament used the noun *agape* liberally while the nouns eros and philia were absent. The biblical verb *agapao* indicates perfect love and the verb *phileo* indicates natural love, but these terms could also function interchangeably.

Anders Nygren exhaustively studied the use of the Greek terms *agape* and *eros* in Scripture and history. Nygren concluded that the Platonic pagan concept of *eros* must remain sharply distinguished from the biblical concept of *agape*. *Agape* is the most basic divine motive.[23]

Systematically, God's perfect love works in four ways: *Agape* derives from God's nature, is not dependent on the object of love, creates worth in the object of love, and is God's way to relate to humanity. The believer first responds to God with love and then reflects God's *agape* to others. Nygren

20. Garrett, *Systematic Theology*, 1:276.

21. C. S. Lewis, *The Four Loves* (New York: Harcourt Brace Jovanovich, 1960).

22. Garrett, *Systematic Theology*, 1:276.

23. Nygren differentiated three opposing "ways to fellowship with God:" The Jewish theology of nomos; the Hellenistic concept of eros, and the Christian motif of agape. Agape is "the Christian *grundmotiv par excellence.*" Anders Nygren, *Agape and Eros: Part I, A Study of the Christian Idea of Love; Part II, The History of the Christian Idea of Love*, transl. Philip S. Watson (1932, 1938, and 1939; reprint, New York: Harper & Row, 1969), xix–xxiii.

found that Paul centered *agape* on Christ's cross and equated love with grace, a grace which knows no boundaries. God loves others through us.[24]

According to the apostolic writings, *agape* derives from God the Trinity who works in selfless grace. Love comes to us from the Father in the Son: "But God proves his own love for us in that while we were still sinners, Christ died for us" (Rom. 5:8). And love engages the human heart intimately through the Holy Spirit: "This hope will not disappoint us, because God's love has been poured out in our hearts through the Holy Spirit who was given to us" (Rom. 5:5).

The love of God in Jesus Christ is without parallel in other religions. For instance, Jesus exemplified a "golden rule" while other religious leaders at best taught various forms of a "silver rule." For instance, the liberal Jewish rabbi Hillel taught, "What is hateful to you, do not do to your neighbor."[25] According to the apostles, Jesus raised love to its highest level. Paul said Christ loved us "while we were still sinners" (Rom. 5:8). John said, "This is how we have come to know love: He laid down his life for us" (1 John 3:16a). Such perfect self-less, self-giving love, a love which has its roots only in God, must characterize his followers too. John thus continued, "We should also lay down our lives for our brothers and sisters" (1 John 3:16b).

Speaking in ontological terms, John twice says, "God is love" (1 John 4:8, 16). This profound statement leads many theologians to affirm the very essence of God is love. This is

---

24. Thor Hall, *Anders Nygren* (Waco: Word, 1978), 167–82. Where Nygren sharply separated *agape* from *eros*, D'Arcy detected a more subtle relationship. Love indicates a harmony of giving and receiving. "Even Eros, if it knows its own nature, can go with Agape." Martin Cyril D'Arcy, *The Mind and Heart of Love: A Study in Eros and Agape* (1954; reprint, Providence: Cluny, 2019), xxix.

25. John Dickson, *Bullies and Saints: An Honest Look at the Good and Evil of Christian History* (Grand Rapids: Zondervan, 2021), 27–29.

doubtless true, for the attributes of God both are one with yet manifest to us the essence of God. Difficulty comes, however, when one opposes or sublimates such attributes as divine holiness and divine wrath to divine love. Millard Erickson tells of how the Swedish Baptist theologian Nels Ferré subordinated the punitive righteousness of God to the love of God, thereby embracing the error of universalism.[26] While we should affirm God is love, we may not divide his essence or diminish other attributes. We know the one perfect God in the richness of his one life through his manifest perfections.[27]

We may summarize the central divine perfection of love this way:

1. The essence of God is love in his eternal triune relations.
2. God loves humanity by creating us, redeeming us, and faithfully drawing us to himself.
3. God is the source and standard of love: "We love because he first loved us" (1 John 4:19). As the source of all true love, God remains both the giver and the measure of true love. We can obey the great commandments only because he loves us with his sufficient, abounding, and everlasting love (Jer. 31:3).
4. It is a nonnegotiable truth that we as God's people are called to reflect God's ontology, loving him with everything we

26. Millard J. Erickson, *Christian Theology* (1983, 1984, 1985; reprint, Grand Rapids: Baker, 1989), 1018–20.

27. Karl Barth, *Church Dogmatics*, Vol. II, *The Doctrine of God*, Part 1, transl. T. H. L. Parker, W. B. Johnston, Harold McKnight, J. L. M. Haire (Edinburgh: T&T Clark, 1957), 322.

are and loving our neighbors as ourselves
(Matt. 22:38–40).[28]

Patience

The first divine attribute related to love is divine patience. Where the Hebrew term *'ap* indicated divine "anger," the Hebrew phrase *'erek 'ap* meant "slow to anger" (Exod. 34:6). The Greek term *makrothumia* literally means "distance of wrath" (1 Tim. 1:16). God delays our punishment so that he might draw his beloved humanity to genuine repentance (2 Pet. 3:16). God called humanity to reflect this divine attribute from the beginning of our traumatic relationships with one another (Gen. 4:15).

Grace

Second, God's perfect patience has a mirror perfection in divine grace. The Hebrew term *chen* indicates the gratuitous attitude of a superior to an inferior (Ps. 84:11). The common Greek noun *charis* is used both of God and Christ (2 Thess. 1:12). *Charis* is the gift of God to unworthy human beings who trust him (Eph. 2:8). The divine attribute of grace grounds every aspect of human salvation.

Faithfulness

Third, God's *chesed* love indicates also his covenant steadfastness. Related terms deepen our knowledge of divine faithfulness. The psalmist praised God for his *'emunah*, "faithfulness" (Ps. 89:1–2, 5, 24, 33). Both Paul and John affirm that God is *pistos*, "faithful" or "steady," to save us (1 Thess. 5:24; 1 John 1:9).

---

28. Please see chapter 2 above.

Kindness, Compassion, and Mercy

Three other terms deepen our knowledge of God's warm emotional love for us. Scripture affirms divine kindness, divine compassion, and divine mercy. The New Testament uses two especially vivid terms to indicate God's awesome mercy toward us: *Splagchnizomai* literally means "yearning bowels" (Mark 1:41) and *oiktirmos*, "merciful bowels" (Rom. 12:1).[29]

Passibility or Impassibility?

The idea that God is passible has generated debate among Christian scholars. Does God suffer with his beloved creatures? Can he feel our emotions? The orthodox church fathers typically denied that God is passible, or even emotional. In this way, they helped preserve his immutability. More recently, many scholars have begun to affirm divine passibility, even that God experiences suffering. They deem God's passibility to be a vital aspect of God's love. I personally know major proponents on both sides of this debate and find their treatments of the matter derive from genuine Christian motives and methods. With Leo Garrett, I commend the doctrine of passibility a matter requiring further study.[30]

Divine Freedom

We conclude our discussion of the divine character by affirming the doctrine of divine freedom as a communicable attribute.

---

29. Garrett, *Systematic Theology*, 1:285.

30. Paul S. Fiddes, *The Creative Suffering of God* (New York: Oxford University Press, 1988); Thomas G. Weinandy, *Does God Suffer?* (Notre Dame, IN: University of Notre Dame Press, 2000); Garrett, *Systematic Theology*, 1:290–92.

Karl Barth oriented his discussion of God's perfections around love and freedom.[31] But Barth's approach to freedom was not without difficulty. Barth unnecessarily delimited freedom by defining it as aseity, an incommunicable attribute.[32] In Barthian Reformed theology, freedom belongs to God alone. Despite this handicap, Barth paradoxically granted humanity freedom under the attribute of patience, wherein God wills "to allow to another . . . space and time for the development of its own existence."[33]

Against those theological philosophies which tend toward mechanical fatalism, we believe that Scripture presumes God may and does communicate his freedom to humanity. Freedom comes to humanity definitively in Christ. "For freedom, Christ set us free" (Gal. 5:1).

Theological wisdom must locate the communication of divine freedom between various extreme positions: On the one hand, the sharing of freedom with humanity does not grant us radical self-determination. On the other hand, aseity belongs to God alone while freedom is shared with humanity.

God shares a measure of his own freedom with us, but only a measure. God has choice with sovereignty. "Man has choice, but not sovereignty."[34] God's gift of freedom[35] allowed human beings a limited authority to be freely creative. When we were made in the image of God, humanity was granted some degree of God's authority (Gen. 1:25, 28), of God's creativity (Gen. 2:19), and therefore also of God's freedom (Gen. 2:16).

---

31. Barth, *Church Dogmatics*, II/1, 257.

32. Barth, *Church Dogmatics*, II/1, 301–2.

33. Barth, *Church Dogmatics*, II/1, 409–10.

34. Abraham J. Heschel, *The Prophets* (1962; reprint, New York: Harper Perenniel, 2001), 242.

35. "Freedom is not a natural disposition, but God's precious gift to man." Heschel, *The Prophets*, 243.

The Fall of humanity in Adam and Eve woefully affected our exercise of this communicable gift.[36] However, God's gift of freedom remained with us, in a limited yet real sense, even in our brokenness (Gen. 4:7). Freedom and its opposite, slavery, became functions of either relationship with God or rebellion to God (Rom. 6:16–21). True human freedom is restored only in union with Christ, obedience to God, and empowerment by the Spirit (Rom. 6:4–7, 22–23; 8:1–2).

Conclusion

While the incomprehensible God has not disclosed his essential nature to humanity, he has disclosed certain great truths about his perfections through the trustworthy revelation of himself. It has taken the last four chapters just to begin painting a portrait of what Scripture teaches God is like. Perhaps a summary of God's identity may help you recall what you have already come to know about God through this great adventure of theology.

A Summary of Divine Identity

In chapter 5, we learned that God is one yet three. The three Persons, God the Father and God the Son and God the Holy Spirit, must be together worshiped and glorified as one God, each sharing equally and eternally in the unity of the divine perfections.

---

36. "The opposite of freedom is not determinism, but hardness of heart. Freedom presupposes openness of heart, of mind, of eye and ear. . . . Hardening of the heart is the suspension of freedom." Heschel, *The Prophets*, 243.

In chapter 6, we learned that God has revealed his common name of "God" and his covenantal name of "Lord," along with many other titles.

We also learned we must receive the revelation of the transcendent God's negative metaphysical attributes of mystery, infinity, simplicity, and aseity. God has also revealed his transcendent self to us in the positive metaphysical attributes of blessedness, sufficiency, spirituality, and personhood. The transcendence and immanence of God must be held together.

In this chapter, we have discovered that among the relative attributes which God shares with his creatures are holiness and love, along with the bridge attribute of righteousness, as well as the divine attribute of freedom.

Alongside God's overarching attribute of holiness, we may consider his eternity, immutability, and wisdom, as well as his universal attributes of omniscience, omnipotence, and omnipresence, and his disconcerting attributes of jealousy, wrath, and anger, and his glorious light.

God's righteousness must be understood not only in its commanding and punitive dimensions, but also as a redemptive gift available to fallen humanity as a grace received by faith.

Deriving from his ontology of love, we must consider his attributes of patience, grace, and faithfulness, as well as his wisdom, kindness, compassion, and mercy, and perhaps passibility.

We noted both that God is eternally free and that he created humanity in his image with a limited freedom.

Finally, we recall the important perfection of God's infinity in time and space that was the major consideration of chapter 4. Such high knowledge threatens to overwhelm us with the weight of his glory.

Overwhelmed by God's Grace

When I consider what God the Trinity is like, I am overwhelmed by the condescension of his grace to reveal himself to me, a mortal man, a sinner, saved by his grace. I agree with the psalmist that, "Such knowledge is too wonderful for me; it is too high; I cannot attain to it" (Ps. 139:6 NASB1995). To begin to know God as his incarnate Word revealed him to the biblical writers, and as his written Word reveals him to us by his Spirit today: This ought to be the cause for our wonder, our witness, and our worship of the eternal Lord.

Study Questions

1. How would you relate God's wrath with God's love? Do you think Garrett's description of divine righteousness as a "bridge" attribute helps to relate these two truths about God?

2. Describe the four ways in which God's love works.

3. Do you agree with the author that divine freedom is, in a limited sense, a communicable attribute?

Suggested Resources

- Rudolf Otto, *The Idea of the Holy*

- Anders Nygren, *Agape and Eros*

- Thomas Weinandy, *Does God Suffer?*

CHAPTER EIGHT

How Do People Know about God?

◆

DOES GOD SHOW HIMSELF TO us? If so, why does God manifest himself? Moreover, how does God give us his revelation? Finally, how do we know whether an idea about God, or about our salvation, came from God rather than from somewhere else? These are just a few of the important questions behind the foundational Christian doctrine of divine revelation.

From the outset, let us humbly recognize we can know nothing about God whatsoever apart from his revelation of himself. "That is, man can know God only as God gives himself to be known: this is the fundamental biblical point of view."[1] Thankfully, Scripture teaches that God has graciously disclosed himself to human beings. God reveals himself so that we might know who he is, what he expects, and how we might be restored to a right relationship with him.

---

1. Emil Brunner, *The Divine-Human Encounter*, transl. Amandus W. Loos (London: SCM Press, 1944), 34.

Revelation and the Nature of God

It is an aspect of God's very nature to reveal himself.[2] The true nature of God's self-revelation is seen in at least three ways: It is seen in revelation's Trinitarian origin, in God's way of working through speech, and in divine revelation's personal location in the third Person of the divine Trinity.

Revelation Is Trinitarian

First, revelation is an eternal movement between the three Persons of the Godhead. For instance, God the Father speaks to the Son (Ps. 110:1–4; Matt. 3:17). In return, God the Son speaks to the Father (Prov. 8:27–30; John 12:28; 17:5, 25–26). And the Father and the Son speak to God the Spirit, who in turn glorifies the Son (John 16:13–15). The Spirit also inspired the written Word of God (2 Pet. 1:20–21), which remains sufficient to reveal our salvation (2 Tim. 3:15–17).[3] The triune nature of God involves the reality of eternal communion between the Father and the Son and the Holy Spirit, and his eternal movement spills over into his relationship with us through his revelation of both his law and his gospel.

Revelation as Speech

Second, when God speaks to his creation, he speaks with power, with authority, and with presence. God always engages

---

2. John Frame says speaking is so fundamental in God that speech is a necessary divine attribute. "Speaking is one of his eternal attributes." "[S]peaking is a necessary attribute of God, an attribute without which he would not be God." John M. Frame, "Foundations of Biblical Inerrancy: Definition and Prolegomena," in John MacArthur, ed., *The Inerrant Word: Biblical, Historical, Theological, and Pastoral Perspectives* (Wheaton, IL: Crossway, 2016), 187.

3. See chapter 12 for a description of biblical sufficiency.

his world through his Word. God originally spoke the world into existence; he maintains it now by the power of his Word; and he will one day bring the world to its final consummation (Rom. 4:17; Ps. 29:1–9; 46:6; Rev. 19:13). God spoke to humanity with authority at creation, commanding our obedience and promising judgment for disobedience (Gen. 1:28; 2:16–17; 3:9–19; John 12:48). He granted his Word all authority and worked the redemption of the world through his Word (Matt. 28:18). Speaking to us personally through his Word, God still makes himself evident to us today. "God's word is his personal presence."[4]

Christ Is Revelation

Third, divine speech is identified with a particular divine Person. The apostle John wrote, "In the beginning was the Word, and the Word was with God, and the Word was God" (John 1:1). This Word, who is both identical with God yet distinct from the Father, "became flesh" in Jesus Christ (John 1:14).[5] John Webster commended our need to remain centered upon Jesus Christ due to his status as the revelation of God. "No reality may pretend to be more fundamental or comprehensive than he. He simply *is*, necessarily and

---

4. "This is also a quality of the Bible, for Scripture is a place where God personally dwells with his people." Frame, "Foundations of Biblical Inerrancy," 191.

5. During the Enlightenment, the doctrine of biblical inspiration was cast into doubt. Even for some conservatives, the written Word was shorn from its connection with the incarnate Word. More recently, theologians on the left, like Robert Jenson and Wolfhart Pannenberg, have begun moving back toward the doctrine of biblical inspiration through their appreciation for Jesus Christ. "The inspiration of Scripture is to be understood in the light of the center of Scripture, in the light of Jesus Christ as its center and criterion." Wolfhart Pannenberg, "Theological Table Talk: The Inspiration of Scripture," *Theology Today* 54 (1997): 214.

underivatively. He is this, of course, in relation to the Father and the Holy Spirit."[6]

Paul's Description of Divine Revelation

The doxology to Paul's great letter to the Romans collects eight basic truths which have been developed by the apostle throughout the entire epistle. An orthodox doctrine of divine revelation must include at least these eight aspects. These aspects extend the three truths about God's self-revelatory nature into God's relation to humanity. Paul's doxology, found in Romans 16:25–27, states,

> Now to him who is able to strengthen you according to my gospel and the proclamation about Jesus Christ, according to the revelation [*apokalypsin*] of the mystery kept silent for long ages but now revealed and made known through the prophetic Scriptures, according to the command of the eternal God to advance the obedience of faith among all the Gentiles—to the only wise God, through Jesus Christ—to him be the glory forever! Amen.

God and Revelation

The first three truths we must learn about the doctrine of divine revelation remind us that divine revelation, like every divine work, involves each person of the Trinity.

---

6. His italics. John Webster, *The Domain of the Word: Scripture and Theological Reason* (New York: T&T Clark, 2012), 35.

First, divine revelation occurs entirely by the gracious will of God the Father. It is "according to the command of the eternal God."

Second, revelation is centered upon the "gospel" which saves believers (cf. Rom. 1:1–4, 15–17). The gospel is received through "the proclamation about the Lord Jesus Christ."

Third, God reveals himself through the work of the Holy Spirit. In Romans, Paul always assigns the application of divine grace to the Holy Spirit (cf. Rom. 1:11; 2:29; 5:5; 8:2, 9, 11, 12–16, 23, 26–27; 12:3–11; 15:16, 19, 30).

Revelation and Humanity

The remaining five aspects taught in Paul's doxology extend the doctrine of revelation in relation to the recipient of divine self-revelation, humanity.

Fourth, revelation discloses God's mysterious will. We would not know the unfathomable "mystery" of the gospel of Jesus Christ in any other way than by the grace of his divine revelation.

Fifth, revelation came to the prophets who wrote Holy Scripture (cf. Rom. 1:2).

Sixth, revelation is for all the nations (cf. Rom. 1:16; 9:17, 24–26; 10:18–20; 11:11–12, 23–24; 15:7–12, 15–16, 20–21, 27; Isa. 52:15; 61:5–6; 62:2; 66:18–23).

Seventh, God's revelation, which again comes only through the proclamation about Jesus Christ, is intended to lead people to faith (cf. Rom. 10:8–13).

Finally, God's revelation of himself in Christ by the Spirit leads ultimately to his "glory." A good Christian doctrine of revelation must incorporate at least these eight basic claims about divine revelation which Scripture itself teaches.

Models of Divine Revelation

Theologians' Models of Revelation

Avery Dulles examined the different models used by theologians to present the doctrine of God's revelation. First, he said, some picture revelation as doctrine, wherein "clear propositional statements [are] attributed to God as authoritative teacher."[7] Others present revelation as history, for "God reveals himself primarily in his great deeds." According to this second model, "the Bible and church teaching are witnesses to revelation."[8]

A third model understands revelation as inner experience, "a privileged interior experience of grace or communion with God."[9] A fourth group portrays revelation as dialectical presence: "Utterly transcendent, God encounters the human subject when it pleases him by means of a word in which faith recognizes him to be present."[10] The fifth model sees revelation as new awareness, "an expansion of consciousness or shift of perspective when people join in the movements of secular history."[11]

Dulles evaluated each model then proposed a sixth model which he called symbolic mediation. He believed it incorporated the best of the other models. "A symbol is a sign pregnant with a plenitude of meaning which is evoked rather than explicitly stated."[12] By appealing to signs, Dulles drew on a long

---

7. Avery Dulles, *Models of Revelation* (Garden City, NY: Doubleday, 1983), 27.

8. Dulles, *Models of Revelation*, 27.

9. Dulles, *Models of Revelation*, 27.

10. Dulles, *Models of Revelation*, 28.

11. Dulles, *Models of Revelation*, 28.

12. Dulles, *Models of Revelation*, 132. Dulles draws upon an unpublished manuscript by Samuel Taylor Coleridge, who wrote, "It is by Symbols alone that we can acquire intellectual knowledge of the Divine." Dulles, *Models of Revelation*, 131.

tradition which goes back at least to Augustine.[13] Theologians have rightly recognized that the eternal God reveals himself in an act of accommodation through analogies, symbols, and metaphors which limited human beings may understand.[14]

A Trinitarian Model of Revelation

While all six of these previous models have something to offer, I prefer a seventh, theologically focused conceptual model. We may call this a *Trinitarian model of revelation.* This model, grounded in biblical revelation and received by the church through its canon and expressed in its creed, states simply that God's revelation of himself comes to humanity in his Word by his Spirit. While this model recognizes the importance, utility, and limits of general revelation, it rejoices in the saving fullness of special revelation. While this model recognizes the truths in the other models of revelation, it is explicitly grounded in the three-in-one Lord God.

The Trinitarian model of revelation considers the source, means, summit, perfection, and end of revelation. The source of revelation is God himself. The means of revelation are first and foremost, Jesus Christ, but also the prophets and the apostles who were inspired by the Holy Spirit. Their inspired writings are preserved and disseminated through the biblical canon. The summit of revelation, toward whom both the Old and New Testament writers point, is the self-revelation of God in our Lord and Savior Christ Jesus. If the perfect triune

---

13. "For a sign is a thing which of itself makes some other things come to mind, besides the impression that it presents to the senses." Saint Augustine, *On Christian Teaching*, transl. R. P. H. Green (New York: Oxford University Press, 1997), 30. Book Two of this classic text is dedicated to a full treatment of interpreting Scripture as composed of signs. Augustine, *On Christian Teaching*, 30–67.

14. Malcolm B. Yarnell III, "Systematic Theology," in *Theology, Church, and Ministry: A Handbook for Theological Education*, ed. David S. Dockery (Nashville: B&H Academic, 2017), 264, 270–71.

God is the source, means, and summit of revelation, then his revelation will also be characterized by perfection. The end of God's revelation displays itself in our human salvation and, ultimately, in his divine glory.

Definitions for Revelation, Reason, and Theology

The New Testament term for *revelation* is the Greek *apokalypsis*, which means to "unveil," "uncover," or "disclose." Millard Erickson defines revelation simply as, "God's manifestation of himself."[15] Avery Dulles says revelation is "a free manifestation by God of that which lies beyond the normal reach of human inquiry. It is the initial action by which God emerges from his hiddenness, calls to man, and invites him to a covenant-existence."[16]

The two major types of revelation are called general revelation and special revelation. In this chapter, we will focus on general revelation. In the next chapter, we will focus on the limited theology which can be derived from general revelation, natural theology. In subsequent chapters, we will consider special revelation and Scripture.

The *special revelation* of God includes that revelation which came first to Israel and its prophets, and then came in Jesus Christ and to the apostles. The special revelation of God includes the law of God which holds humanity accountable and the gospel of God which brings salvation to believers.

By *general revelation* we mean God the Trinity's disclosure of certain truths to all human beings about himself.

---

15. Millard J. Erickson, *Christian Theology*, 2nd ed. (Grand Rapids: Baker, 2001), 178.

16. Avery Dulles, *Revelation Theology: A History* (New York: Herder and Herder, 1969), 9.

These truths deal with God, humanity, and God's relation to humanity. These truths come to us via both external evidence through nature and internal evidence in the human conscience. General revelation is focused upon God's law rather than his gospel.

We must also distinguish the law from the gospel: The *law* of God brings condemnation and is available to the Jews through the Mosaic law and to everyone through conscience. The *gospel* of God is available to those who hear about the person and work of Jesus Christ and believe in him. Every person is condemned by means of the law, which highlights our sin. The redeemed are justified by means of the gospel, which makes forgiveness available to those who believe in Christ.

In *natural theology*, we are concerned with the human being's intellectual, moral, and spiritual response to God's general revelation. Natural theology is also sometimes referred to as rational theology or, rather simply, as reason. In natural theology, human reason is put in service of thinking about what God reveals through nature and in the human conscience. Natural theology is not concerned with man's entire set of curiosities. Instead, it is focused upon God and humanity's relationship with God.

Human *reason* participates in divine reason in a limited way. God is himself supremely reasonable, and he created us in his image to be reasonable too. The Greek term *logos* means "word," "reason," or "meaning." John wrote that Jesus Christ is the divine Logos who came into the world (John 1:1, 14). He also said, "The true light that gives light to everyone was coming into the world" (John 1:9). We know by this that all human beings have been given reason. But the human ability to reason is only a "representation" of the second Person of the Trinity, who is the divine Logos. Human reason is derivative of divine reason. Our reason works incompletely due to our createdness, and it works fallibly due to our fallenness.[17]

In contrast to natural theology, human theological reflection which is based on special revelation is typically referred to as *revealed theology* or *supernatural theology* and sometimes simply as *revelation*. Since the early church, theologians have affirmed that "although the Christian revelation is above reason, it is not contrary to reason."[18] We necessarily use reason when we reflect upon divine revelation, whether that revelation comes to all people generally or whether it comes as a special revelation.

In summary, the terms *revelation*, *reason*, and *theology* must remain carefully distinguished from one another: Revelation is what God manifests about himself, while theology is what we as human beings do with our reason in response to his revelation. Moreover, the concepts of general revelation and special revelation, and the various human responses of natural theology and revealed theology, must also remain distinct. The law and the gospel must also be delineated from one another, even as both have their necessary purposes.

The Bible Affirms General Revelation

Holy Scripture indicates what it means to say that God reveals himself to everyone. First, the Old Testament

---

17. Emil Brunner carefully correlates the abstract Greek idea of human reason with the personal biblical idea of divine reason. Yes, we are enabled to "see light" by means of God's light (Ps. 36:9). This light is ours because we were created in his image. The universal light compels humanity to seek truth and goodness, but we are unable to come to God apart from the Light who is God incarnate, Jesus Christ. Emil Brunner, *Revelation and Reason: The Christian Doctrine of Faith and Knowledge*, transl. Olive Wyon (Philadelphia: Westminster Press, 1946), 311–21.

18. Brunner, *Revelation and Reason*, 310.

establishes that some knowledge about God has been granted to all human beings: The Lord's name is magnified "throughout the earth," both in "the mouths of infants" and in "your heavens" (Ps. 8:1–3). Again, "the heavens declare the glory of God," pouring out "speech" and communicating "knowledge" (Ps. 19:1–2).

The prophets continued to affirm the truth of general revelation alongside the psalmists. The idolater knows intuitively he needs salvation, but he makes a worthless idol rather than worshipping the true God (Isa. 44:17). The Lord gave both life and order to nature, such that its regularity testifies to the certainty of his gifts of life and goodness (Jer. 31:35–36).

The New Testament likewise affirms general revelation. As mentioned above, John said our ability to reflect on truth was given by the One who later came into the world (John 1:9). Barnabas and Paul told the pagans of Lystra that God "did not leave himself without a witness" (Acts 14:17). The provision of life through nature demonstrates there is a God and that he is good.

Preaching to the academy of Athens, Paul taught that God providentially guides human history. He sets the variable times and boundaries of nations (Acts 17:26), and these phenomena too reveals him. God guides human history so that people "might seek God, and perhaps they might reach out and find him, though he is not far from each one of us" (Acts 17:27). God reveals his providence, not only in nature but also in human history.

In his famous epistle to the Romans, the apostle Paul divided the revelation of God into two parts: The righteousness of God "is revealed" (Greek *apokalypsetai*) in the gospel of Jesus Christ (Rom. 1:17), while the wrath of God "is revealed" (Greek *apokalypsetai*) against all human unrighteousness (Rom. 1:18).

Special revelation conveys the righteousness, which can be appropriated by faith (Rom. 1:16–17). By way of contrast, general revelation is universal and brings condemnation on all people, for we are all unrighteous (Rom. 3:23). The general revelation of God comes "among" us in creation (Rom. 1:18–20) and to the human "heart" or "conscience." The conscience witnesses to God's law even apart from the written revelation of God's law (Rom. 2:14–16).

Scripture clearly affirms the reality of general revelation. God's revelation of himself, particularly in the law, comes to human beings in nature, in human history, and in human hearts and consciences.

The Bible Limits General Revelation

Scripture affirms general revelation, but Scripture also ascribes various limitations to general revelation.

Unheard

The first limitation with general revelation is that it is not intended to heal but to expose the sinful nature of the human being. And human beings do not listen carefully enough even to the general revelation we are given. General revelation may be said to speak without clarity, because its "voice is not heard" on the side of the recipient (Ps. 19:3). The human heart has "deceived" itself (Isa. 44:20). The unrighteous "suppress the truth" of general revelation (Rom. 1:18). The human being's general deafness toward God must be overcome by the grace of special revelation.

False Prophets

The second limitation with general revelation is that false prophets propagate both false revelation and the false interpretation of true revelation. Jeremiah warned that "the lying pen of scribes has produced falsehood" by proclaiming peace when God intended judgment (Jer. 8:8–12). One group of prophets is doubly deceptive. On the one hand, they propagate false revelation (Jer. 23:32) by relaying "visions from their own minds, not from the LORD's mouth" (Jer. 23:16). On the other hand, the same prophets also pervert true revelation with false interpretation (Jer. 23:28–30).

Jeremiah condemned the prophet Hananiah, "The Lord did not send you, but you have led these people to trust in a lie" (Jer. 28:15). False claims to revelation and false interpretations of revelation abound. This is as true for all revelation, both general revelation and special revelation.

Partial

The third limitation to general revelation is that it draws only a partial portrait of God. Romans 1:18–2:16 offers a series of truths about God which are available through general revelation. These include that God is hidden from our sight, has eternal power, and has a divine nature (Rom. 1:20). He is also incorruptible, deserves glory (Rom. 1:21), and is truth (Rom. 1:25). God is our Creator (Rom. 1:25), should be known (Rom. 1:28), and should be loved (Rom. 1:21). He is also angry at us (Rom. 1:18; 2:2–6), because he gave us his law (Rom. 2:12–14), which we disobeyed (Rom. 2:8). Remember also that Scripture teaches God's providential goodness is revealed. Despite all these truths about God's character and ways which are revealed to all people, Scripture provides no hint whatsoever that the ultimate theological truth of God as Trinity and the saving truth of Jesus as the Lord Christ are available through general revelation.

Suppressed

The fourth limitation of general revelation concerns what it says about man in his relationship to God. In Romans 1, Paul taught that humanity is granted an inclination to worship God (Rom. 1:25), but humanity invariably suppresses this truth in unrighteousness (Rom. 1:18). Although a human person might perceive some truths, he or she perverts these truths. Idolatry and sexual impurity are two characteristic self-centered sins against general revelation (Rom. 1:22, 24). It is increasingly evident from such texts that human beings could never build a holistic doctrine of God or of humanity with only general revelation.

Insufficient for Redemption

The fifth limitation to general revelation concerns its insufficient soteriology. General revelation lets us know we can expect the sentence of judgment and that we need salvation (Rom. 1:32; 2:15–16; Isa. 44:9–11, 17). Alas, however, general revelation reveals nothing about the identity of the Lord Jesus Christ, including his incarnation, teaching, death, resurrection, and coming judgment. Neither does it reveal the Trinity in a sufficient manner. Because of its incomplete portrait of God and of the way of salvation, general revelation remains incapable of justifying sinners. In affirming our condemnation, the law of general revelation exhibits a preparatory function, but it can never solve the root problem, our deserved judgment by God.

Worldly Wisdom

A sixth limitation with general revelation concerns the errant worldviews it generates. In his Corinthian correspondence, the apostle Paul contrasted "the world's wisdom" with

"God's wisdom" (1 Cor. 1:20–21). Jews and Greeks pursue wisdom in different ways (1 Cor. 1:22), but neither can attain the wisdom of God. God's wisdom is displayed in "Christ crucified," but the cross is a "stumbling block" and "foolishness" to those in the world (1 Cor. 1:23). The proclamation which saves people seems "weak," "insignificant," and "despised" to carnal people (1 Cor. 1:27–28; 2:1). However, Christ on the cross is "the power" and "the wisdom" of God (1 Cor. 1:24). God's wisdom, prepared from eternity, was hidden until it was manifested in Christ (1 Cor. 2:7–8, 16). Only those who are specifically led by the Spirit have access to this divine wisdom (1 Cor. 2:10–14).

The Bible Reveals More Than General Revelation

Scripture clearly teaches that there is a revelation of God made available to all human beings. All human beings know through nature, history, and conscience of the existence of God, of certain attributes of God, and of our impending judgment by God. However, the Bible also places limits upon general revelation. These limits are especially critical regarding its restricted purpose of making God's law known and regarding humanity's propensity to pervert general revelation. The limits of general revelation demonstrate the need for another type of revelation if humanity will be saved.

Special Revelation Overcomes the Limits of General Revelation

In his second epistle to Timothy, Paul showed how the limits of general revelation can be overcome. Most importantly, he argued, we must focus on the apostolic teaching about the special revelation of Jesus Christ (2 Tim. 2:2). We should avoid unnecessary worldly entanglements, although we necessarily continue to live and witness in the world (2 Tim. 2:3–5). Rather than being infatuated with the world, we must let the Word of God work in our midst (2 Tim. 2:6–13), by reminding others of God's Word (2 Tim. 2:14) and rightly interpreting it according to the gospel (2 Tim. 2:8, 11, 15).

We must also beware of false teachers who are "always learning and never able to come to a knowledge of the truth" (2 Tim. 3:7). In conclusion, Paul tells us we must have continual resort to the special revelation of Scripture, for it sufficiently brings salvation (2 Tim. 3:14–15). Scripture is divinely inspired (2 Tim. 3:16a) and is also thus "profitable" for teaching a disciple how to live (2 Tim. 3:16b).

If God did not reveal himself to us in a saving way, we would be devoid of all hope in this life. However, by virtue of his loving will, God has revealed not only his law but also his salvation to us. He has supremely revealed himself in the person of Jesus Christ, his only begotten Son, to atone for our sins and offer us salvation through union with him. This revelation is offered for us to believe personally by the work of the Holy Spirit through the written and proclaimed Word of God. The divine gift of salvation is a special revelation which requires the proclamation of the gospel of Jesus Christ.

General Revelation Remains a Reality

Yet the truth remains that God also reveals himself to all human beings in general through both nature and conscience, and in human history. This general revelation is verified by Scripture. This general revelation has been the subject of many interesting treatises by both believers and nonbelievers. However, as we have seen, general revelation has definite limits. General revelation teaches everyone about God, about humanity, and about the need for human salvation. However, general revelation does not offer the knowledge which leads to salvation.

How Can We Use General Revelation?

We must now turn to the question about whether we should use general revelation. And, even if we may use general revelation, how can we craft a natural theology from it? Finally, if general revelation is incapable of bringing someone into a saving relationship with the Lord, what could possibly be its purpose? In the next chapter, we will explore the various ways Christians have conceived of general revelation and constructed natural theology.

Study Questions

1. Are all three Persons of the Godhead involved in the work of revelation? If so, what does God the Father do? What is God the Son's work? And what is God the Holy Spirit doing?

2. Of the seven models of revelation described above, which do you believe is the best? Is there an even better way to conceive of divine revelation?

3. What truths about God would you say general revelation provides? What important truths about God does general revelation not provide?

Suggested Resources

- Emil Brunner, *The Divine-Human Encounter*

- Avery Dulles, *Models of Revelation*

- Augustine, *On Christian Teaching*

CHAPTER NINE

What about Natural Theology?

◆

In the previous chapter, we explored both divine revelation and that category of revelation known as general revelation. We found that the Bible affirms that some revelation about God is available to all human beings. However, we also learned Scripture ascribes definite limits to general revelation. In this chapter, we explore the discipline of natural theology. Natural theology is comprised of doctrines derived through human reasoning about God and his creation.

We will first look at how theologians in the early church answered the question of whether we can even use secular learning in theology. Second, we consider three proposals from the Medieval, Reformation, and Modern periods of the church for how natural theology may be incorporated into theology. Third, we criticize Karl Barth's strident denial of both general revelation and natural theology. Finally, we offer a systematic definition for the utility of general revelation in the construction of natural theology.

Early Christians Confront Pagan Learning

In the history of Christianity, two major types of questions have confronted Christians as they considered the truth of general revelation and its possible use for the construction of a natural theology. First, logically came the questions about general revelation: Does God truly reveal himself to all creatures? And if so, how does he do so? Second, came the questions about human reception or certainty: How proficient is human reason in perceiving general revelation? And how adequate is human reason for reflecting upon general revelation in the construction of natural theology?

During the church's early centuries, contradictory answers were given to the first question in the form of asking whether theologians might employ pagan philosophy alongside Scripture. On the optimistic side, the Jewish philosopher Philo used Stoic ideas about the Logos to link biblical theology with pagan philosophy.[1] Early Christian apologists followed in train and correlated the New Testament Son of God with the fundamental principle of Logos, universal reason. Justin Martyr believed pagans who lived reasonably could, therefore, perhaps be seen as "Christians before Christianity."[2] Theologians in the second and third centuries thus appropriated pagan reason for a compelling witness to Christ.

However, some theologians soon overstepped their bounds and began fashioning theology according to pagan philosophy. Most famously, Arius of Alexandria was condemned for using the Logos tradition to separate the Son from the Father

---

1. John Norman Davidson Kelly, *Early Christian Doctrines*, revised ed. (San Francisco: Harper Collins, 1978), 9–11.

2. Kelly, *Early Christian Doctrines*, 96. Ülrich Zwingli in the sixteenth century similarly placed Hercules, Socrates, and other distinguished men in heaven. Francis Turretin, *Institutes of Elenctic Theology*, ed. James T. Dennison Jr., transl. George Musgrave Giger, 3 vols. (1696; Philipsburg, NJ: P&R Publishing, 1992), 1:15.

by the council of Nicaea in 325 and by orthodox theologians thereafter. Arius's fundamental error was to make the Son subordinate to God.[3] The greatest heresy ever to confront the church thus arose through the enthusiastic employment of Greek philosophy.[4]

Negative reactions to such optimistic use of pagan classics by Christian thinkers came from Julian the Apostate, Tertullian of Carthage, and Jerome of Dalmatia. Julian reigned as Emperor over the Roman Empire centered in Constantinople for a short period (361–363). He renounced his former identification with Christianity, sought to reinstate paganism, and banned Christians from teaching the classics. According to his former Christian classmate, Gregory of Nazianzus, Julian believed only pagans have "the right to speak, write, and think in Greek."[5]

Tertullian, a lifelong believer, is today widely known for certain dismissive comments toward pagan learning. For instance, he asked, "Therefore, what of Athens and Jerusalem? What of the academy and the church?"[6] However, Tertullian's declamations were obvious rhetorical flourishes. While he recognized paganism could lead to idolatry or heresy, he also argued Christianity was supremely reasonable and appropriated the philosopher's pallium.[7]

---

3. Rowan Williams, *Arius: Heresy and Tradition*, revised ed. (Grand Rapids: Eerdmans, 2002), 175–78.

4. For Arius's idiosyncratic use of Platonic philosophy, see Williams, *Arius*, 181–232.

5. Julian argued Christians "ought to refrain from teaching what they themselves do not believe to be true." Jaroslav Pelikan, *Christianity and Classical Culture: The Metamorphosis of Natural Theology in the Christian Encounter with Hellenism* (New Haven: Yale University Press, 1993), 12.

6. He also once said, "I believe it because it is absurd." Geoffrey D. Dunn, *Tertullian* (New York: Routledge, 2004), 31.

7. The pallium originated as the Greek philosopher's cloak but was later adopted by Christian bishops. Dunn, *Tertullian*, 32–33.

Like Tertullian, the famous Bible translator and early commentator, Jerome, was trained in the classics. However, Jerome came to adore them uncritically, especially the writings of the Roman philosopher, Cicero. The heavenly judge in a dream convicted Jerome for his misplaced enthusiasm, so Jerome forswore their use.[8] This early church father kept his promise for over a decade, but he later contended the classics might be used if they were purified and consecrated.[9]

Later fourth and fifth century theologians in the Roman Empire spurned the uncritical employment of pagan philosophy on the one side and avoided the entire renunciation of classical culture on the other. Leading Christian theologians in the Greek East and in the Latin West used the secular classics after stripping them of their pagan religion.

In the East, the Cappadocians distinguished Greek language and philosophy from Greek religion, appropriating the former while rejecting the latter: Basil of Caesarea reminded his readers the human mind was created in the image of God but had fallen. The Trinity transforms our reason and our will so we might truly perceive him.[10] Macrina taught her younger brother, Gregory of Nyssa, to employ classical philosophy wisely when constructing his doctrine of God.[11] Nyssa appealed to the example of Moses, who judiciously utilized his Egyptian education.[12] Gregory of Nazianzus first differenti-

---

8. In this dream, Jerome appeared before the divine Judge, who asked for his identity. After stating he was a Christian, he was condemned, "You are lying. You are a disciple of Cicero, not of Christ; for your heart is where your treasure is." Jerome swore in response, "Lord, if I ever again possess worldly books, if I ever read them, I shall have denied you." John Norman Davidson Kelly, *Jerome: His Life, Writings, and Controversies* (1975; reprint, Peabody, MA: Hendrickson, 2000), 42.

9. Kelly, *Jerome*, 43–44.

10. Pelikan, *Christianity and Classical Culture*, 282–87.

11. Pelikan, *Christianity and Classical Culture*, 216.

12. Pelikan, *Christianity and Classical Culture*, 10, 22.

ated faith from reason, then elevated faith above reason, and finally affirmed "faith as the fulfillment of our reasoning."[13]

In the West, Augustine of Hippo divided pagan learning between those ideas established by demons and those established by humans. Demonic institutions must be evaded as idolatrous superstition,[14] but human discoveries may be used with due care. "This whole area of human institutions which contribute to the necessities of life should in no way be avoided by the Christian; indeed, within reason, they should be studied and committed to memory."[15] These life necessities include truths about the body, the mind, and history; the natural sciences, the arts, and crafts; and logic, rhetoric, and math.[16]

Like the Cappadocians, Augustine applied the Israelite experience in Exodus to the Christian use of classical learning. Augustine argued that Christians should use classical learning just as the Israelites took with them the moral and spiritual truths which the Egyptians had previously dug from "the mines of providence."[17]

In the end, however, even the best of paganism's gold, silver, and clothing pale into "insignificance" when "compared with the knowledge contained in the divine scriptures." Augustine exalted Scripture and strived to keep pagan learning subordinate.

> For what a person learns independently of scripture is condemned there if it is harmful, but found there if it is useful. And when one has found there all the useful knowledge

---

13. Pelikan, *Christianity and Classical Culture*, 216–17.

14. Saint Augustine, *On Christian Teaching*, transl. R. P. H. Green (New York: Oxford University Press, 1997), 48–53.

15. Augustine, *On Christian Teaching*, 54.

16. Augustine, *On Christian Teaching*, 54–62.

17. Augustine, *On Christian Teaching*, 65.

that can be learnt anywhere else, one will also find there, in much greater abundance, things which are learnt nowhere else at all, but solely in the remarkable sublimity and the remarkable humility of the scriptures.[18]

Three Ways to Incorporate General Revelation into Theology

Following on the heels of the lessons learned in the early church, orthodox Christians have typically distinguished human reason from special revelation. They have also elevated revelation over natural reason. Christian theologians invariably employ their reason while explaining revelation to their audiences.

Four major proposals have been put forward for the construction of natural theology from general revelation. Each proposal involves divergent attitudes toward both the possibility of general revelation and the measure of certainty with which humanity may craft a theology from such general knowledge about God, humanity, and God's relationship to humanity.

The first three major proposals regarding the possibility and usage of natural theology derive from medieval Thomism, the Reformers, and post-Reformation dogmatics. The fourth proposal, a dissenting report offered by Karl Barth, will be considered in the next section.

---

18. Augustine, *On Christian Teaching*, 67.

Medieval Thomism

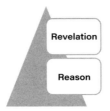

Thomas Aquinas drew on the legacies of the Christian theologian Augustine and the pagan philosopher Aristotle to create a relatively optimistic, intellectually sophisticated, yet biblically sensitive natural theology. This thirteenth-century theologian used general revelation as "a sort of preamble" to revealed theology.[19] It has become axiomatic to represent Aquinas as having constructed a two-story building, with special revelation founded upon natural reason.[20] His large systematic works, *Summa Contra Gentiles* and *Summa Theologia*, routinely place philosophical demonstration prior to revelation.

> There is a twofold mode of truth in what we profess about God. Some truths about God exceed all the ability of the human reason. Such is the truth that God is triune. But there are some truths which the natural reason also is able to reach. Such are that God exists, that

---

19. Anton C. Pegis, "General Introduction," in Saint Thomas Aquinas, *Summa Contra Gentiles*, 5 vols., transl. Pegis (Notre Dame, IN: Doubleday, 1955–1957), 1:23.

20. Denys Turner, *Thomas Aquinas: A Portrait* (New Haven: Yale University Press, 2013), 104–6. This structure does not mean Aquinas was uncritical of natural theology nor that he was less interested in Scripture. Turner, *Thomas Aquinas*, 107–9; *Aquinas on Scripture: An Introduction to His Biblical Commentaries*, ed. Thomas G. Weinandy, Daniel A. Keating, and John P. Yocum (New York: T&T Clark, 2005).

He is one, and the like. In fact, such truths
about God have been proved demonstratively
by the philosophers, guided by the light of
the natural reason.[21]

Aquinas, like John Wycliffe and many other medieval
theologians, was a philosophical realist who linked human
language with the reality it represented. Realist theologians
agreed with Plato regarding the existence of universals and
with Aristotle regarding the utility of categories. Realists
believed "universals" are metaphysical realities which lie
behind such common phenomenal categories as color, solidity,
and humanity.

Philosophical nominalists, including not only William of
Ockham but Martin Luther, strongly disagreed with this optimistic realism. They denied the realist construal of universalist
language. For instance, realists said certain things participate
in a form called redness and therefore look red. Nominalists
denied these ideas participate in eternal reality. Rather, universal terms are "merely conceptual tools manufactured by
the mind to explain commonalities between individuals."[22]
Nominalists denied divine reality was undermined by their
razor logic; only human descriptions were. However, realists
deemed nominalism a threat to theological certainty.

---

21. Aquinas, *Summa Contra Gentiles*, 1:63.

22. Malcolm B. Yarnell III, *Royal Priesthood in the English Reformation*
(New York: Oxford University Press, 2013), 19.

The Reformers

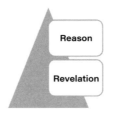

Martin Luther both elevated the authority of Scripture and attacked the use of Greek philosophy. Luther wanted to separate the gospel from the accretions of scholastic tradition, especially when it speculated about human free will, the presence of good works in soteriology, and the sacrifice of the Mass. He used the logic of nominalism to slice away theological conclusions constructed during a millennium of optimism about language and tradition.[23]

Reformers like Philip Melanchthon in Wittenburg, Ülrich Zwingli in Zürich, and John Calvin in Geneva soon began systematizing this new theology. The Reformers explicitly grounded their systems in biblical revelation. They also expounded their ideas about biblical faith affectively and reasonably. The Reformers were skeptical about human reason, but they nonetheless utilized reason.

Calvin believed humanity inevitably misconstrues the universal knowledge that God is Creator. The human heart perverts general revelation into "a perpetual factory of idols."[24] "[I]f men were taught only by nature, they would hold to

---

23. Bernhard Lohse, *Martin Luther's Theology: Its Historical and Systematic Development*, transl. Roy A. Harrisville (Minneapolis: Fortress Press, 1999), 37, 48–49, 98–99, 187–95.

24. John Calvin, *Institutes of the Christian Religion*, ed. John T. McNeill, transl. Ford Lewis Battles, 2 vols. (Philadelphia: Westminster Press, 1960), 1:108; idem, *Commentaries on the Epistle of Paul the Apostle to the Romans*, transl. John Owen (reprint, Grand Rapids: Baker, 1996), 73.

nothing certain or solid or clear-cut but would be so tied to confused principles as to worship an unknown god."[25] Instead of nature, people can hear God speak clearly in Scripture alone[26] as they become convinced of its truth by the witness of the Spirit.[27] Calvin agreed that reason must yield to the supremacy of revelation.[28]

The medieval culture of epistemological certainty was undermined by nominalist Reformers like Luther. Establishing different trajectories for both Reformed theology and Anabaptist theology, Zwingli originally argued for the existence of a common intellectual certainty when people approach the interpretation of Scripture.[29] However, repelled by the way that more radical reformers used promiscuous certainty, Zwingli backed away from his universal optimism. Calvin long expressed misgivings about the availability of certainty to various interpreters. Nevertheless, Calvin ascribed certainty to the proclamation of Reformed pastors due to the Word's divine origin.[30]

---

25. Calvin, *Institutes of the Christian Religion*, 1:66.

26. Calvin, *Institutes of the Christian Religion*, 1:70.

27. Calvin, *Institutes of the Christian Religion*, 1:79.

28. Calvin, *Institutes of the Christian Religion*, 1:80–81.

29. "God's Word brought with it its own clarity and enlightenment." Ülrich Zwingli, *On the Certainty and Clarity of the Word of God* (1522), in *Zwingli and Bullinger*, ed. G. W. Bromiley (Philadelphia: Westminster Press, 1953), 77. On the basis of the universal priesthood, all Christians may judge the teaching of priests through dependence on the Spirit, prayer, reading of Scripture, and faith. Zwingli, *On the Certainty and Clarity of the Word of God*, 88–89.

30. "Calvin participated in its [certainty's] erosion, but even as he did so, he also clung to it." William J. Bouwsma, *John Calvin: A Sixteenth-Century Portrait* (New York: Oxford University Press, 1988), 71–72.

Post-Reformation Dogmatics

Human reason attained a prominent role in Christian theology during the subsequent modern period. Toward the end of the Reformation, radical Socinian theologians "fenced" revelation with *recta ratio* (Latin, "right reason").[31] Socinians denied the Trinity, demoted both Christ and the Spirit, and said the atonement worked merely by example. With roots in Italy, their movement flourished for a time through religious tolerance in Poland and in Transylvania, but its greatest influence came in Holland and England over the next several centuries.[32]

A leading Protestant scholastic theologian of the seventeenth century, Francis Turretin, detected a spectrum of views regarding the relationship of reason to faith. He distinguished the Reformed yet located them next to the Socinians on one side while lumping together the Roman Catholics, Lutherans,

---

31. *The Racovian Catechism with Notes and Illustrations* (1609), ed. Thomas Rees (London: Longman et al., 1818), ciii. Similarly, the 1659 editors of this Socinian confession employed language from the 1646 preface of the First London Confession. But where the Particular Baptists asked for opponents to offer the "friendly part" of correcting them "from the word of God," the Socinians asked their opponents to offer "friendly admonition" by correcting them "from just and solid reasons." Cf. *Baptist Confessions of Faith*, ed. William L. Lumpkin (Valley Forge, PA: Judson Press, 1969), 149; *The Racovian Cathecism*, ed. Rees, cv.

32. Arthur J. Long, "Socinianism," in *The Dictionary of Historical Theology*, ed. Trevor A. Hart (Grand Rapids: Eerdmans, 2000), 522–24.

and Anabaptists with others on the opposing side. Turretin argued the Socinians overrated reason while the rest of Christianity, other than the Reformed, underrated reason.[33] He admitted other Christians perceived the Reformed "as if we made ourselves the judges and final arbiters" of faith due to their optimism about reason.[34]

Echoing medieval Thomism, natural theology thereby became the basis "upon which supernatural theology is built" in Reformed dogmatics.[35] Revelation and reason were closely correlated. Although Reformed scholastic theologians like Turretin found reason very useful, they argued that natural theology nevertheless remained insufficient. The special revelation of the Lord Jesus Christ remains necessary to know salvation.[36]

Turretin classified the certainty attributable to human reasoning as either "solid," "probable," or "corrupted."[37] Although human reason has been blinded by sin, it can become "sound and healed by grace" through the Spirit's enlightenment.[38] People should submit their reason both to Scripture and to "pastors appointed in the church."[39] Reformed scholastics positioned their rational ability lower than Socinianism but above the laity and above rival clerics.

The Roman Catholic Church codified the certainty of natural theology at Vatican I: "If anyone says that the one, true

---

33. Turretin, *Institutes of Elenctic Theology*, 1:24, 28.

34. Turretin, *Institutes of Elenctic Theology*, 1:29.

35. Turretin, *Institutes of Elenctic Theology*, 1:11.

36. Turretin, *Institutes of Elenctic Theology*, 1:18, 24.

37. Turretin, *Institutes of Elenctic Theology*, 1:18, 27, 31.

38. Turretin, *Institutes of Elenctic Theology*, 1:31. "Reason is perfected by faith," became an axiom for Reformed theologians. Cf. Herman Bavinck, *Reformed Dogmatics*, vol. 1, *Prolegomena,* ed. John Bolt, transl. John Vriend (Grand Rapids: Baker Academic, 2003), 322.

39. Reformed pastors have a "subordinate judgment" to Scripture but a superior judgment to the laity. Turretin, *Institutes of Elenctic Theology*, 1:29.

God, our creator and lord, cannot be known with certainty from the things that have been made, by the natural light of human reason: let him be anathema."[40] The council, however, also subordinated reason to revelation and deemed supernatural revelation necessary for redemption.[41] The Anabaptists, the Moravians, and the Pietists, among many others, were less sanguine than either the Roman Catholics or the Reformed scholastic theologians about the capabilities of human reason and the utility of natural theology.[42]

Despite such diversity, all orthodox Christians from Rome to Geneva to Nashville continued to affirm the certainty of Scripture even as they differed over its level of authority, its theological interpretation, and the incorporation of general revelation into natural theology. Alas, however, as the Modern period progressed many began to follow the example of the earlier Socinians and challenge every orthodoxy. Radical philosophers like Baruch Spinoza elevated nature above God and reason above Scripture.[43] Protestant liberals like Friedrich Schleiermacher developed a high view of human experience.[44]

---

40. *Dogmatic Constitution on the Catholic Faith* (1870), in *Decrees of the Ecumenical Councils*, ed. Norman P. Tanner, 2 vols. (Washington, DC: Georgetown University Press, 1990), 2:810.

41. *Dogmatic Constitution on the Catholic Faith*, 2:810–11.

42. Bavinck, *Prolegomena*, 161–62, 184; Malcolm B. Yarnell III, *The Formation of Christian Doctrine* (Nashville: B&H Academic, 2007), 49–70.

43. Baruch Spinoza, *Theological-Political Treatise* (1670), in *The Collected Works of Baruch Spinoza*, ed. Edwin Curley, vol. 2 (Princeton: Princeton University Press, 2016), 65–354.

44. Friedrich Schleiermacher, *On Religion: Speeches to its Cultured Despisers* (1799), ed. Richard Crouter (New York: Cambridge University Press, 1988).

A Dissenting Report: Karl Barth

Karl Barth (1886–1968) mounted a full-scale offense against any use of natural theology by denying general revelation. He defended his rejection in his heated response to a former colleague and in his exhaustive *Church Dogmatics*.[45] Barth said the utterly transcendent God knows himself and reveals himself to humanity, but God moves entirely by grace. Because revelation is a grace, we cannot move upward from the sphere of humanity's knowledge into the sphere of God's self-knowledge. Rather, God must especially "encroach" upon human beings.[46]

Unlike Anselm, Aquinas, or Calvin, Barth said natural analogies never reveal God as Lord and Creator, much less Reconciler and Redeemer.[47] Barth assumed natural theology always creates an abstract God, an idol. Knowing God "apart from grace and therefore from faith, or which thinks and promises that it is able to give such a guarantee—in other words, a 'natural' theology—is quite impossible within the

45. Emil Brunner and Karl Barth, *Natural Theology: Comprising "Nature and Grace" by Professor Dr. Emil Brunner and the Reply "No!"* ed. John Baillie, transl. Peter Fraenkel (1946; reprint, Eugene, OR: Wipf and Stock, 2002), 65–128; Karl Barth, *Church Dogmatics*, Vol. II, *The Doctrine of God,* Part 1, ed. G. W. Bromiley and T. F. Torrance, transl. T. H. L. Parker et al (Edinburgh: T&T Clark, 1957), 63–128.

46. Barth, *Church Dogmatics*, II/1, 67–69, 73–74.

47. Barth, *Church Dogmatics*, II/1, 75–79.

Church, and indeed, in such a way that it cannot even be discussed in principle."[48]

Even attempts to ground general revelation in Scripture show the impossibility of its existence, because Scripture is the record of special revelation. Barth reviewed select biblical passages regarding general revelation. He emphasized texts teaching that nobody understands or seeks God (Ps. 14:2–3) and that there is no clarity in speech from nature (Ps. 19:3). Like Job, we must repent of efforts to build a natural theology from general revelation (Job 42:3–6).[49]

However, the biggest problem, Barth argued, is that the natural theology derived from general revelation has sundered itself from the special revelation of God in Jesus Christ. "Incontestably, because from the very outset a theology of this kind looks in another direction than where God has placed Himself, and therefore involves, from the very outset, a violation of the Christian concept of God. Why, then, is all this not so simple and self-evident?"[50]

Karl Barth's protest should make us step back and question the use of general revelation in the construction of Christian doctrine. After all, Barth was motivated to offer his negative report after witnessing his liberal teachers use natural theology to support German nationalism during the first world war. Subsequently, the National Socialist regime and the fawning of the so-called "German Christians" over the Fuhrer proved the troubling extent to which natural theology might be applied.[51]

---

48. Barth, *Church Dogmatics*, II/1, 85.

49. Barth, *Church Dogmatics*, II/1, 99–116.

50. Barth, *Church Dogmatics*, II/1, 126.

51. For a fuller discussion of the debate between Barth and Brunner, see David S. Dockery and Malcolm B. Yarnell III, *Special Revelation and Scripture* (Brentwood, TN: B&H Academic, 2024), ch. 3.

Although Barth protested for good reasons, his theological exegesis of the biblical text is obviously partial. Moreover, the biblical and historical warnings about false interpretation of revelation apply as much to special revelation as to general revelation.[52] Barth did not entirely abandon the book of divine Scripture due to egregious interpretation. Neither may we entirely abandon the books of nature and of conscience. False interpretations of revelation abound, so every claim to revelation or to its interpretation must be tested thoroughly. The "more noble" Bereans exemplify how every claim to revelation and every interpretation of revelation (Acts 17:11), whether that revelation is special or general, must be tested.

Carl F. H. Henry, the late twentieth century's leading evangelical proponent for the truthfulness of divine revelation, was likewise uncomfortable with certain types of natural theology. But Henry, unlike Barth, never proscribed general revelation. He believed general revelation says important things about God, humanity, and humanity's relationship to God. Henry corrected Barth's error: "Barth's denial and repudiation of general divine revelation was just as costly an error as the scholastics' espousal of natural theology."[53]

Systematic Conclusions

What truths can we garner from the general revelation of God to all human beings? Seven conclusions immediately come to mind.

---

52. See the discussion about false prophecy and false interpretation in chapter 8.

53. Carl. F. H. Henry, *God, Revelation and Authority*, vol. 2, *God Who Speaks and Shows: Fifteen Theses, Part One* (1976; reprint, Wheaton: Crossway, 1999), 89.

Affirm the Truths of General Revelation

First, we should affirm the limited truths which general revelation teaches about God, humanity, and humanity's broken relation to God.[54] James Madison Pendleton agreed, "heathen nations are not ignorant of the existence of a Supreme Being." However, "it cannot be maintained that they have sufficient knowledge of his character to render them intelligent and acceptable worshippers." Human beings "have conceptions of his wisdom, power, greatness, and of other natural attributes. But what can we say of his moral perfections? The light of nature does not reveal it, and the deductions of man's reason do not disclose it."[55] Geerhardus Vos similarly concluded that general revelation "cannot teach believers anything unto salvation that is not contained in Scripture."[56]

Is All Truth God's Truth?

Second, we must evaluate the common proverb that "All truth is God's truth." Augustine famously argued, "A person who is a good and true Christian should realize that truth belongs to his Lord, wherever it is found."[57] Moreover, Jesus claimed that he himself is "the way, the truth, and the life" (John 14:6). All truth comes from God in one way or another. However, caution is needed when men ascribe their ideas to God. Christians should never grant theological authority to mere human innovation. Every truth about God descends from God either through natural revelation or by supernatural revelation, but human beings consistently practice deception

---

54. See chapter 8 above.

55. James M. Pendleton, *Christian Doctrines: A Compendium of Theology* (1906; reprint, Valley Forge: Judson Press, 1985), 25.

56. Geerhardus Vos, *Natural Theology*, transl. Albert Gootjes (Grand Rapids: Reformation Heritage Books, 2022), 5.

57. Augustine, *On Christian Teaching*, 47.

(Rom. 1:18–3:20). The common proverb must be coupled with a qualification: "All truth is God's truth, but human beings deceive and are deceived."[58]

Reject False Claims of Revelation

Third, building on the previous point, we must reject spurious revelations and false interpretations of true revelation. All human beings reflect upon general revelation, but we must be careful about human constructions and conclusions. For example, the speculations of unbelieving psychologists, or the religious teachings of the holy books of Islam and Hinduism, must never be classified with revelation. The teachings of Sigmund Freud and Carl Rogers are not general revelation, though they reflect upon the psychology of humanity.[59] The Koran must not be identified as revelatory, though it sometimes reflects on prior revelation. Mohammed mixed truth with error and directly denied truths taught in the Holy Scriptures of the Old and New Testaments. The Koran does not merely lack inspiration; it directly denies non-negotiable truths regarding Christianity's central figure.[60]

---

58. Augustine in the same sentence therefore warned us to reject "superstitious vanities." Augustine, *On Christian Teaching*, 47.

59. Their ideas are considered yet criticized by Christian counselors. Gordon Lynch, "Pastoral Counseling and Pastoral Theology," in *The Blackwell Reader in Pastoral and Practical Theology*, ed. James Woodward and Stephen Pattison (Malden, MA: Blackwell, 2000), 226–28.

60. Russell Moore, "Natural Revelation," in *A Theology for the Church*, ed. Daniel L. Akin, revised ed. (Nashville: B&H Academic, 2014), 97-98. The attitude of Mohammed and the Koran toward Jesus Christ will be considered in volume two of this series, Theology for Every Person.

Truths about God, Humanity, and Their Relationship

Fourth, we may work carefully toward seeing certain ideas about God, humanity, and humanity's relation to God as made available through general revelation. Besides the knowledge of guilt, which general revelation offers to all human beings, other truths may be derived from the general revelation of God's law. For instance, because of the witness of the human conscience to universal law, the conscience can provide the impetus for recognizing basic human rights.[61] Barrett Duke argues both that the first freedom of religious liberty can be derived from secular arguments, and that Scripture clearly supports this most fundamental of human rights.[62] Likewise, the discipline of "natural law" argues that all human beings have access to basic moral truth. Natural law theorists cite the ancient and continuing widespread evidence of moral discourse among human beings. Natural law and its derivatives in civil law have been asserted by theologians ranging from Thomas Aquinas to Martin Luther King Jr.[63]

The Existence of God

Fifth, what about efforts to prove the existence of God? In the third chapter of this book, I argued that God is real by appealing to general revelation. The various philosophical proofs for the existence of God appear to be useful in their

---

61. Paul Strohm, *Conscience: A Very Short Introduction* (New York: Oxford University Press, 2011), 84-88.

62. Barrett Duke, "The Christian Doctrine of Religious Liberty," in *First Freedom: The Beginning and End of Religious Liberty*, ed. Jason G. Duesing, Thomas White, and Malcolm B. Yarnell III, 2nd ed. (Nashville: B&H Academic, 2016), 87–105.

63. Ralph McInerny, "Ethics," and Paul E. Sigmund, "Law and Politics," in *The Cambridge Companion to Aquinas*, ed. Norman Kretzmann and Eleonore Stump (New York: Cambridge University Press, 1993), 208–14, 222–29.

totality for helping to remove intellectual stumbling blocks toward faith. But these arguments derive primarily from reason, so they cannot ultimately save a person. Proofs for God's existence can help destroy mental falsehoods, but they cannot introduce a person to saving faith. Philosophy is incapable of regenerating the human heart. The Holy Spirit necessarily uses the special revelation of the Word of God to bring people to saving faith in the gospel of Jesus Christ (John 3:5–8; 2 Cor. 3:1–6). The special revelation of the gospel emphasizes both Christ's unique death for our trespasses and his miraculous resurrection for our justification (Rom. 4:25; 1 Cor. 15:3–5).

A Summary of Natural Theology

Sixth, those major truths which general revelation teaches about God, humanity, and humanity's relationship to God may be summarized as follows: God reveals his existence, yet he remains invisible to us. God is powerful, and he governs his universe providentially. God is good, and God is just. God will judge the wicked, and his law reveals the guilt of all human beings in their hearts and consciences. All human beings have some reliable knowledge of God and should worship him, but we consistently pervert God's general revelation of himself. Every human being remains personally responsible to God through the witness of the conscience.

Salvation Awaits Special Revelation

Finally, while well-meaning Christians may disagree over exactly whether and how to incorporate general revelation into natural theology, we should agree that the general revelation of God does not offer humanity the saving gospel of Jesus Christ. The gospel is the special revelation that God loves us and has sent his only begotten Son to become a man, die on the cross for our sins, and arise from the dead to justify believers. God wants his special revelation in his Son's redeeming work made known to the entire world, and that is our responsibility as the church. We begin our survey of God's special revelation in the next chapter.

Back to the Bible

Whichever method you employ to incorporate general revelation into natural theology, it is the mark of Christian wisdom to check every idea against Scripture repeatedly. My daughter once asked me about how she might tame her vivid imagination, especially when she is tempted by evil. I told her the only way I found to conquer evil ideas was to "take every thought captive to obey Christ" (2 Cor. 10:5). The trusted method I follow is to read his Word, pray for the Spirit's guidance, and submit to God's revealed will. Whether we are tempted by moral sin or intellectual sin, we can trust Jesus to help us. Our Savior knows your struggles, and he will never fail your heart or your mind. Come to him in prayer.

Study Questions

1. Who do you think had the proper attitude toward Christian use of the pagan classics: Julian the Apostate, Arius of Alexandria, or Augustine of Hippo? Write down the primary reason why you chose this person's viewpoint.

2. Who do you think has the best model for incorporating general revelation into theology: Thomas Aquinas, John Calvin, or Francis Turretin? Write down the primary reason you chose this person's viewpoint.

3. What do you think is a positive aspect of Karl Barth's denial of natural theology? What do you think is a major problem with Barth's denial of general revelation?

Suggested Resources

- Geerhardus Vos, *Natural Theology*

- Emil Brunner and Karl Barth, *Natural Theology*

- Jason Duesing, Thomas White, and Malcolm Yarnell, *First Freedom*

CHAPTER TEN

How Can We Know God as Savior?

◆

W E   K N O W   T H A T   G O D   R E V E A L S limited information about himself to everyone through nature, with history, and in the human conscience. General revelation discloses that God exists, that he is powerful, and that he will judge our sin. In other words, the law of God against sin has been revealed to everyone. However, the law has a limited purpose and a limited utility for salvation.

The good news that God wants to save us and restore us to a right relationship with him comes in a different way, a special way. What is God's special revelation? How does it convict us and save us? And how does that news come from the eternal God to us today? These are some of the questions to which the doctrine of special revelation provides answers.

Because God pursues a personal relationship with us, and we are bodily, temporal creatures, God works with and through history. This chapter therefore follows a generally historical approach. First, we must consider God's special revelation as personal. God the Father revealed his Word through the prophets by the inspiration of the Holy Spirit but he personally reveals himself through his incarnate Son, who is the Word of God.

Second, we will rehearse God's historic acts of revelation in the Old Testament. There, we learn God walked with our parents in the garden of Eden, delivered his covenantal promises to the patriarchs, and gave the Law through Moses and his promise of redemption through Moses and various other prophets.

Third, we must reflect on God's personal revelation of himself in the New Testament. This latter testament teaches us that God sent his eternal Son as a human being, that he died for our sin and arose from the dead for the justification of believers. God in Christ then sent his Holy Spirit to establish the church and prepare for Christ's second coming.

We will conclude this chapter with some important personal questions for you. These will be the most important questions you have ever been asked. I pray you answer them well!

God's Personal Revelation

Even before we discuss the historical progress of our eternal God's saving disclosure to humanity, note that God's revelation establishes, restores, and preserves a living personal relationship with his people. God is personal, so by creating us in his image, he demonstrated his intention for us to engage him personally. God's Spirit breathed life into the first human being (Gen. 2:7).[1] God gave humanity freedom (Gen. 2:16) and responsibility (Gen. 2:17), granting him the privilege to speak freely and creatively (Gen. 2:19). God also blessed

---

1. God continually sustains human life through the breath of his Spirit, and when he withdraws his Spirit, humanity perishes (Ps. 104:29–30).

Adam with a complementary human being (Gen. 2:18) and walked with both the man and the woman in intimacy (Gen. 3:8). God's original encounter with his human creatures was marked by the blessing of personal relationship. After our relationship with God was broken by humanity's choice to sin, he has worked to restore it.

The difficulties stemming from our Fall include the temptation to substitute for a personal relationship with God our own abstract ideas about God. J. I. Packer lamented how evangelical theologians often lack "the gaiety, goodness, and unfetteredness of spirit which are the marks of those who have known God."[2] He argued against "knowing notions" rather than "knowing God." As a professional theologian Packer reminded himself, "over and over again, 'What a difference there is between knowing notions, even true notions, and knowing God.'"[3] Woeful figures know about God without knowing God, for knowing God is supremely "a personal matter." "You can have all the right notions in your head without tasting in your heart the realities to which they refer." Only one "full of the Holy Spirit" can develop a "deeper acquaintance with his God and Saviour."[4]

The different levels of knowing God can be arranged on a scale from partial knowledge to fuller knowledge. We know God only incompletely through general revelation and typically pervert that knowledge with our natural theology. However, we can know God in a growing way through his restoration of a personal relationship with us by his Word and in his Spirit. And one day, believers will know God in an even

2. J. I. Packer, *Knowing God: Twentieth-Anniversary Edition* (Downers Grove, IL: InterVarsity Press, 1993), 25.

3. Packer, "Knowing Notions or Knowing God" (1982), in *Honouring the Written Word of God*, vol. 3, *The Collected Shorter Writings of J. I. Packer* (Carlisle: Paternoster Press, 1999), 246.

4. Packer, *Knowing God*, 39.

more complete way, for we shall see him "face to face." "Now I know in part, but then I will know fully, as I am fully known" (1 Cor. 13:12). Just as there are different levels of knowing God, there are also different types of doubt about God.[5]

Some doubt the existence of God, others his goodness or love, and yet others his power. Epicurus summarized these three forms of denial: "Is God willing to prevent evil, but not able? Then he is impotent. Is he able, but not willing? Then he is malevolent. Is he both able and willing? Whence, then, is evil?"[6] The congregational leader of Israelite worship, Asaph, struggled with such questions. He saw the wicked cast doubt on God's omniscience, and wondered why, "They are always at ease, and they increase their wealth" (Ps. 73:12b). Asaph doubted his own piety, "Did I purify my heart and wash my hands in innocence for nothing?" (Ps. 73:13). His internal crisis generated hopelessness (Ps. 73:16).

But an important shift occurs in the middle of Psalm 73. A personal structure lies behind the formal structure of the Psalm. At first, Asaph spoke about God primarily in an abstract way, with studied, judgmental distance (Ps. 73:1–16). In the second part of the Psalm, he shifts dramatically toward speaking to God in a very personal way, with heartfelt prayer (Ps. 73:18–23). In verse 17 Asaph exchanged his discourse of abstraction and doubt for an intimacy and certainty. Asaph

---

5. For an audio-visual presentation of the material focused on Psalm 73 in the next few paragraphs, see Malcolm Yarnell, "Knowing God," Southwestern Baptist Theological Seminary Chapel (November 2, 2016; http://media.swbts.edu/item/2249).

6. David Hume, *Dialogues and Natural History of Religion*, ed. J. C. A. Gaskin (New York: Oxford University Press, 2008), 100. Hume, a rather notorious Enlightenment skeptic (1711–1776), failed to perceive that the answer lies not in an abstract discussion about God providing natural verification for his miraculous work, but in God's personal engagement with us in our history and eschatology.

doubted God until he "entered God's sanctuary" and, through congregational worship, "understood."

Theology may be toppled by doubt until it finds stability in the congregation who serves the Lord in word and in action. The theologian must exercise his faith in the context of a living congregation which worships a living God to gain epistemological certainty and orthodoxy. Two movements seem to be necessary for the development of a true understanding of God: First, God must reveal himself to a person in a saving way through his special revelation of himself in Jesus Christ by his Spirit. Second, the theologian must receive with a humble mind and faithful heart the relationship which God offers those who worship him.

Anselm of Canterbury demonstrated this progression. He learned from reading Scripture with his monastic teachers how humanity was made for relationship with God, then we rebelled. Anselm admitted his personal efforts to regain personal knowledge of God were futile, "I strove toward God, and I stumbled on myself."[7] So he appealed for grace, "Lord, I am bowed down and can only look downward; raise me up that I may look upward."[8] Anselm's humble dependence upon God's illumination has become an axiomatic aid to theologians ever since. "For this also I believe—that unless I believed, I should not understand."[9] *Cogito ut intelligam*: "I believe that I may understand." Theological understanding depends upon humble personal prayer.

Because of our creation in God's image, God's special revelation entails a personal relationship. Because of our sinful departure from God, yet God's continuing love for us, it also entails the restoration of a personal relationship. The

---

7. Anselm, *Proslogium*, in *Basic Writings*, 2nd ed., ed. Charles Hartshorne, transl. S. N. Deane (La Salle, IN: Open Court, 1962), 51.

8. Anselm, *Proslogium*, 52.

9. Anselm, *Proslogium*, 53.

relationship between God and humanity is comprised of one who is eternal and spiritual on the one hand and creatures who are temporal and bodily as well as spiritual on the other hand. Emil Brunner noted that "in this encounter there can be no question of ignoring man, as the human partner in the process of revelation."[10]

Brunner advocated a focus on reason, for we were created in the image of a reasonable God. We considered human reason above, but now we must recall the bodies of humanity. Because humanity was created as both spiritual and embodied (Gen. 2:7), and bodies are bound in time and space, God's special revelation necessarily worked with history. To the historical account of God's self-disclosure we now turn, remembering God's special revelation of himself to humanity requires that it take in a personal dimension.

The Revealed Mystery

According to James Leo Garrett Jr., two major phases dominate God's special revelation of himself to humanity. God especially disclosed himself "to and through the people of Israel," as recorded in the Old Testament, and "in and through Jesus Christ," as recorded in the New Testament.[11] The older revelation was recorded in the sacred writings of those called "prophets," while the newer revelation of God in Christ was recorded in the sacred writings of the "apostles." The prologue of the epistle to the Hebrews correlates the two phases of God's special revelation:

10. Emil Brunner, *Revelation and Reason: The Christian Doctrine of Faith and Knowledge*, transl. Olive Wyon (Philadelphia: Westminster Press, 1946), 48.

11. James Leo Garrett Jr., *Systematic Theology: Biblical, Historical, and Evangelical*, vol. 1, 2nd ed. (North Richland Hills, TX: BIBAL, 2000), 105.

Long ago God spoke to our ancestors by the prophets at different times and in different ways. In these last days, he has spoken to us by his Son. God has appointed him heir of all things and made the universe through him. The Son is the radiance of God's glory and the exact expression of his nature, sustaining all things by his powerful word. After making purification for sins, he sat down at the right hand of the Majesty on high. So he became superior to the angels, just as the name he inherited is more excellent than theirs. (Heb. 1:1–4)

The revelation of God came to the Hebrew Christians' ancestors, Israel, "by the prophets," who were situated "at different times" and worked "in different ways." This emphasis on variety and multiplicity does not allow us to conclude God's revelation was haphazard, piecemeal, or divided. Rather, the biblical canon signals that God followed an integral plan to reveal himself through his prophets and apostles. The biblical doctrine of revelation as "mystery" (Aramaic *raz*; Greek *mysterion*) indicates continuity between eternity and time, between the various times and ways of revelation, and between the old and the new covenants. It also indicates that God worked progressively, through the administration of covenants centered on the Messiah.

In their study of "mystery," Gregory Beale and Benjamin Gladd work through the biblical materials exhaustively, demonstrating their interconnection. In the book of Daniel, a threefold pattern emerges: First comes a fearful and partial revelation about God's mystery; second came further revelation with important details; third will come fulfillment of the prophetic revelation of the mystery.[12] In the synoptic Gospels, *mysterion* occurs "at pivotal points" regarding Jesus's teaching about how his kingdom comes in two stages, the "already" and the "not yet."[13] The Apocalypse of John treats the mystery as something both in progress and awaiting final fulfillment in the eschaton (Rev. 1:20; 10:7; 17:5, 7).

The apostle Paul's doctrine of *mysterion* is particularly thick. First, as previously mentioned, the doctrine of mystery is central to divine revelation (Rom. 16:25–26; Eph. 3:3). Second, while God revealed himself first to Israel, the Gentiles must be incorporated prior to the conclusive salvation of Israel (Rom. 11:25). Third, revealing the mystery previously hidden in eternity and partially revealed to the prophets constitutes God's way of wisdom (1 Cor. 2:1, 7; Eph. 3:9; Col. 1:26). Fourth, Jesus Christ centers the revealed mystery, for in him all things are summed up according to the rightly timed "plan" of God (Eph. 1:9; 6:18–19; Col. 1:27). Fifth, the New Testament apostles are now "managers of the mysteries of God" (1 Cor. 4:1). Sixth, the mystery will be more fully revealed in the events surrounding the Second Coming of Jesus Christ (2 Thess. 2:7). Seventh, the bodily resurrection which will transform the saints culminates the mystery (1 Cor. 15:51). Finally, the gospel of Jesus may be abridged as "the mystery of godliness" (1 Tim. 3:16).

The Prophetic Revelation of God to Israel

As the author of Hebrews stated, God revealed himself through the prophets to Israel "at different times" and "in different ways." The special revelation of God "at different times"

---

12. G. K. Beale and Benjamin L. Gladd, *Hidden but Now Revealed: A Biblical Theology of Mystery* (Downers Grove, IL: IVP Academic, 2014), 41.

13. Beale and Gladd, *Hidden but Now Revealed*, 58.

began with God's personal encounters with the Patriarchs, from Adam (Gen. 1–5) and Noah (Gen. 6–10) to Abraham, Isaac, and Jacob (Gen. 11–35) as well as the sons of Judah (Gen. 36–50). God continued to deal directly with the tribes of Judah as his covenantal people through the prophet Moses, as recorded in the remaining four books of the Torah (Exodus, Leviticus, Numbers, and Deuteronomy). Moses led the nation in their escape from Egypt, mediated the legal covenant (Exod. 19), conveyed the Ten Commandments (Exod. 20:1–17), and the rest of the Law, oversaw the construction of the Tabernacle, and established the Levitical Priesthood. While the Torah, or Pentateuch, remains the initial, substantial, and indispensable corpus of written revelation, it did not complete revelation.

Continuing to reveal himself to Israel, God also manifested himself and his will "in different ways." While Moses was a unique "prophet" to Israel (Deut. 34:10), God used other intermediaries to speak to the Israelites as they inhabited the Promised Land. The Lord at first spoke to the conquering Israelites through Moses's successor, Joshua, and various "judges" (Joshua, Judges, and Ruth). The greatest and last judge was Samuel, who was also a prophet and priest (1 Sam. 1–16). Samuel, himself not a king, consecrated the first kings of Israel, including her greatest Old Testament king, David (1 Sam. 16–31; 2 Sam.; 1 Kings 1–2). David, while anointed a king, also served as prophet and priest (2 Sam. 23:1–2; 1 Chron. 15:16–24; Ps. 3, 4, 5; Acts 2:30). Those who inhabited the offices of judge, king, and priest might receive revelation from God, but a "prophet" mediated divine revelation.[14] David received the covenantal promise that his descendent,

---

14. Even critics recognize "the essence of prophecy involves the transmission of messages from God." Konrad Schmid and Jens Schröter, *The Making of The Bible: From the First Fragments to Sacred Scripture* (Cambridge, MA: Harvard University Press, 2021), 90.

who would also be God's son, would reign forever upon the throne of Israel (2 Sam. 7:12–16).

God veiled his glorious presence in the darkness of the Temple built by David's immediate son and successor, Solomon (1 Kings 8:10–13). God continued to reveal his will through various prophets, some unknown to us by name. God's sayings and actions through some prophets were recorded by others (as with Nathan, Elijah, and Elisha in the historical books). Other prophets recorded their prophecies in writing or had them recorded, as with the "major" prophets (Isaiah, Jeremiah with Lamentations, Ezekiel, and Daniel) and the "minor" (Hosea, Joel, Amos, Obadiah, Jonah, Micah, Nahum, Habakkuk, Zephaniah, Haggai, Zechariah, and Malachi). These prophets worked in both the northern and southern kingdoms through the centuries, calling God's people to trust and obey God, but the people rebelled. The prophets continued prophesying even as the nation was overthrown and the people were exiled (1–2 Chronicles).

The diversity of divine revelation continued after the fall of Jerusalem. Prophecy took a decidedly apocalyptic turn during Israel's exile (Daniel, Ezekiel, Zechariah). Divine revelation could become instructive and allusive, failing even to mention God (Esther). During the return from exile, rebuilding of Jerusalem, and reestablishment of the cult, a civil servant could join a priest in revealing God's will (Nehemiah, Ezra). From the earliest times (Gen. 3:15) through the final prophetic books of the Hebrew canon (Mal. 4:1-4), promises regarding the messianic king provided the hope for the people of God to have their nation and themselves restored to a right relationship with God. Jesus Christ taught that the messianic promises, fulfilled in himself, could be found in "all the

Scriptures," permeating its three divisions (Luke 24:25–27, 44).[15]

B. B. Warfield, the great evangelical defender of the doctrines of revelation and inspiration at the turn of the twentieth century, identified three general "modes" or ways that God revealed himself. First, there was the way of "external manifestation," typically a theophany or visible manifestation of God or his work, as in miracles. Second was the way of "internal suggestion," as with dreams or visions. The third mode involved "concursive revelation," as when God inspired the writing of a psalm, history, or epistle. These diverse modes of revelation are found throughout the Old Testament and the New Testament.[16]

We must recognize that all these revelations at different times and in various ways are necessarily contextual. The eternal God revealed himself in or through unique historical events to specific people at certain times in particular places. Unlike general revelation, the unique events of special revelation must employ written and oral means if they are to be communicated to others who did not directly experience these revelations. The necessary use of communicative means also characterizes the ordinary proclamation of the highest revelation, the personal self-revelation of God in human flesh.

---

15. The Jews arranged their sacred writings according to Torah or Pentateuch (the first five books, the books of Moses), the Nevi'im (the Prophets, including the historical books from Joshua through 2 Kings and most of the writing prophets), and the Ketuvim (the poetic writings plus Daniel). Schmid and Schröter, *Making of the Bible*, 8.

16. Benjamin Breckinridge Warfield, *Revelation and Inspiration* (New York: Oxford University Press, 1932), 15.

The Perfect Revelation
of the Eternal Christ

The incarnation of the Son of God in Jesus the Christ is the unique, unparalleled, and ultimate revelation of God. The message of the New Testament is focused on Christ and his work and teaches that he is the Messiah whom the Old Testament promised. "The New Testament and the Primitive Church united in the declaration that God has finally and completely revealed the secret of His being and His will in the Person of Jesus, in His life, death, and resurrection."[17] The truth that the perfect revelation of God has come in the divine-human person of Jesus Christ and that he has risen from the dead for the redemption of believers remains non-negotiable for orthodox Christianity.

The Synoptic Gospels weave both common and unique outlooks on Christ's life into their various reports.[18] All three trace the disciples' increasing realization of God the Father's revelation to them that, as Matthew wrote, Jesus is "the Messiah, the Son of the Living God" (Matt. 16:16; cf. Mark 8:29; Luke 9:20). Matthew and Luke begin with his royal genealogy and virgin birth then review his early years. Mark joins with them in rehearsing his baptism, temptation, and miraculous works and teachings, as well as his transfiguration. Approximately half of these Gospels focuses on the profound events of his final week of earthly life, including his trial, his vicarious death, and his victorious resurrection. "It is not too much to say that the Gospels are books about the

---

17. Brunner, *Revelation and Reason*, 95.

18. For a helpful comparative apparatus, see Burton H. Throckmorton Jr., *Gospel Parallels: A Synopsis of the First Three Gospels*, 4th ed. (Nashville: Thomas Nelson, 1979).

atonement."[19] The Synoptic Gospels conclude with Christ's commission to the church, that his disciples should make disciples (Matt. 28:16–20; Mark 16:15–16; Luke 24:46–49).

The Synoptic Gospels generally follow the method of a "Christology from below," focusing on the history of the human life of Christ, gradually making it clear that this one is also divine.[20] The Gospel of John pursues a "Christology from above," amplifying the deity of Jesus Christ. Reflecting these diverse methods of the Gospel writers, Garrett affirmed that whether theologians today begin "from below" with the humanity of Christ or "from above" with the deity of Christ, we must profess he is both God and Man.[21]

John commences with a theological exposition which uses simple statements to convey stunning meanings: "In the beginning was the Word [*logos*], and the Word was with God, and the Word was God" (John 1:1). The Logos is thereby both identified with God yet distinguished from God, just as later the "Son" is both identified as one with God yet eternally proceeds from the Father by generation (John 1:18; 10:30; cf. Heb. 1:5). The Word is the Son who takes upon himself human nature, becoming "flesh" in Jesus and dwelling "among us" (John 1:14). Jesus Christ, the original Creator of the world (John 1:3), was embodied to become "the Savior of the world" (John 4:42). Through his subsequent death and resurrection, followed by his gift of his Holy Spirit to his church, Christ obtained the way for our return to the Father's presence and empowered the church's witness (John 7:37–39; 20:22). His claims for himself are wonderful: "I am the way, the truth,

---

19. Leon Morris's focus when saying this was on the Gospels of Matthew and Mark in particular. Leon Morris, *The Cross in the New Testament* (Grand Rapids: Eerdmans, 1965), 13.

20. Daniel L. Akin, "The Person of Christ," in *A Theology for the Church*, revised ed. (Nashville: B&H Academic, 2014), 391, 411–19.

21. Garrett pursued a Christology from below. Garrett, *Systematic Theology*, 1:609–11.

and the life. No one comes to the Father except through me" (John 14:6).

The New Testament verifies that Jesus Christ is indeed God's perfect revelation in so many ways. He unites the Old and the New Testaments: "For the law was given through Moses; grace and truth came through Jesus Christ" (John 1:17). The former's "ministry that brought condemnation had glory," but the latter's "ministry that brings righteousness overflows with even more glory" (2 Cor. 3:9). Jesus was a great teacher and miracle-worker, but he fundamentally exceeded all others. The prophets conveyed messages from God, about God, for God; Jesus is God and brings his own message. The prophet's authority was never located in the prophet but in the divine Word; Jesus has divine authority because he is that Word.

The offices of prophet, priest, and king were typically divided in the Old Testament, but Jesus assumed and completed them all. Jesus is more than the holder of an office or offices, for all offices and their lesser authorities derive from the one who has "all authority" (Matt. 28:18; John 19:11). First, speaking of royal power, the New Testament pronounces Jesus is "King of kings and Lord of lords" (Rev. 19:16). Second, speaking of prophetic proclamation, Christ exceeds the one who is "more than a prophet," John the Baptist (Matt. 11:9–15). Third, speaking of priestly mediation, Jesus is a priest of an infinitely higher order than Levi, for he "passed through the heavens" (Heb. 4:14). Christ provided the once-for-all sacrifice of himself and "perfected forever those who are sanctified" (Heb. 7:11–14). Where prophetic revelation was limited by their inability to see God, Jesus himself has seen God (John 6:46). Indeed, those who wish to see God must see in Jesus the personal face of God (John 14:9).

On the one hand, the relationship between Jesus Christ and God the Father is distinguishable, for in his eternal personhood, he is the Son of God, and in his adoption of human

nature, he became a creature. On the other hand, the relationship between Jesus Christ and God the Father is also identical
in every way except for his eternal relation of generation and
his adoption of humanity. Jesus proclaims of himself, "I and
the Father are one," and his disciples confess of Jesus, "My
Lord and my God!"(John 10:30; 20:28). Paul joined this chorus of apostolic praise for the eternal Son who became incarnate and was crucified and arose (Phil. 2:4–11; Col. 1:15–20).
He confessed the works of Christ and God are one, "In Christ,
God was reconciling the world to himself" (2 Cor. 5:19). If
we want to see God, we must look in the face of Jesus Christ.
"When He speaks, God Himself speaks; when He acts, God
Himself acts; in His personal presence the personal presence
of God has become real."[22]

Jesus Christ became the revelation of God to humanity,
perfecting all previous revelation when he became a human
being. The author of Hebrews, after affirming prior revelation,
thus proceeded to praise the superiority of Jesus: "In these
last days, he has spoken to us by his Son"(Heb. 1:2a). Unlike
Moses, a mere man who passed on the words of God, "The
Son is the radiance of God's glory and the exact expression of
his nature, sustaining all things by his powerful word" (Heb.
1:3a). Jesus Christ unites all prior revelation of God in himself. "Above all," David Baker concludes, we must "recognize
the centrality of Jesus, the Christ of the Old Testament and of
the New, the descendant of Abraham and David and firstborn
of a new creation, who in his person and coming unites the
two Testaments into one Bible."[23]

Not only is Christ superior in his person; he is superior
in every aspect of his work. "In comparison to everything else

---

22. Brunner, *Revelation and Reason*, 113.
23. David L. Baker, *Two Testaments, One Bible: The Theological
Relationship Between the Old and New Testaments*, 3rd ed. (Downers Grove,
IL: InterVarsity Press, 2010), 281.

in the divine plan for creation and redemption, Jesus Christ is superior."[24] For instance, he is superior to the angels in his person and in his work. "After making purification for sins, he sat down at the right hand of the Majesty on high. So he became superior to the angels, just as the name he inherited is more excellent than theirs" (Heb. 1:3b–4). Through his strategic and prolific use of the Greek word *kreitton* ("more excellent," "superior," or "better"), the author of Hebrews makes abundantly clear that Jesus excels in every single way, including his priesthood, his covenant, and his sacrifice (Heb. 7:1–10:39).

One day, all shall know the truth of the ultimate superiority of Jesus Christ. "Look, he is coming with the clouds, and every eye will see him, even those who pierced him" (Rev. 1:7a). "Every knee will bow" and "every tongue will confess, 'Jesus Christ is Lord!'" (Phil. 2:10b, 11). The eternal Christ has always been, is now, and always will be the perfect revelation of God in his person and his work (Rev. 1:17–18; 22:13). The special revelation of Jesus Christ as Lord, once granted to the apostles and the church, will become a general revelation on the last day.

The Good News and the Bad News

We learned in this chapter that God's desire is to establish a personal relationship with us, even after our sinful rebellion. In the Old Testament, God revealed not only that we rebelled, but that he did not leave us on our own. God established his covenant with Abraham, delivered his Law through Moses, and sent his prophets with the promise of a redeeming Messiah. The New Testament makes it clear that Jesus is this

---

24. Malcolm B. Yarnell III, "Hebrews: Introduction," in *HCSB Study Bible: Holman Christian Standard Bible, God's Word for Life* (Nashville: Holman Bible Publishers, 2010), 2113.

expected Messiah. Jesus is the Christ, eternal Word of God, who has come in human flesh. Through his death and resurrection, he accomplished our redemption, and his Spirit now applies the grace of God to humanity through the witness of his church. The work of God the Trinity in special revelation is to offer humanity salvation.

The most important issues in this life can be reduced to two questions and their answers. The first important question concerns our response to God's general revelation of the bad news: Will we recognize the truth of God's existence, God's law, and our culpability? The second important question concerns our response to God's revelation of the good news: Will we receive the truth of God's special revelation in Jesus Christ, God's love, and our need to respond with faith?

Will You Recognize the Bad News?

The first unavoidable question for you and me, and indeed for every person, is this: How will you respond to the bad news that the final judgment will see you rightly condemned for your sins? Due to his holiness on the one hand and our wickedness on the other hand, the Old Testament Law and the law available to every human conscience reveal the bad news that we face. Each of us languish in this human life under the general knowledge that we face the judgment of God and deserve his wrath for our sins. Will you admit these truths, or will you deny and pervert them?

Will You Receive the Good News?

The special knowledge of God's offer of salvation is thoroughly tied up with the second question: How will you respond to the good news that God loves you? Despite our sin, God has provided a way to restore the broken relationship we have with him. Due to his love, God the Father sent God the Son to become a human being, to die on the cross, and to arise from the dead. Will you receive this good news (*gospel* means "good news") that God loves you in his Son? Will you receive the Holy Spirit's conviction and offer of faith in Jesus Christ? Your eternal future depends upon a positive response of personal trust in him. Will you come and drink freely of the water of life (Rev. 22:17)?

Study Questions

1. Is God's special revelation necessarily personal, in the sense that it is intended for a relationship? On what basis would you make such a claim?

2. What are the two major phases in God's special revelation of himself? Which one occurred first? What was revealed in the second phase?

3. How does Jesus Christ unite the Old Testament and the New Testament? List three Bible verses which support your perspective.

Suggested Resources

- J. I. Packer, *Knowing God*

- B. B. Warfield, *Revelation and Inspiration*

- David Baker, *Two Testaments, One Bible*

CHAPTER ELEVEN

Does Scripture Continue Special Revelation?

◆

IN THE LAST CHAPTER, OUR review of the way God revealed himself for our salvation in the Old and the New Testaments made it clear that, from the perspective of divine eternity, special revelation is a Trinitarian work. Each of the one God's works necessarily involve all three Persons, the Father and the Son and the Holy Spirit,[1] and this includes God's work of self-disclosure. God the Trinity knows himself perfectly, but we have no knowledge of God apart from his condescension by grace. God revealed himself by accommodating his perfect self-knowledge to our limited capabilities and by mediating his Word through his Spirit to the prophets of Israel. Subsequently, God revealed himself immediately and personally in Jesus Christ.[2]

---

1. See chapter 5 above.

2. God's perfect knowledge of himself has been called "archetypal theology." This intra-Trinitarian knowledge of God is too great for humanity and is thus hidden from us. When God reveals himself to us, he accommodates his revelation to fit our limited capacity. Theologians call theology

Besides being a Trinitarian grace from eternity, the special revelation of God also necessarily works in and through history. Accommodating himself to our limitations of being bodily located in time and space, God elected to use history to bring us our salvation through the only mediator who is simultaneously God yet man (1 Tim. 2:5). The eternal Son entered our history. Sent by the eternal Father, the eternal Word embodied himself in Jesus of Nazareth through the eternal Spirit's work upon the Virgin Mary. He taught. He healed. He worked our salvation for us in his atoning death and justifying resurrection. With his ascension, he began interceding for us at the right hand of the Father. The Lord Christ will one day return to bring in the fullness of his kingdom on earth as in heaven.

The eternal ontological truths about God the Trinity and the God-Man Jesus Christ undergird the economic work of the gospel. The gospel of Jesus Christ is the eternal plan of God for our salvation. Formerly a mystery determined by the eternal God yet veiled to humanity, the gospel was disclosed in the person and work of Jesus Christ. Our Savior manifested himself and his atoning work on our behalf to particular people at special times in specific places. God's gift of salvation is intended for all people everywhere (Matt. 28:19). However, it is not available to all through the universally available forms of general revelation. Special revelation, manifested in history, requires its own special historical means of transmission.

How is this special revelation, especially the saving disclosure of the once-for-all time perfect sacrifice of the Lord

---

constructed from the accommodation of revelation, "ectypal theology." Archetypal theology is God's exalted perfect knowledge of his transcendent self; ectypal theology is our human response to his accommodated revelation of himself to us. This distinction, developed in medieval scholasticism, was later adopted by Protestant theologians. Richard A. Muller, *Prolegomena to Theology*, vol. 1, *Post-Reformation and Reformed Dogmatics: The Rise and Development of Reformed Orthodoxy, ca. 1520 to cas. 1725*, 2nd ed. (Grand Rapids: Baker, 2003), 229–38.

Jesus, made available to others who were not personally there on the hill called Golgotha? What about all those who did not personally see, hear, and touch Christ after his resurrection from the tomb? How can they come to know that Christ was also raised for their salvation? God the Father and God the Son chose to preserve and disseminate this special revelation of the gospel, which contains historical truth necessary for human salvation, through the work of God the Holy Spirit. This special revelation of the gospel must be proclaimed and believed to bring salvation.[3] God chose to continue disclosing the special saving revelation of himself to all human beings through the Spirit's work of inspiration.

In this chapter, we first survey the modern debate over divine revelation through biblical inspiration. Next, we review the Bible's presentation of how knowledge about these unique acts of God were recorded by the prophets and the apostles under the inspiration of the Holy Spirit, so that subsequent generations might also know God's saving revelation of himself. Third, we evaluate the various theories of biblical inspiration which have been put forward by theologians. Finally, we offer a sevenfold definition of the Holy Spirit's work of biblical inspiration.

---

3. The difference between the universal availability of God's law and the exclusive availability of God's gospel may be compared to the geography of God's sacred work. God's law was revealed externally and especially on the mountain called Sinai, yet it was also revealed diffusedly to all people through the inner human conscience. The gospel of God was revealed particularly on the hill called Golgotha and at the empty tomb, but his revelation of our salvation is not available except through the witness of the disciples who were there and saw their risen Lord.

The Modern Debate over
Revelation through Inspiration

God's offer of salvation works in, with, and through history. God revealed himself through the prophets in diverse ways and at various times to Israel. God then revealed himself personally in his Son Jesus Christ, who atoned for human sin upon the cross and arose from the dead. Because there is "no other name under heaven given to people by which we must be saved" (Acts 4:12), the personal identity and saving work of Jesus Christ must be proclaimed to those who did not see and hear Christ after his resurrection. In other words, the proclamation given to the apostles must be mediated to the rest of humanity through historical instruments chosen by God. This is the role granted by God in Christ to the church and its Scriptures.

Despite Scripture's claims regarding its own inspiration, claims which we shall review in the next section, debate over inspiration intensified during the modern period. The Enlightenment of the eighteenth century elevated the certainty of human reason. Influenced by humanity's increasing self-certainty, liberal theologians in the nineteenth century began to doubt the certainty and authority of divine revelation. They also developed methods of reading the Bible in increasingly critical ways. Liberal opposition was particularly directed against the traditional doctrine that Scripture was inspired by the Holy Spirit.[4]

---

4. "The underlying presuppositions of both neo-liberalism and neo-orthodoxy are derived from this source; however diversely they interpret the meaning and function of revelation, they unite in rejecting the identification of God's truth with any formulation given in the Scriptures. For that reason, we can group them together in opposition to the evangelical doctrine of inspiration." R. A. Finlayson, "Contemporary Ideas of Inspiration," in *Revelation and the Bible: Contemporary Evangelical Thought,* ed. Carl F. H. Henry (Grand Rapids: Baker, 1958), 221–22. Finlayson was criticizing J. K. S. Reid, John Baillie, and Karl Barth, among others.

The opponents of biblical inspiration undermined the doctrine in many ways: Some drove a wedge between divine revelation and the scriptural text. Others narrowed the meaning of revelation to saving encounter and denied revelation was the communication of truth propositions. Still others denied the identity of Scripture with God's Word.

Presuming he could preserve the special revelation of Christ as the Word by downplaying the special revelation of Scripture as the Word, Karl Barth retained some liberal views even as he sought to recover theological orthodoxy. Barth and other neo-orthodox theologians argued that the Bible is merely the record of revelation and that it "becomes" God's Word by grace when God reveals himself in a saving way to the elect.[5] Evangelical theologians, however, have refuted both liberal and neo-orthodox theologians and defended the doctrine of inspiration. Evangelicals also note that Scripture claims for itself inspiration by the Holy Spirit.

The leading evangelical expositors of the doctrine of biblical inspiration and its meaning have been, successively, Benjamin Breckenridge Warfield, Carl F. H. Henry, and David S. Dockery. Writing at the turn of the twentieth century, the early scholar "best known as the theologian of the doctrine of inspiration" was Warfield. He wrote some 1,500 pages to construct from Scripture and history a strong defense for it.[6] Henry, friend of evangelist Billy Graham, founder of *Christianity Today*, and cofounder of the Evangelical Theological Society, was deemed the architect of twentieth-century evangelicalism.[7] Henry's *magnum opus*, the six-volume

---

5. Karl Barth, *The Doctrine of the Word of God*, Vol. I, Part 1, 2nd ed., *Church Dogmatics*, ed. G. W. Bromiley and T. F. Torrance (Edinburgh: T&T Clark, 1975), 113.

6. Fred G. Zaspel, *The Theology of Warfield: A Systematic Summary* (Wheaton, IL: Crossway, 2010), 63, 114.

7. David S. Dockery, "Introduction," in *Architect of Evangelicalism: Essential Essays of Carl F. H. Henry* (Bellingham, WA: Lexham, 2019), 1–7.

God, Revelation and Authority, exhaustively defended a high doctrine of Scripture.[8] More recently, Dockery has dedicated much of his influential theological career to explaining and defending the truth of Scripture in countless books, articles, and presentations.[9] His most recent contribution, *Special Revelation and Scripture*, builds on Warfield and Henry while crafting a sophisticated doctrine of inspiration for the next generation.[10]

The Biblical Basis for Biblical Inspiration

Warfield defined biblical inspiration summarily as "a supernatural influence exerted on the sacred writers by the Spirit of God, by virtue of which their writings are given Divine trustworthiness."[11] Both Dockery and I follow Warfield in stressing three primary texts: 2 Peter 1:19–21; 2 Timothy 3:14–17; John 10:34–36.[12] However, several other biblical texts

8. Carl F. H. Henry, *God, Revelation and Authority*, revised ed., 6 vols. (Wheaton, IL: Crossway, 1999).

9. A representative but very partial list of his contributions may be found in *Convictional Civility: Engaging the Culture in the 21st Century: Essays in Honor of David S. Dockery*, ed. C. Ben Mitchell, Carla D. Sanderson, and Gregory A. Thornbury (Nashville: B&H Publishing, 2015), 177–86. A partial theological review of Dockery's contribution may be found in James Leo Garrett Jr., *Baptist Theology: A Four-Century Study* (Macon, GA: Mercer University Press, 2009), 704–10. Enterprising doctoral students will find research in Dockery's corpus beneficial.

10. David S. Dockery and Malcolm B. Yarnell III, *Special Revelation and Scripture* (Nashville: B&H Academic, 2024). His earliest contribution was the popular *The Doctrine of the Bible* (Nashville: Convention Press, 1991).

11. Warfield, *Revelation and Inspiration* (New York: Oxford University Press, 1932), 77–78.

12. Garrett evaluated "two principal texts" for his doctrine of inspiration. James Leo Garrett Jr., *Systematic Theology: Biblical, Historical, and Evangelical*, vol. 1, 2nd ed. (North Richland Hills, TX: BIBAL Press, 2000),

are also helpful for constructing a biblical doctrine of biblical inspiration and the Holy Spirit's perfection of Scripture. These other texts, worthy of consultation for a fuller portrait of the important doctrine of biblical inspiration, include 2 Samuel 23:2; Matthew 5:17–18; John 14:26; 15:26–27; 16:12–15; Galatians 3:16; 1 Timothy 5:18; 2 Peter 3:14–16; Revelation 22:18–19.

The three primary biblical texts, written by three leading apostles, provide a full-orbed Trinitarian doctrine of divine inspiration in which the Holy Spirit takes a leading role: Paul explains that inspiration is a work of God, that he grants his attribute of holiness to Scripture, that his inspiration is plenary and includes the choice of words, and that the resultant text is sufficient both to bring personal salvation and to guide the Christian life. John demonstrates that Scripture participates by grace in the perfections of God through the Son of God. Peter shows clearly how the Holy Spirit is involved not only in the inspiration of the original authors but also in the illumination and interpretation of the text by its readers.

2 Timothy 3:15–17

> And you know that from infancy you have known the sacred Scriptures, which are able to give you wisdom for salvation through faith in Christ Jesus. All Scripture is inspired by God and is profitable for teaching, for rebuking, for correcting, for training in

---

125–27. Feinberg evaluated many texts but did not include the text from John 10. John S. Feinberg, *Light in a Dark Place: The Doctrine of Scripture*, Foundations of Evangelical Theology (Wheaton: Crossway, 2018), 113–15, 116–49. Bavinck found all three texts useful. Herman Bavinck, *Prolegomena*, vol. 1, *Reformed Dogmatics*, ed. John Bolt, transl. John Vriend (Grand Rapids: Baker, 2003), 394–97, 422–28.

righteousness, so that the man of God may
be complete, equipped for every good work.

The apostle Paul describes the Bible as *hiera grammata*,
"holy scriptures" or "sacred writings" (2 Tim. 3:15). Ligon
Duncan calls this "a wonderful two-word description of the
Bible's view of itself."[13] Paul also connects the sufficiency of
Scripture with both personal salvation (2 Tim. 3:15) and the
Christian life (2 Tim. 3:17).

In this *locus classicus*, the first three Greek words of verse 16
get to the heart of biblical inspiration. Each term is individu-
ally significant for a theological exposition of Paul's doctrine:
Pasa grapha theopneustos: "All Scripture is inspired by God."

First, Paul ascribes inspiration to "every" Scripture or "all"
Scripture. The Greek term *pasa* has been curiously mistrans-
lated by some liberal theologians, who seek to make inspiration partial. But such an intricate reading contradicts Paul's
stated priority.[14]

Exposing the second Greek term, Dockery points out,
"There are fifty occurrences of *graphe* in the New Testament,
all of which refer to Holy Scripture."[15] This indicates that the
words written down, and not just the authors of those writings, are inspired.

---

13. J. Ligon Duncan III, "The Nature, Benefits, and Results of Scripture,"
in *The Inerrant Word: Biblical, Historical, and Pastoral Perspectives*, ed. John
MacArthur (Wheaton, IL: Crossway, 2016), 93.

14. Garrett, *Systematic Theology*, 1: 126. Dockery notes that I. Howard
Marshall argued such partial readings "can be confidently rejected." David
S. Dockery, "Special Revelation," in *A Theology for the Church*, revised ed.,
ed. Daniel L. Akin, Bruce Riley Ashford, and Kenneth Keathley (Nashville:
B&H Academic, 2014), 114.

15. Dockery, "Special Revelation," 114. "Paul isn't talking about the act of
the Holy Spirit in carrying along the writers of Scripture; he is talking about
the product." "He is saying that the Bible is objectively inspired—the words
themselves are the product of inspiration." Duncan, "The Nature, Benefits,
and Results of Scripture," 96.

Third, *theopneustos* (literally, "God-breathed) is typically translated as "inspired." However, this less-than-literal translation has led liberal theologians to adopt a Romantic notion of inspiration, as if the writers are merely like poets. For this reason, Dockery prefers "spiration" as a translation. However, Dockery settles for "inspiration," due to the established tradition of translation.[16] The Greek term indicates God breathes life-giving reality into the biblical text through a creative act akin to the original gift of life to humanity.[17]

John 10:34–36

> Jesus answered them, "Isn't it written in your law, I said, you are gods? If he called those to whom the word of God came 'gods'—and the Scripture cannot be broken—do you say, 'You are blaspheming' to the one the Father set apart and sent into the world, because I said: I am the Son of God?"

Referring to the Psalmist's prophecy that a human being will be called divine (Ps. 82:6), Jesus said, "Scripture cannot be broken." He claimed that written prophecy is inviolable. Even those texts that theologians find difficult to understand, such as this one, must be fulfilled. Doubly reinforcing the doctrine of biblical inspiration, Jesus also claimed this prophecy came from and in the person standing before them.

First, the word *luthenai*, "broken," is derived from *luo*. In Rabbinic and New Testament literature, *luo* is often paired with *deo* to convey a formal binding or loosing before and by

---

16. Dockery, "Special Revelation," 114.

17. God breathed life into humanity in Genesis 2:7; God breathes into Scripture in 2 Timothy 3:16.

God.[18] Jesus's use of the term *luthenai* indicates God determined from eternity to proclaim and fulfill Psalm 82. When God promises to act, he will necessarily fulfill the words he inspired the prophet to speak and write.

Second, Jesus is the God who inspires Scripture. He is the eternal Word who gave the prophecy in the genre of a psalm to the ancient Israelite prophet. He later personally fulfilled the very prophecy he himself previously provided. Jesus is the man who can be called "God" in fulfillment of prophecy.[19] The prophecy of Psalm 82 was inspired by the eternal Word and fulfilled by the incarnate Word. Jesus knew "the Scripture cannot be broken," because he is "the word of God" who originally inspired the ancient prophets.[20]

2 Peter 1:19–21

> We also have the prophetic word strongly confirmed, and you will do well to pay attention to it, as to a lamp shining in a dark place, until the day dawns and the morning star rises in your hearts. Above all, you know this: No prophecy of Scripture comes from the prophet's own interpretation, because no prophecy ever came by the will of man; instead, men

18. Cf. Matthew 16:19; 18:18. Friedrich Büchsel, "*deō,*" in *Theological Dictionary of the New Testament,* ed. Gerhard Kittel, Geoffrey W. Bromiley, and Gerhard Friedrich, 10 vols. (Grand Rapids, Eerdmans, 1964–1976), 2:60.

19. He had just claimed deity for himself with the controversial statement, "I and the Father are one" (John 10:30).

20. A. T. Hanson, "John's Citation of Psalm LXXXII," *New Testament Studies* 11, no. 2 (January 1965): 158–62; idem, "John's Citation of Psalm LXXXII Reconsidered," *New Testament Studies* 13, no. 4 (July 1967): 363–67.

spoke from God as they were carried along
by the Holy Spirit.

In the verses immediately preceding these, Peter recalled
his experience on the mount of transfiguration, where Jesus
manifested the light of his divine glory to a few disciples.
Moses, representing the Law, and Elijah, representing the
Prophets, were also there (Mark 9:1–4). God the Father
reminded Peter of the worship uniquely due his beloved Son
(Mark 9:7). In his second epistle, Peter now discussed the
Holy Spirit's role in the revelation of God's light (cf. Ps. 36:9;
John 1:9; James 1:17; 1 John 1:5).

Five truths about God's revelation through the inspiration of Scripture are clearly stated in this passage. I arrange
these truths in a systematic format to stress revelation's divine
origin and the process of human reception: First, Scripture has
its origin in the will of God (2 Pet. 1:21a). Second, the Holy
Spirit is the efficient cause of the revelation of God's glorious
light (2 Pet. 1:21c). Third, the prophets were "carried along"
(Greek, *pheromene*) in the process of inspiration as instrumen-
tal agents (2 Pet. 1:21b). The Greek term indicates the Holy
Spirit's "initiating role in inspiration," not human inaction.[21]
Fourth, the prophet's words, having derived from God and
his Spirit, subsequently illuminate the human heart, bringing
divine knowledge (2 Pet. 1:19). Fifth, just as prophecy origi-
nates with God, so does its interpretation originate with his
Spirit (2 Pet. 1:20).

Theories of Biblical Inspiration

Scripture makes it clear that God the Trinity inspired
Scripture and that the Holy Spirit is the divine agent who

---

21. Dockery and Yarnell, *Special Revelation and Scripture*, 164.

guided the human writers to disclose God's identity and works. Theologians in the Enlightenment period began to reconsider the human contribution to the production of the biblical text. In their conclusions, they generally split into two major camps, with some emphasizing the human role while others retained divine agency in the authoring of Scripture. Kevin Vanhoozer discerned four primary ways in which modern theologians have related divine inspiration to the human authors.[22]

Arranging Vanhoozer's categories along a spectrum emphasizing humanity on the one side and God on the other, we first note "naturalism." The naturalist approach, exemplified by Baruch Spinoza, removes God entirely from the process. Three other ways emphasize the divine role variously. Those views which ascribe a role both to God and to humanity in the writing of the biblical text include, "weak divine authorship," which judges that God allowed human error to come into the text; "strong divine authorship," which argues God guided the human writers such that their writings really are God's Word; and "extreme divine authorship," which says God acted dictatorially. The strong divine authorship view, sometimes called "confluent" or "concursive" inspiration,[23] best fits the biblical evidence.[24]

The various theological models which diverse theologians have used to describe biblical inspiration may be arranged into four categories: dictation theories, partial theories, dynamic theories, and verbal plenary theories. It should be noted that there remains variety among those who hold to the same class of theory.

---

22. Kevin Vanhoozer, "Holy Scripture," in *Christian Dogmatics: Reformed Theology for the Church Catholic*, ed. Michael Allen and Scott R. Swain (Grand Rapids: Baker, 2016), 31–34.

23. Warfield, *Revelation and Inspiration*, 96–99, 106; Dockery and Yarnell, *Special Revelation and Scripture*, 8–9, 237.

24. Dockery and Yarnell, *Special Revelation and Scripture*, 150–52.

Dictation Theories

Advocates of dictation follow the extreme divine authorship view. Dictation theorists like John R. Rice often portray the human authors as amanuenses or secretaries.[25] Because of their tendency to use mechanical terminology and coercive descriptions of inspiration, these theories have been compared to the docetic heresy, wherein Christ only appeared as human.[26]

Partial Theories

The various proponents of partial inspiration have been heavily influenced by philosophical naturalism's prioritization of nature and the elevation of human reason. Partial theorists like Charles Briggs argue that the biblical writings contain various degrees of inspiration.[27] Because these partial theories diminish divine agency, they have been compared to the Ebionite heresy, wherein Christ was a mere human.[28]

Dynamic or Organic Theories

Developed in the twentieth century by moderate evangelical theologians like Edgar Young Mullins and Donald G. Bloesch, these theories retain the divine impetus in inspiration but emphasize the contribution of the human agent in the process of inspiration. Some reviewers believe this movement is conservative, arguing they believe, "The biblical authors were 'moved' by the Spirit in such a way that their own character, style, and context remained visible but without any

---

25. Garrett, *Systematic Theology*, 1:131.
26. Dockery, "Special Revelation," 128–29.
27. Zaspel, *The Theology of B. B. Warfield*, 122–23.
28. Dockery, "Special Revelation," 129.

errors."[29] Others, however, state these theories may underplay the product of inspiration.[30]

The Verbal Plenary Theory

The verbal plenary view grants the initiative in inspiration to the Holy Spirit as divine author. The human author, moreover, remains fully involved in the process of writing as a particular human being with distinct experiences shaped by a definite context using personal expression. Due to the supervising authority of the Holy Spirit, the writings retain the quality of inspiration. Proponents of this theory, such as Dockery, ascribe inspiration to the original autographs as written in their entirety, or plenarily, and not just to portions.[31] This theory also affirms that the Spirit led the writers in their choice of certain words. The verbal aspect of verbal plenary inspiration honors the distinctive context, thoughts, and style of the writers. It also recognizes meaning occurs not merely with the choice of particular words but at the levels of sentence, genre, and purpose.[32]

A Systematic Summary of Biblical Inspiration

After examining the biblical basis, the historical evidence, and the systematic debates, David Dockery and I recently collaborated to outline seven aspects in our doctrine of the inspiration of Scripture.

---

29. Cornelis van der Kooi and Gijsbert van den Brink, *Christian Dogmatics: An Introduction*, transl. Reinder Bruinsma and James D. Bratt (Grand Rapids: Eerdmans, 2017), 544.

30. Dockery and Yarnell, *Special Revelation and Scripture*, 155.

31. Dockery, "Special Revelation," 131.

32. Dockery and Yarnell, *Special Revelation and Scripture*, 155–58.

First, we believe "the Bible was inspired by the Holy Spirit as the executor of the will and the word of the Triune God."

Second, "the human authors were fully involved in the process of writing." We refer to this aspect of the doctrine as "concursive inspiration," highlighting the cooperation between the divine and human authors of Scripture.

Third, not only the writers but "the resultant text is also inspired." Unlike liberal and neo-orthodox theologians, we believe inspiration applies both to the producers and the product of the biblical text.

Fourth, "Scripture must always be accorded the status of being the perfect Word of the living God in written form."

Fifth, "God's written Word speaks to us today with the same divine power as it spoke to its original hearers."

Sixth, we agree with Warfield that the Bible may be called both "'the crystallized voice of God' and 'living words still speaking to us,'" for the Bible's inspiration by the Holy Spirit renders it always valuable, beautiful, dynamic, and incontestable." We really believe God was present to the original recipients when he acted before them in past events, and that he is present to and active now in the biblical text.

Seventh, "the best existing theological model for explaining biblical inspiration remains the verbal plenary theory."[33]

Listen to Him

Like many others, I have been driven to a high doctrine of biblical inspiration because this is the teaching of Scripture about itself. In addition, Christians often testify how they hear God's voice palpably through the biblical text. I can attest that, sometimes against my own preferences, God speaks transformative truth to me in his Word. God's Holy Spirit convicts

---

33. Dockery and Yarnell, *Special Revelation and Scripture*, 171–72.

me, instructs me, and renews my heart with hope every time I read Scripture.

Therefore, I have come to read God's Word as often as possible. I open the Bible every day on my own in prayer. I use it regularly in congregational worship. I use it to witness to others, hoping to bring them to salvation or to enhance their walk with the Lord. I study it deeply for my mind and for my heart. I cannot get enough of the Bible because I meet God in it. Would you join me in hearing God through his Spirit's inspiration of his Word?

Study Questions

1. Choose one of the three major biblical texts that teach the doctrine of biblical inspiration and explain its meaning regarding inspiration.

2. Which one of the above views of inspiration would you defend? Describe your primary reason for adopting that view.

3. Describe one time when you heard God speak clearly through his Word. Did he speak his convicting law to you? Did he speak his saving gospel to you? Please share your answer with a friend.

Suggested Resources

- B. B. Warfield, *Revelation and Inspiration*

- Carl Henry, *God, Revelation and Authority*, vol. 4

- David Dockery and Malcolm Yarnell, *Special Revelation and Scripture*

CHAPTER TWELVE

What Is Scripture?

◆

WHEN CHRISTIANS SPEAK OF THE church's canonical text, we often use terms like *Sacred Scripture*, *Holy Bible*, even *Word of God*. In the last chapter, we rehearsed the inspiration of Scripture. We also pondered how Scripture works. We have more to discover about the work of Scripture in the next chapter. But, at this point, we must consider the identity of Scripture.

While we previously emphasized the work of the Holy Spirit in biblical revelation, we have spoken only some about the Son's work in biblical revelation. To rectify that situation, we will first demonstrate the need to incorporate the Word of God into our doctrine of Scripture in the first major section of this chapter. While doing so, we must contemplate the close correlation between the Word and the Spirit. We must also compare the words of men with the Word of God and show how the phrase, "Word of God," evinces both unity and diversity.

The second major section of this chapter will explore the nature or ontology of Scripture by considering its perfections or attributes. These attributes have been granted to Scripture by

God so that it will effectively accomplish his purposes. The Bible's perfections include the inerrancy of the original autographs, the infallibility of the textual tradition, the clarity of the Bible, the authority of God's Word, and the sufficiency of Scripture.

A *Logos-Pneuma* Ontology of Scripture

Systematic theologians in the modern period have treated the doctrine of Scripture in three ways. Some treat the Bible as an introductory matter before engaging in theology, typically for apologetic reasons.[1] Others subsume the written Word of God in the doctrine of Jesus Christ, who is the personal Word of God.[2] Some exposit the doctrine of Scripture within their doctrine of the Holy Spirit, who inspired Scripture.[3] On the one hand, each method has its obvious benefits. On the other hand, either method on its own can lead to error.[4]

I locate the doctrine of sacred Scripture in this first volume to honor its priority in the construction of all theology and its importance in contemporary apologetics. Yet I also

---

1. Wayne Grudem, *Systematic Theology: An Introduction to Biblical Doctrine*, 2nd ed. (Grand Rapids: Zondervan, 2020), 31–168.

2. Wolfhart Pannenberg, *Systematic Theology*, vol. 2, transl. Geoffrey W. Bromiley (Grand Rapids: Eerdmans, 1994), 463–64. Pannenberg speculated far more about "revelation as history" than about biblical revelation. Departing from his teacher, his most prominent American Evangelical student located the doctrine of Scripture in his prolegomena. Millard J. Erickson, *Christian Theology*, 2nd ed. (Grand Rapids: Baker, 2001), 224–287.

3. Cornelis van der Looi and Gijsbert van den Brink, *Christian Dogmatics: An Introduction*, transl. Reinder Bruinsma and James D. Bratt (Grand Rapids: Eerdmans, 2017), 533–71.

4. Telford Work argues a Word-dominant bibliology can lead to a form of Apollinarianism, where humanity is a mere carrier of divine truth, whereas a Spirit-dominant bibliology treats the incarnate Word as a mere messenger. Work, *Living and Active: Scripture in the Economy of Salvation* (Grand Rapids: Eerdmans, 2002), 122.

intentionally place Scripture after our exposition of God the Trinity and his attributes, thereby reasserting the supremacy of God as Trinity over his elect means of revelation. This method retains the benefits of the other methods while equally recognizing the Father sending the Son and the Spirit, and the leading roles of both the divine Word and the divine Spirit in Scripture. I, therefore, locate the ontology of Scripture in the Trinitarian economy through its dependence upon the God who is and who acts as *Logos*, "Word," and *Pneuma*, "Spirit."

The apostolic doctrine of Scripture likewise recognized the agency of both the Word and the Spirit. As we saw in chapter 11, the apostle Peter focused on the role of the third Person of the Trinity, the Holy Spirit, near the beginning of his second epistle. He taught about inspiration, illumination, and interpretation of revelation.[5] At the beginning of his first epistle, Peter also recognized the role of the second Person of the Trinity, the Word of God, in revelation. He demonstrated that "the Word of God," a title which the New Testament ascribes to Christ and the written and oral message about him, even now actively works for our salvation. The leading apostle reminded his believing readers of their regeneration by the Word.

> Because you have been born again—not of perishable seed but of imperishable—through the living and enduring word of God. For all flesh is like grass, and all its glory like a flower of the grass. The grass withers, and the flower falls, but the word of the Lord endures forever. And this word is the gospel that was proclaimed to you. (1 Pet. 1:23–25)

---

5. See the exposition of 2 Peter 1:19–21 in chapter 11 regarding the Spirit's role in inspiration and the exposition in chapter 13 regarding the Spirit's role in illumination and interpretation.

Peter, pursuing the teaching of Jesus Christ (Matt. 13:1–23; Mark 4:1–20; Luke 8:4–15), drew upon Isaiah's description of the Word as simultaneously a living, an active, and an eternal agent (Isa. 40:6–8). Peter used the metaphor of a "seed" to portray how God's word possesses divine power to generate life. In the New Testament, God's "word" or "message" (Greek *logos* or *rhema*) is powerful enough even to re-create life. This regenerating Word from God is "the gospel" which has been "proclaimed to you" (1 Pet. 1:25). Peter conveyed this truth to them, at first through oral proclamation, but now through written proclamation.

Through two accounts (1 Pet. 1:23–25; 2 Pet. 1:19–21), Peter demonstrated the soul transforming power of divine revelation is equally the work of the Word and the Spirit. Peter offers a rich Trinitarian doctrine of revelation through this correlation. A proper theology of Scripture today requires emphasis upon both the Word (*Logos*) and the Spirit (*Pneuma*). We advocate, therefore, a Logos-Pneuma ontology of Scripture. The Bible's nature lies within the Trinitarian economy of revelation.

The Word with the Spirit

One of the ablest proponents of a Trinitarian understanding of Scripture was the sixteenth-century Evangelical Anabaptist theologian, Pilgram Marpeck. Influenced both by the classical Trinitarianism of the Athanasian Creed and by the Reformers' recent emphasis upon biblical authority, Marpeck held to the coinherence of the Word with the Spirit. He navigated between various theological extremes to maintain an ecumenical faith deeply conversant with both Scripture and tradition.

The classical confession of Trinitarian theology by Marpeck's community states, "It is our Christian faith that there are not three Gods, but only one God in three persons and that each holy Person of the Godhead, the Son as well as the Father, and the Holy Spirit as well as the Son, are truly God in nature; and are of like authority, might, honor, glory, and magnificence."[6]

Regarding the Trinity's work of divine revelation, Marpeck's dictum was both simple and deep: "God's Word and Spirit work together."[7] He argued that the Word and the Spirit always work with one another, never apart from one another, and never against one another. Stressing the Word, Marpeck said, "Only by means of the word of truth does the Holy Spirit generate faith." Stressing the Spirit, he said, "Even today, God will reveal his art and wisdom only through the Holy Spirit."[8]

Of course, this Word and Spirit theology of revelation is based upon Scripture: God sent the Son and the Spirit to bring us salvation (Gal. 4:4–6). The Spirit works inwardly as the incarnate, crucified, and risen Word is proclaimed outwardly. Saving faith comes through the proclamation of the revealed Word of God (Rom. 10:14; 1 Cor. 1:18), that Jesus Christ is the only begotten Son of the living God, the eternal Word (Matt. 16:16; John 1:1, 14; 3:16). Saving faith simultaneously comes as an internal grace through conviction and regeneration by the Holy Spirit (John 3:5–8; 16:8–11).

Like Marpeck, Christians today can avoid various errors by sustaining the Trinitarian work of revelation. We can avoid the error of spiritualism by upholding the proclamation of the

---

6. Pilgram Marpeck, *Verantwortung* (1542), in *Quellen und Forschungen zur Geschichte der oberdeutschen Taufgesinnten im 16. Jarhundert: Pilgram Marbecks Antwort auf Kaspar Schwenckfelds Beurteilung des Buches der Bundesbezeugung* von 1542, ed. J. Loserth (Vienna: Carl Fromme, 1929), 551; translated in Malcolm B. Yarnell III, *The Formation of Christian Doctrine* (Nashville: B&H Academic, 2007), 84.

7. Marpeck, *Verantwortung*, 516; Yarnell, *The Formation of Christian Doctrine*, 83.

8. Yarnell, *The Formation of Christian Doctrine*, 88.

Word of God. We can avoid the error of legalism by honoring the necessity of the internal work of the Spirit. We must refuse to diminish the sovereign and free work of the Holy Spirit. We can avoid yet other errors by refusing to add to Scripture's message or to take away from it.

The Eternal and Effective Word of God

The words of men and the Word of God must be differentiated from one another, although God also uses the words of men to carry his Word. Paul reminded the Thessalonian believers, "when you received the word of God that you heard from us, you welcomed it not as a human message, but as it truly is, the word of God, which also works effectively in you who believe" (1 Thess. 2:13). The CSB chose "human message" to translate *logon anthropon*, which literally means, "word of man." Paul juxtaposed this word of man against the Word of God (Greek, *logon theou*).

From a merely descriptive perspective, the words of men are used to communicate knowledge. Basic knowledge is communicated via words as signs which convey propositions about truth. The failure or success of communication depends on the speaker's ability to convey a proposition that the hearer will receive and, by these words, understand the same proposition about truth. Human words can communicate information well, but breakdowns in communication can and do occur at numerous points in the process.

From a moral perspective, the words of men are intended to sway minds toward truth or error. Alas, however, human words may be intentionally employed by people not to convey truth but to misrepresent it. James, the brother of Jesus, lamented, "Blessing and cursing come out of the same mouth. My brothers and sisters, these things should not be this way" (James 3:10).

The Eternal Word of God: The Word of God is different from the words of men in at least two ways. First, truth is a divine attribute, so the Word of God is eternally truthful by nature. John said the Son of God, the Word who became flesh, was "full of grace and truth" (John 1:14). Jesus prayed to the Father, "Your word is truth" (John 17:17b). The Spirit, like the Father and the Son, is identified with truth. He is the "Spirit of truth" (John 14:17; 15:26; 16:32). God is truth, so he "cannot lie" (Titus 1:2). The Word of God conveys truth without error, because this is God's very nature.

The Effective Word of God: The second way in which the Word of God differs from the words of men is that it effectively causes whatever it speaks. Human words and arguments can be empty, useless (Eph. 5:6; Col. 2:8; Titus 1:10). To the contrary, Moses reported that when God spoke, the world wondrously came into existence out of nothing (Gen. 1:3, 6–7, 9).[9] Isaiah prophesied that when God sends his Word, it will "accomplish" his will and "prosper" (Isa. 55:11). Paul said the Word of God "works effectively" to bring salvation (1 Thess. 2:13). The author of Hebrews agreed that the Word of God is "living and effective" (Heb. 4:12). Peter said the Word causes the regeneration of believers (1 Pet. 1:23). The Word of God will triumph totally in the end.[10]

The Threefold Word of God

The Word of God is different from the words of men, but the Word of God may and does employ the words of men. God uses the prophets and the apostles as instruments

---

9. The second volume of *Theology for Every Person* shall consider the doctrine of *creatio ex nihilo*, that God created the world out of nothing, in more detail.

10. Revelation 19:11–15. On the dynamic nature of Scripture, see Telford Work, *Living and Active.*

to communicate his truth propositions through them. God thereby accommodates himself to us, speaking to us in terms and concepts we understand.

Scripture uses the terminology, "Word of God," in three intimately related ways. I have often spoken of the threefold nature of the Word as incarnate, intoned, and inscripturated. The incarnate Word is the Son of God. The intoned Word is the oral proclamation of God's special revelation, which is focused on the incarnate Word. The inscripturated Word is the perfect written record of the revelation of God to Israel and in Jesus Christ. Scripture clearly teaches the threefold unity of the Word and helpful theology maintains this biblical way of speaking about the Word.

The Incarnate Word: First, there is the person of the Word, the eternal Son of God who became flesh in Jesus Christ (John 1:14). The eternal Word was with God and is God (John 1:1) and is worthy of our worship. All three divine Persons speak from heaven, including the Father (Rev. 21:5–8), the Lamb (Rev. 22:7, 12–16, 20), and the Holy Spirit (Rev. 22:17). While the Father and the Spirit also speak, the Son of God is particularly named "the Word of God."

The Intoned Word: Second, there is the oral proclamation of the Word of God. The message of God was delivered at first to the prophets and the apostles. As Jeremiah discovered, however, this Word ought never be kept silent.[11] This oral Word of God was then proclaimed to others by the prophets and the apostles who heard it. The prophetic refrain, "Hear the Word of the Lord," appeared some 3 dozen times in the former and latter prophets (cf. 1 Kings 22:19; Isaiah 1:10). The oral Word of God continues to be proclaimed wherever

---

11. The prophet declared that when he decided to keep God's Word for the people to himself, "his message becomes a fire burning in my heart, shut up in my bones." He could not hold it in, for it "prevailed" over him. Jeremiah 20:9.

the words of the prophets and the apostles are repeated (Matt. 16:13; 1 Pet. 1:25).

The Inscripturated Word: Third, we must also speak of the written Word of God. Sacred Scripture is the Word of God too (John 10:35; 2 Tim. 2:15; Heb. 4:12). God gave the written Word of God to his church to serve as the source for its oral proclamation of the Law and the Gospel. The Holy Spirit inspired the prophets and the apostles to convey his inspired word in script. The written Word of God, as we shall see below, participates in the perfections of God by grace.

As a careful reader of Scripture, Pilgram Marpeck also confessed "the Word of God" was properly understood in three ways, first personally in Christ, then as mediated through oral or written proclamation. Regarding the written Word in the holy Scriptures, Marpeck said of the apostles, "Their script was God's script engraved." "Therefore, they are the writing of God or the Holy Spirit."[12]

However, Marpeck warned against efforts to separate the Word from God, to divorce the proclamation of the Word from Christ as the Word. "Namely, we mean that there is only the unique word of the Father, which comes to us from the human Word, the Lord Jesus Christ." "Through himself and his apostles this word was brought to us through the gospel, and now it still speaks in believers' hearts by the Holy Spirit, as a living word or speech of God."[13] The incarnate Word speaks effectively through the intoned Word and the inscripturated Word.

The oral and written forms of the Word of God are the communicative means by which God continues to make his personal Word present to humanity by grace. After the ascension of Jesus Christ to the right hand of the Father, he is made

---

12. Marpeck, *Verantwortung*, 298; Yarnell, *The Formation of Christian Doctrine*, 83.

13. Marpeck, *Verantwortung*, 298; Yarnell, *The Formation of Christian Doctrine*, 83–84.

known to human beings through the written and oral forms of his Word. There is an insurmountable difference between human words, flawed by temporal imperfections, and the divine Word, fruitful with God's eternal perfections. God overcomes the imperfections of human words by graciously displaying himself through them. We now provide an ontological description of Scripture through its perfections.

The Perfections of Holy Scripture

We learned in chapter 5 that the Holy Spirit, the third person of the Trinity, is fully divine. One with God, the Spirit participates in all the divine perfections, which were surveyed in chapters 6 and 7. The Spirit of God is perfect, so his work also possesses perfection.[14] We, therefore, affirm that Scripture is trustworthy because God the Holy Spirit, who inspired Scripture, is trustworthy. "God is towards his people the same as the words he speaks to them."[15] In the same way, we must say that because God is living and powerful, so his Word also possesses life and power.[16] Again, because God is

---

14. Jesus Christ argued that diminishing the Holy Spirit's work is sinful, even a blasphemy which is unforgiveable (Matt. 12:22–32 and parallels). Other sins against the Holy Spirit include lying to him (Acts 5:3, 5), testing him (Acts 5:9), and grieving him (Eph. 4:30). The third volume of Theology for Every Person will discuss the person and work of the Spirit in more detail.

15. Paul Helm and Carl R. Trueman argue this is the "recurring theme" of Scripture. Helm and Trueman, "Introduction," in *The Trustworthiness of God: Perspectives on the Nature of Scripture*, ed. Helm and Trueman (Grand Rapids, Eerdmans, 2002), x.

16. "For the word of God is living and effective and sharper than any double-edged sword, penetrating as far as the separation of soul and spirit, joints and marrow. It is able to judge the thoughts and intentions of the heart." Hebrews 4:12 appears to refer to "the Word of God" in all three of its related theological senses: the personal Word of Jesus Christ, the written

characterized by oneness, so his Word receives and manifests the integrity of his unity.[17] In other words, because God the Holy Spirit is perfect by nature, the written Word of God is perfected by the grace of his inspiration of it.

Scripture possesses trustworthiness, dynamic power, and unity because God graced it with his perfections. Although Scripture is characterized by yet many other perfections, such as holiness, we limit our current review to five perfections which have required careful reaffirmation due to the doctrinal recoveries of the Reformation and the acidic challenges of the Enlightenment. The perfections of holy Scripture include the inerrancy of the original autographs, the infallibility of the copies in the surviving textual tradition, the clarity of the Bible, the authority of God's written Word, and the sufficiency of Scripture. God has certainly graced the holy Bible as his written Word with his perfections, such that we may even speak of Scripture as having a "dogmatic ontology."[18]

The Inerrancy of the Original Autographs

The doctrine of biblical inerrancy was likely the default position in the history of the church.[19] As late as 1833, the

---

Word of Holy Scripture, and the proclaimed Word of the Law and the gospel.

17. Matthew Y. Emerson says the Bible has unity because it has "one subject" and "one story." Biblical unity is reinforced by its narrative context, method of recapitulation, intertextuality, covenants, and canonical structure. Emerson, *The Story of Scripture: An Introduction to Biblical Theology* (Nashville: B&H Academic, 2017), 10–16.

18. John Webster, *Holy Scripture: A Dogmatic Account* (New York: Cambridge University Press, 2003), 2. Telford Work refers to this ontology more pointedly as a "divine-human ontology." Work, *Living and Active*, 11.

19. Garrett cites statements by both Augustine and Luther. James Leo Garrett Jr., *Systematic Theology: Biblical, Historical, and Evangelical*, vol. 1, 2nd ed. (North Richland Hills, TX: Bibal Press, 2000), 184.

New Hampshire Confession said the Bible has "God for its author, salvation for its end, and truth, without any mixture of error, for its matter."[20] However, the need for a detailed definition of inerrancy became necessary during the late twentieth century, as evangelicals addressed the crisis of epistemological certainty caused by the rising dominance of historical critical methods of Bible study.[21] The Chicago Statement on Biblical Inerrancy of 1978 offered a detailed description.[22]

Carl Henry, the leading evangelical exponent of the doctrine, argued that Scripture's inerrancy derives from its inspiration and that it refers to the original autographs rather than the subsequent copies. He believed inerrancy applies equally to the historical and scientific claims of Scripture, although they are not as central as its theological and soteriological teachings.[23] Henry argued strongly for inerrancy, deeming it

---

20. William L. Lumpkin, *Baptist Confessions of Faith*, revised ed. (Valley Forge, PA: Judson Press, 1969), 361–62. This language was borrowed from the early modern Christian philosopher, John Locke, and has been incorporated into subsequent statements like the first article of *The Baptist Faith and Message* (1925, 1963, 2000). Malcolm Yarnell, "The Baptists and John Locke," in *Baptist Political Theology*, ed. Thomas S. Kidd, Paul D. Miller, and Andrew T. Walker (Brentwood, TN: B&H Academic, 2023), 97–122.

21. James Leo Garrett Jr. noted the Southern Baptist conversation over inerrancy arose around 1970 with a publication by Clark Pinnock warning against the ideas being taught in seminaries and colleges. Garrett, "The Teaching of Recent Southern Baptist Theologians on the Bible" (1987), in *The Collected Writings of James Leo Garrett Jr. 1950–2015*, Vol. 1, Part I, ed. Wyman Lewis Richardson (Eugene, OR: Wipf and Stock, 2017), 212.

22. "The Chicago Statement on Biblical Inerrancy," in Carl F. H. Henry, *God, Revelation and Authority*, revised ed., 6 vols. (Wheaton, IL: Crossway, 1999), 4:211–19.

23. "The Holy Spirit superintended the scriptural writers in communicating the biblical message in ways consistent with their differing personalities, literary styles and cultural background, while safeguarding them from error." Henry, *God, Revelation and Authority*, 4:167–68.

helpful for preserving biblical authority, but he did not consider it essential for salvation.[24]

While there have been various definitions, David Dockery helpfully defined biblical inerrancy as, "When all the facts are known, the Bible (in its original writings), properly interpreted in light of the culture and communication means that had developed by the time of its composition, will be shown to be completely true (and therefore not false) in all that it affirms, to the degree of precision intended by the biblical authors, in all matters relating to God and his creation."[25] Leo Garrett preferred the positive language of "dependability," but employed "inerrancy," too.[26]

The Infallibility of the Textual Tradition

Henry differentiated infallibility from inerrancy. The original manuscripts, which we no longer possess, were without error by virtue of the Holy Spirit's inspiration. The ancient copies of those original manuscripts, which are now encompassed in a large textual tradition, may be said to be infallible. Infallibility means the textual tradition is "not prone to error."[27] The question regarding the copies concerns whether "they reliably convey the Word of God, or are they undependable?"[28]

---

24. Henry, *God, Revelation and Authority*, 4:171; "The Battle for the Bible: An Interview with Dr. Carl F. H. Henry," *Scribe* (1976): 3, cited in Robert K. Johnston, *Evangelicals at an Impasse: Biblical Authority in Practice* (Philadelphia: John Knox Press, 1979), 35. "We deny that such confession is necessary for salvation." *Chicago Statement on Biblical Inerrancy*, "Affirmations and Denials," Article XIX.

25. David S. Dockery and Malcolm B. Yarnell III, *Special Revelation and Scripture* (Brentwood: B&H Academic, 2024), 229–34.

26. Garrett, *Systematic Theology*, 1:182–92.

27. Henry, *God, Revelation and Authority*, 4:220.

28. Henry, *God, Revelation and Authority*, 4:220.

I believe the copies are, indeed, reliable. The Holy Spirit's superintendence of revelation through the Bible did not cease with the inspiration of the human authors and their manuscripts. According to Henry, the Spirit's work includes at least "inspiration, illumination, regeneration, indwelling, sanctification, guidance."[29] He also placed his doctrine of revelation on a pneumatic foundation and warned evangelicals against neglecting the Holy Spirit.[30] We shall have more to say about Henry's robust contribution in this matter in this volume's final chapter.

Citing critical textual scholarship, Henry noted that the textual tradition comes "within 99.9% accuracy." "Whatever uncertainties copying has contributed, the Bible remains virtually unchanged and its teaching undimmed."[31] Garrett similarly concluded the copies we have in the original languages are "dependably accurate reproductions of the originals or autographs." He also noted that evangelicals, despite their great diversity, agree the Bible's doctrines are secure. Christian Scripture remains dependable "in respect to its basic religious and moral message."[32]

The Clarity of the Bible

Scripture affirms that it is not difficult to understand. "For this commandment which I command you today is not too difficult for you, nor is it out of reach. It is not in heaven, that you should say, 'Who will go up to heaven for us to get it for us

29. Henry, *God, Revelation and Authority*, 4:273.

30. Malcolm B. Yarnell III, "Whose Jesus? Which Revelation?" *Midwestern Journal of Theology* 1 (2003): 41–46. R. Albert Mohler Jr. criticized Henry for giving "little attention" to the Holy Spirit. Mohler, "Carl F. H. Henry," in *Theologians of the Baptist Tradition*, ed. Timothy George and David S. Dockery (Nashville: Broadman & Holman Publishers, 2001), 292.

31. Henry, *God, Revelation and Authority*, 4:235.

32. Garrett, *Systematic Theology*, 1:186.

and make us hear it, that we may observe it?' Nor is it beyond
the sea, that you should say, 'Who will cross the sea for us to
get it for us and make us hear it, that we may observe it?' But
the word is very near you, in your mouth and in your heart,
that you may observe it" (Deut. 30:11–14 NASB1995). Moses
hereby declared that the clarity of the Law to its hearers constituted a divine grace.

The apostle Paul employed this text from the Law of
Moses when explaining the effectiveness of the Word of God
in bringing salvation through the gospel. Paul first explained,
"Christ is the end of the law" for the believer (Rom. 10:4).
Divine righteousness comes when we have faith in the Word
proclaimed (Rom. 10:5–8). The message of the gospel, that
Jesus is Lord and arose from death, must be received inwardly
and confessed outwardly (Rom. 10:9–10). Salvation occurs
as the Word of the gospel is returned in confession (Rom.
10:12–13). Salvation comes by means of the proclamation
of the Word of God, so the church must set aside preachers
(Rom 10:14–15). Like Moses, Paul credited effective agency
to the Word proclaimed rather than to its hearer: "So faith
comes from what is heard, and what is heard comes through
the message about Christ" (Rom. 10:17).[33]

During the Middle Ages, the clarity of Scripture was
compromised. Scripture was seen as dark, even dangerous. The
clergy, responsible for safeguarding Scripture from misinter-
pretation, in places denied the laity access to it. Late medieval
Lollards, for instance, were violently persecuted as heretics for
possessing vernacular translations.[34] The Reformers, following
the lead of Erasmus of Rotterdam, recovered the concept of

---

33. The psalmist likewise illuminating agency to the Word (Ps. 119:105).

34. As with the Oxford Constitutions of 1409. Malcolm B. Yarnell III,
Royal Priesthood in the English Reformation (New York: Oxford University
Press, 2013), 31, 80–83.

the clarity of Scripture, advocated its translation into the vernacular, and wanted to see it made available to the milkmaid and the plowboy as well as the professional theologian.[35]

Ülrich Zwingli denied Scripture was inherently dark, judging it both clear and certain. To overcome any confusion about Scripture's meaning, he counseled Christians to "consult the Spirit of God" in humble prayer.[36] Reformers like Zwingli were optimistic about believers' ability to understand the text and judge their teachers, at least at first.[37] Although there will remain difficulties for all readers, the lighter portions of Scripture clarify the darker parts. "Scripture interprets Scripture" became a key hermeneutical slogan for the Reformation.[38]

The clarity of Scripture does not mean readers will never have questions about its meaning and application. Even the apostle Peter admitted he had difficulty understanding the apostle Paul (1 Pet. 3:16). Neither does scriptural clarity negate the need for careful Bible study, interpretation, and instruction (Acts 17:11; 2 Tim. 2:15; 3:15). The doctrine of biblical clarity says the primary theological, moral, and soteriological teachings of Scripture are available to the prayerful reader through God's gracious and effective revelation in the biblical text.

---

35. Erasmus, *Paraclesis*, in *Christian Humanism and the Reformation*, 3rd ed. by John C. Olin (New York: Fordham University Press, 1987), 101–4; Yarnell, *Royal Priesthood in the English Reformation*, 86–89.

36. Ülrich Zwingli, *On the Clarity and Certainty of the Word of God* (1522), in Zwingli and Bullinger, ed. G. W. Bromiley, Library of Christian Classics (Philadelphia: Westminster Press, 1953), 88–89.

37. Zwingli, *On the Clarity and Certainty of the Word of God*, 93–95. The Reformers reduced their "exegetical optimism" after encountering more radical reformers. Alister E. McGrath, *Reformation Thought: An Introduction*, 3rd ed. (Malden, MA: Blackwell, 1999), 161–65. On Luther's changes in these matters, see Yarnell, *Royal Priesthood in the English Reformation*, 90–96.

38. Bernard Ramm, *Protestant Biblical Interpretation: A Textbook of Hermeneutics*, 3rd ed. (Grand Rapids: Baker, 1970), 55.

The Authority of God's Word

All power belongs to God, as does the authority which enables its proper use.[39] All authority was given to the Son (Matt. 28:18). All authority derives from above (John 19:11; Rom. 13:1). Everyone must use their authority according to the Lord's command (Luke 6:46). Believers must honor and pray for human authorities, simultaneously recognizing their divine authorization (Rom. 13:1–7; 1 Tim. 2:1–4; 1 Pet. 2:13–17) and their sinful rebellion (Rev. 13). But believers must serve divine revelation above all (Acts 4:19–20; 5:29). Christ will one day hold everyone accountable for their use of his gifts of power and authority (Rev. 20:13).

In the garden, God described the authority he granted with his image (Gen. 1:26). He revealed the blessings of the gift of authority (Gen. 3:16) and the consequences for disobeying his commands about our actions (Gen. 3:17). God's own authority accompanies his revelation. God and his Word work together. The New Testament exemplified how we must view biblical authority by stating, "God says," or "the Holy Spirit says," when quoting the Old Testament (Acts 4:24–25; 2 Cor. 6:16). God's Word speaks with God's authority. And God will hold the hearers of his Word accountable for their various responses (Rom. 10:16, 18–21). The Bible has authority, simply because it is God's Word.

The authority of Scripture became a major point of discussion during and after the Reformation. The Reformers argued Scripture has authority over the church because it is the Word of God inspired by the Spirit. Theological authority comes primarily through God's Word rather than from the church's officers or the doctrinal tradition. Scripture stands in judgment of the church.[40]

---

39. *Power* is the ability to perform an act. *Authority* concerns the right to use that power.

40. McGrath, *Reformation Thought*, 152–57.

Alas, the authority of Scripture has been repeatedly challenged in the Modern period. As noted in the last chapter, some theologians limited or denied the Spirit's inspiration. And as the Chicago Statement on Inerrancy indicated in its opening sentence and paragraph, the inerrancy of Scripture became the "key issue" for supporting biblical authority.[41] Post-modernism and post-liberalism, which developed in reaction to philosophical modernism and theological liberalism, likewise present challenges to biblical truth and authority when they unduly and respectively elevate individual human authority and communal human authority.[42]

The Sufficiency of Scripture

While Scripture's perfection of authority affirms our need to believe and obey God's written Word, Scripture's perfection of sufficiency speaks to its purpose. Evangelicals emphasized Scripture's inspiration, authority, and inerrancy during the late twentieth century, but they have increasingly begun to address the sufficiency of Scripture.[43] There are five aspects in a healthy doctrine of the sufficiency of Scripture. We should speak of its origin, relevance, comprehensiveness, dynamism, and above all, its purpose.

First, Scripture is sufficient because God is himself sufficient. God's Word participates in God by grace. In a short passage, Paul refers to sufficiency three times: "It is not that we are competent in ourselves to claim anything as coming from ourselves, but our adequacy is from God. He has made us

---

41. Henry, *God, Revelation and Authority*, 4:211.

42. Dockery and Yarnell, *Special Revelation and Scripture*, 99, 170–71, 224–25.

43. Noel Weeks, *The Sufficiency of Scripture* (Edinburgh: Banner of Truth, 1998); *The Authority and Sufficiency of Scripture*, ed. by Adam W. Greenway and David S. Dockery (Fort Worth: Seminary Hill Press, 2022).

competent to be ministers of a new covenant, not of the letter, but of the Spirit. For the letter kills, but the Spirit gives life" (2 Cor. 3:5–6). He establishes that humanity lacks sufficiency, that God is the origin of sufficiency, and that the sufficiency of the apostles' ministry is a gift of the Spirit. The apostles' ministry and thus their sufficiency are made available to us today through their writings.

Second, Scripture does not require us to "make it relevant." Scripture is relevant whether we immediately see it or not. Neither the church nor the culture can make Scripture relevant. Scripture is eternally relevant, and it makes us relevant through transforming our hearts when it is proclaimed. Third, everything which the Christian needs to know about how to think and about how live in relation to God is available from Scripture. The sufficiency of Scripture refers to its comprehensive spiritual utility.

Fourth, sufficiency encompasses Scripture's dynamism. As discussed in chapter 11, the Holy Bible continues the proclamation of the gospel about his eternal, personal Word who became human, died, and arose. The biblical canon is God's choice instrument for proclaiming his saving Word through the voice of the preacher. The Word is the powerful agent of God, a "grace" of the Holy Spirit (2 Cor. 12:9). It has living power to discern our hearts, convict of sin, and inculcate life through faith (Heb. 4:12; Rom. 10:17).

Fifth, God gave Scripture for a particular set of his purposes, rather than our purposes. The Bible is intended as God's instrument to accomplish two primary tasks. The written Word of God was given to be the ordinary means to foster saving faith and to show Christians how to live out their salvation. Paul said the sacred Scriptures are "able [*dunamena*] to make you wise for salvation through faith in Christ Jesus" (2 Tim. 3:15 NIV). Moreover, Scripture is "profitable [*ophelmos*] for teaching, for rebuking, for correcting, for training in righteousness, so that the man of God may be complete, equipped for every good work" (2 Tim. 3:16–17).

The doctrine of sufficiency does not mean Scripture addresses all our questions, especially the mundane matters of life. It also doesn't contradict the usefulness of teaching our faith with creeds and confessions.[44] We affirm the sufficiency of Scripture when we recognize it is God's own Word, that it is intended to renew and sustain our relationship with him, and that it serves his purposes.[45] We deny the sufficiency of Scripture when we try to use his Word for our purposes, when we elevate our tradition of interpretation above his Word, or when we try to impose "a widely disputed interpretation" or non-essential aspect of faith upon other believers.[46]

The Blessing of God's Written Word

One of the first songs I learned as a child was the simple hymn, "Jesus Loves Me." I heard it at Vacation Bible School at the age of seven. Receiving the grace of its truth claim about the blessing of sacred Scripture, I was soon after converted by faith in Jesus. These easily memorable lyrics encouraged me to hold a high view of God, Christ, and the Bible.

True Christians do not believe the Bible is God, nor do we worship the Bible. But we do honor it, for we know the Bible is a special gift of God for us. And we have experienced the truth that the Lord speaks effectively in, through, and by Scripture. The Old and New Testaments comprise God's Word. Both testaments testify to the promise and fulfillment

---

44. David S. Dockery and Malcolm B. Yarnell III, "Introduction," in *The Authority and Sufficiency of Scripture*, 10.

45. Dockery and Yarnell, "Introduction," 11–12.

46. Dockery and Yarnell, "Introduction," 12–13.

of God's love in the beautiful Messiah, Jesus. He died for my sins, and he arose from the dead for my justification.

Listen to the first verse of this hymn, learn it, and repeat it. My wife and I sang it to our babies each night before bed, and we have continued to do so with our grandchildren. Perhaps you might share the same gift with your little loved ones. It will bless them, and it will bless you. May both of you remember forever that Jesus loves you, simply because the Bible told you so.

> Jesus loves me! This I know, for the Bible
>   tells me so;
> Little ones to Him belong; They are weak,
>   but He is strong.
> Yes, Jesus loves me, Yes, Jesus loves me.
> Yes, Jesus loves me, The Bible tells me so.[47]

Study Questions

1. How would you answer somebody's argument that the Bible should not be identified with the Word of God?

2. Does the Holy Spirit ever contradict the Bible? Or does the Spirit work together with the Word? What biblical text might you use to prove your point?

3. What is the difference between biblical inerrancy and biblical infallibility? How would you defend the doctrine of biblical inerrancy?

---

47. Anna B. Warner, "Jesus Loves Me," in *The Baptist Hymnal*, ed. Wesley L. Forbis (Nashville: Convention Press, 1991), 344.

Suggested Resources

• John Webster, *Holy Scripture*

• *The Baptist Hymnal*

• Malcolm Yarnell, *The Formation of Christian Doctrine*

CHAPTER THIRTEEN

How Does the Church Serve the Word in the World?

◆

WE STARTED OUR GRAND TOUR of theology by surveying the dogmatic loci of God and revelation. In the last several chapters, we discovered important truths about his revelation: that God reveals his law to everyone; that he revealed himself redemptively in the Messiah; and that the Spirit inspired the prophets and apostles to record his special revelation in their writings. To bring this volume to a close, we must now consider how God calls the church to deliver his saving Word to the rest of humanity.

First, we will discuss the church as the servant of the Word of God to the world. The church was commissioned by Jesus Christ and is guided by the Holy Spirit. Second, we consider the canon as the rule of faith and how the Spirit led God's people to recognize and preserve the inspired writings. Third, we discuss the Trinity's role and then the church's role in the theological interpretation of Scripture. Fourth, we conclude this volume by considering the church's fulfillment of our mission of proclamation through generosity toward Christian diversity while treasuring a common core of truth.

The Church as Servant of the Word to the World

The Mission of the Christ

We have seen that Jesus Christ is the Second Person of the Trinity. He is fully God in every way.[1] He is also fully human in every way, except that he committed no sin.[2] As a human being, Jesus understood that he was sent by the Father to proclaim the gospel, and that his gospel concerns God's inbreaking rule. "It is necessary for me to proclaim the good news about the kingdom of God to the other towns also, because I was sent for this purpose" (Luke 4:43).

In his humanity, Jesus understood the Spirit also called him. At his baptism, the Spirit descended on him in the form of a dove. The Spirit next drove him into the wilderness to prepare him for his ministry (Mark 1:9–13). The inaugural preaching of Jesus confessed the powerful presence of the Holy Spirit, his sending by the Father, and his intimate possession of God's words. Jesus simultaneously confessed the fulfillment of the Old Testament's messianic prophecies in his own person and in his power to give the Spirit to others (Mark 1:14; Luke 4:17–21; John 4:34).

The Son's mission to bring the kingdom of God, as sent by the Father and empowered by the Spirit, undergirds the witness of his Evangelists. Jesus exorcised the demonic enemies of his kingdom and celebrated his recovery of lost

---

1. See chapter 5 above.

2. The humanity of Christ and the sinlessness of Christ will be considered in more detail in volume two of Theology for Every Person.

human beings.[3] He witnessed to the mercy and goodness of the Father, yet he warned of impending judgment upon the wicked.[4] The grace and generosity of God was the solution he offered them.[5] Mark summarizes the whole message of the Son in his own words, "The time is fulfilled, and the kingdom of God has come near. Repent and believe the good news!" (Mark 1:15).

The "kingdom of God," or "kingdom of heaven," "pervades the entire proclamation of Jesus recorded in the gospels and appears largely to have determined the course of his ministry."[6] George R. Beasley-Murray concluded Jesus mediates our salvation in three great acts. Christ is "the Mediator" of salvation, "alike in its initiation in his ministry, in its powerful 'coming' in the cross and resurrection, and in its consummation at the parousia."[7] Regarding the doctrine of divine revelation, Beasley-Murray established that "in these deeds the revelation of God reached its perfection."[8]

Death did not bring to an untimely end the person of Jesus Christ. Rather, the trauma of the cross fulfilled the atoning mission of his first coming. Jesus therefore confessed, "Now my soul is troubled. What should I say—Father, save me from this hour? But that is why I came to this hour" (John 12:27). Christ's atoning death on Friday obtained the gift of propitiation for us, and his bodily resurrection on Sunday obtained the gifts of justification and bodily resurrection for

---

3. Marianne Meye Thompson, "Jesus and His God," in *The Cambridge Companion to Jesus*, ed. Markus Bockhuehl (New York: Cambridge University Press, 2001), 44–45.

4. Thompson, "Jesus and His God," 47–49.

5. Thompson, "Jesus and His God," 50–51.

6. G. R. Beasley-Murray, *Jesus and the Kingdom of God* (Grand Rapids: Eerdmans, 1986), x.

7. Beasley-Murray, *Jesus and the Kingdom of God*, 344.

8. Beasley-Murray, *Jesus and the Kingdom of God*, 344. Cf. chapter 10, section 4 above, "The Perfect Revelation of the Eternal Christ."

those united with him by faith—this is his glorious gospel (1 John 2:2; Rom. 4:25; 1 Cor. 15)! Jesus then ascended after giving his disciples the promise that he would come again to bring the final consummation of his kingdom (Acts 1:11). The Revelation of John provides details concerning the coming fulfilment of Christ's promise of his final victory over sin, death, and Satan.[9]

The Mission of the Church

Jesus was not the only one with a mission according to the eternal plan of God. The Lord also commissioned a people to be the external agent for the preservation, interpretation, and proclamation of his Word. "The people of God," which is comprised of Israel and the church, are united through the same faith in the same promise of the same Messiah.[10] Fulfilling the promise of the Old Testament prophecies, Jesus commissioned his church as the people of God. He sent his disciples to make disciples out of the nations by proclaiming his gospel. The Synoptic Gospels conclude with a report on this commission to the church prior to Christ's ascension (Matt. 28:16–20; Mark 16:15–16; Luke 24:46–48).

Luke and John also report on the Holy Spirit's relation to the church and its mission. Jesus said, "And look, I am sending you what my Father promised. As for you, stay in the city until you are empowered from on high." These were the final words of Jesus in the Gospel of Luke (Luke 24:49). Continuing in the book of Acts, Luke says Jesus promised the disciples

---

9. Richard Bauckham argues "conquering" is "Revelation's key concept." Bauckham, *The Theology of the Book of Revelation* (New York: Cambridge University Press, 1993), 69.

10. "There is only one 'People of God' in both Testaments." Walter C. Kaiser Jr., "Israel as the People of God," in *The People of God: Essays on the Believers' Church*, ed. Paul Basden and David S. Dockery (Nashville: Broadman, 1991), 100.

immediately before his ascension, "But you will receive power when the Holy Spirit has come on you, and you will be my witnesses in Jerusalem, in all Judea and Samaria, and to the end of the earth" (Acts 1:8).

Beginning with the advent of the Holy Spirit at Pentecost, the book of Acts records the work of the Holy Spirit in growing the church through the witness of Christ's disciples. In Acts 2, Jews from many places were converted in Jerusalem through faith and regeneration by the Holy Spirit. In Acts 8, Samaria saw the concurrent witness of the Spirit with the witness of the apostles. In Acts 10, the Spirit won Gentile God-fearers through the preaching of the apostles. In Acts 19, followers of John the Baptist were also brought to faith in Jesus by the concurrent witness of Paul and the Holy Spirit.[11]

The book of Acts reports on the mission of the church to convert the nations through making disciples as the apostles proclaimed the Word empowered by the Spirit. However, what about the generations in the church after the apostles? How might they continue the mission given by Christ to the church? The mission of the church, I would argue, continues to be empowered by the presence of the Holy Spirit.

According to the apostle John, when Jesus commissioned his church, he gave the Holy Spirit. Unlike the Synoptic Gospels, the Gospel of John's version of the Great Commission explicitly includes the giving of the Holy Spirit to effect salvation through the apostles' proclamation: "'As the Father has sent me, I also send you.' After saying this, he breathed on them and said, 'Receive the Holy Spirit. If you forgive the sins of any, they are forgiven them; if you retain the sins of any, they are retained'" (John 20:21–23). The Evangelists agree that the

---

11. Malcolm B. Yarnell III, "The Person and Work of the Holy Spirit," in *A Theology for the Church*, revised ed., ed. by Daniel L. Akin, Bruce Riley Ashford, and Kenneth Keathley (Nashville: B&H Publishing, 2014), 490–93.

church has a mission from Christ, and the Spirit empowers their fulfillment of that mission.

The Mission of the Spirit

The Gospel of John discloses Jesus's method for continuing the apostolic witness to future generations. In his Paraclete sayings, Jesus said he was giving "the Spirit of truth" as a permanent gift to overcome the natural blindness of the world (John 14:16–17a). The Spirit will reside within the disciples of Christ during his bodily absence from them (John 14:17b–18). Jesus spoke to his disciples while he was with them. But he promised that after his departure, the Spirit "will teach you all things and remind you of everything I have told you" (John 14:25–26).

Jesus said the Spirit whom he and the Father will send to his disciples "will testify about me," and "you also will testify" (John 15:26–27). In other words, the Spirit was given to the first disciples to ensure the truth of their testimony. The Spirit-guided apostolic witness included both those things Christ taught in the flesh and "what is to come" (John 16:12–13). Finally, the Paraclete sayings make it clear the Spirit will come specifically to bring conviction to the world regarding their sin, God's impending judgment, and the righteousness available through faith in Christ (John 16:7–10).

The Spirit guided the apostles and prophets in their witness, including in their writings, as both Peter and Paul testified (2 Pet. 1:19–21).[12] Peter specifically classified the writings of the apostle Paul among "the rest of the Scriptures" (2 Pet. 3:15–16). The empowering work of the Holy Spirit did not, moreover, cease with the apostles, who were directly commissioned by the risen Jesus Christ.

---

12. See chapter 11 above.

Other disciples shared in the promise of the Spirit's inspiration when they recorded the apostles' testimony, like Luke on behalf of Paul or Mark on behalf of Peter. The same applied to chosen amanuenses like Tertius, Sosthenes, and Timothy (Rom. 16:22; 1 Cor. 1:1; 2 Cor. 1:1). While the initial activity of inspiration certainly ceased with the writings of the apostles and their commissioned disciples, the products of inspiration remained the gift to and responsibility of the early churches.

The Lord gave the Holy Spirit to his people to lead them in the task of sharing the revelation of God with other peoples of their own day, as well as with future generations. Jesus specifically had in mind those future generations when he prayed both for the apostles and for those who would believe *through* their witness. Christ conveyed to the apostles the "words" which were given to him by the Father (John 17:8). He then prayed for those who would believe in him "through their word" (John 17:20).

Jesus prayed to the Father for Trinitarian unity among his disciples "so that the world may believe you sent me" (John 17:21). Christ concluded his high priestly prayer by saying he had "made your name known." But he will also "continue to make it known," so that believers might enter communion with the Trinity (John 17:26). God the Trinity intends the self-revelation of the Trinity to continue to change the world through the continuing witness of the apostles via the Scriptures as empowered by the Holy Spirit.

The Church and the Canon

After Inspiration

The Trinity as the Source of Wisdom. The beginning of Paul's first letter to the church of Corinth grounds wisdom in the Trinity and ascribes the transference of wisdom to the church as the work of the Holy Spirit. First, God's mysterious plan to send Christ to the cross stems from God's exclusive wisdom (1 Cor. 1:18–21). Second, Christ participates onto-logically in God's perfections of "wisdom" and "power" (1 Cor. 1:24). Third, God's wisdom is accessible also to "the Spirit of God" (1 Cor. 2:10–11). True wisdom, which descends from eternity to embrace creation and redemption, belongs exclu-sively to the one God who is the Father and the Son and the Holy Spirit.

The Spirit and the Church. Regarding the transference of God's hidden wisdom to humanity, Paul ascribed that work particularly to the Holy Spirit. The Spirit takes wisdom from God and gives it to believers, "so that we may understand what has been freely given to us by God" (1 Cor. 2:12). Believers, having received that wisdom internally, are then compelled to "speak" to others these "spiritual things" (1 Cor. 2:13). The only way the recipient of the church's proclamation can adequately "receive" and "evaluate" spiritual claims is under the guidance of the Holy Spirit (1 Cor. 2:14–15).

Through this entire chain of divine communication, the Spirit remains the agent who obtains wisdom from God and exclusively opens human minds to enable them to receive, understand, and in turn proclaim God's wisdom. The content of divine wisdom glorifies Christ and makes known his gospel. The receptacle of this wisdom which saves humanity is not the individual Christian's mind on its own, but the church as a whole. Paul concludes his teaching about the Spirit's work of illumination with the confident claim, "We have the mind of Christ" (1 Cor. 2:16b). Here is a vivid epistemological image: "We," the church, can lay claim, via the Holy Spirit, to have unique access to "the mind" of the Lord.

The Testimony of the Holy Spirit. John Calvin attrib-uted the church's enlightenment to the Spirit's "testimony," which "illumines" Scripture. Calvin meanwhile placed a check on hubris in the church. "Hence the Scriptures obtain full authority among believers only when men regard them as having sprung from heaven, as if there the living words of God were heard."[13]

This realization involves a process. The hearer recognizes authority in the church's proclamation of God's Word, which prompts faith in Christ.[14] Agency belongs not to the church's reasoning, but to "the testimony of the Spirit." "The same Spirit, therefore, who has spoken by the mouths of the prophets must penetrate into our hearts to persuade us that they faithfully proclaimed what had been divinely commanded."[15]

Both Inspiration and Illumination. The dual role of the Spirit and the church in continuing humanity's access to divine revelation explains why evangelicals today distinguish between the Spirit's works of inspiration and illumination. The Holy Spirit's "original inspiration" applied to the biblical authors and their writings, whereas the Spirit's "ongoing illumination" concerns the readers of those writings.[16]

Inspiration was "technically concluded with the completion of the New Testament and the death of the apostles."[17] Illumination occurs when the Spirit "empowers us to receive

---

13. John Calvin, *Institutes of the Christian Religion*, ed. John T. McNeill, transl. Ford Lewis Battles, 2 vols. (Philadelphia: Westminster Press, 1960), 1:74.

14. "Those who have not yet been illumined by the Spirit of God are rendered teachable by reverence for the church, so that they may persevere in learning faith in Christ from the gospel." Calvin, *Institutes of the Christian Religion*, 1:77.

15. Calvin, *Institutes of the Christian Religion*, 1:79. Scripture's authority does not depend upon the church, but upon the Spirit, which is also to say, "Scripture indeed is self-authenticated." Calvin, *Institutes of the Christian Religion*, 1:80.

16. Carl F. H. Henry, *God, Revelation and Authority*, 2nd ed., 6 vols. (Wheaton, IL: Crossway, 1999), 4:259.

17. Henry, *God, Revelation and Authority*, 4:259.

and appropriate the Scriptures, and promotes in us a norma-
tive theological comprehension for a transformed life."[18]

The Process of Revelation. The Holy Spirit's work of illumination concerns the granting of saving knowledge to the
church. Carl Henry summarized the process which God follows in conveying salvation through history, both during the
age of the apostles and subsequently. He touched successively
upon the economy of the Word and the Spirit in special revelation, inspiration, the sacred Scriptures, illumination, interpretation, and proclamation:

> Special revelation came to and through the
> apostles by the Spirit, and by the Spirit it
> comes through their inspired word to us;
> revelation comes to us through their words
> illumined and interpreted by the Spirit; and
> through our witness in turn, revelation pro-
> ceeds to others who like us must depend for
> its normative cognitive content upon the
> inspired writings.[19]

The Church's Preservation of Revelation in the Canon

The Hebrew term *qaneh* indicated a "stick," and by meta-
phorical extension, a "measuring rod." The Greek term *kanon*
carried the same meanings, but "canon" was extended to mean

18. Henry, *God, Revelation and Authority*, 4:273.

19. Henry, *God, Revelation and Authority*, 4:276. Henry's "Fifteen
Theses," summarized in volume 2 and detailed in volumes 2–4 of his magnum opus, constituted the premiere evangelical system of revelation in the
late twentieth century.

a "rule" or "list."[20] The post-apostolic church assigned the word to various standards.

The Canon as "The Rule of Faith." The earliest use of canon was as a rule, standard, or norm for teaching the Christian faith. Two second-century fathers, Irenaeus of Lyons and Tertullian of Carthage, derived the canon as "the rule of faith" from Scripture. This rule of truth was subsequently taken up by Origen, Augustine, and many others to indicate the basic teachings of the faith which should guide interpreters and teachers in the church.

The rule of faith focused on the central truths proclaimed in the Christian church. These foundational truths include God's identity as Father and Son and Holy Spirit, and God's works, particularly his redemption of sinful humanity through faith in the gospel of Jesus Christ.[21]

The Canon as "The Collection of Sacred Scriptures." Soon after, Christians also began to use canon to indicate "the list of writings acknowledged by the Church as documents of divine revelation."[22] The term "canon" applies both to the central teachings of the Christian faith, "the rule of faith," and to the books of the prophets and the apostles that convey those

---

20. Lee Martin McDonald, *The Origin of the Bible: A Guide for the Perplexed* (New York: T&T Clark, 2011), 14.

21. For example, Irenaeus defined "the rule of truth" received at baptism, "the faith," as belief in "one God, the Father Almighty, . . . and in one Christ Jesus, the Son of God, . . . and in the Holy Spirit, who proclaimed through the prophets, . . . the birth from a virgin, and the passion, and resurrection from the dead. . . ." Irenaeus, *Against Heresies*, in *The Apostolic Fathers and Justin Martyr and Irenaeus*, ed. A. Cleveland Cox, The Ante-Nicene Fathers, vol. 1 (1885; reprint Peabody, MA: Hendrickson, 1994), 330. For basic treatments of the rule of faith, see David S. Dockery and Malcolm B. Yarnell III, *Special Revelation and Scripture* (Brentwood, TN: B&H Academic, 2024), 277–83; Everett Ferguson, *The Rule of Faith: A Guide* (Eugene, OR: Wipf and Stock, 2015).

22. After R. P. C. Hanson; F. F. Bruce, *The Canon of Scripture* (Downers Grove, IL: IVP, 1988), 17.

central teachings. The dual use of the term indicates their mutually reinforcing nature. The canon as the rule of faith derives from the biblical canon; and the biblical canon is to be interpreted by the rule of faith.

The foundational concepts behind the Christian textual canon were already at play in the biblical text. Paul asked Timothy to bring him the *biblia*, the Hebrew Scripture rolls, and the *membranae*, the codex form of his own writings (2 Tim. 4:13). Christ, the Spirit, and the apostles intended the apostolic writings to be read as messages from God during the churches' gatherings (1 Cor. 5:9; 2 Cor. 7:8; Col. 4:16; Rev. 2:1, 7, 8–9, 11). Divine commands in both testaments warn against altering the written texts in any way (Deut. 4:2; 12:32; Rev. 22:18–19).

The Old Testament Canon. Focusing on the Old Testament as Law, Jesus proclaimed that every part of the inspired Hebrew writings would be fulfilled by God (Matt. 5:18). Jesus affirmed the totality of the Hebrew Scriptures in its three traditional divisions of the law, the prophets, and the writings (Luke 24:44). Christ's high regard for Israel's canon was continued by his disciples, who treated the Old Testament writings as sacred. The New Testament apostles alluded to, cited, and quoted the Old Testament canon profusely.[23]

Jewish tradition held that the Hebrew canon was compiled in the fifth century BC by Ezra for the purposes of hearing, interpreting, and renewing the covenant (Ezra 10:1–4; Neh. 7:73–8:18). Scholars today date the Old Testament canon's final form between the second century BC and the first century AD.

Two canon traditions developed during this early period: The Palestinian canon included the books comprising the Protestant Bible's current form, while the Hellenistic

---

23. See the massive *Commentary on the New Testament Use of the Old Testament*, ed. G. K. Beale and D. A. Carson (Grand Rapids: Baker, 2007).

canon added several more. These additional books, called Deuterocanonical or Apocrypha by Christians, are never explicitly treated as canon in the New Testament. They have been honored though not fully embraced by the Christian churches.[24]

The New Testament Canon. The earliest churches read both the Old Testament writings and the apostolic books in worship, sharing the latter with one another.[25] By the end of the second century, the bulk of the current New Testament was being used in worship. Church fathers like Irenaeus defended the apostolic writings against diverse alternative gospels, acts, and epistles.[26]

Modern scholars identify various principles which seem to have driven the early church to receive only certain books. These principles may be classified as the worship, gospel, and apostolic tests: Is it used in public worship? Does it preserve the rule of faith? Was it written by an apostle or close associate?[27] The current New Testament canon list was universally accepted by the late fourth century, although it was largely and effectively in use well before that date. A Festal Epistle of 367, written by Athanasius of Alexandria, is a key closing point.[28]

Recognizing the Whole Biblical Canon. During the Reformation debates over the authority of Scripture, the Reformers argued the church did not make the canon. Instead, the Reformers said the early church was led by the Holy Spirit

---

24. Roman Catholics honor the Apocrypha, but not as inspired. Protestants typically consult them but not as if they were inspired.

25. Justin Martyr, *The First Apology*, in *The Apostolic Fathers*, 185–86.

26. Hans von Campenhausen, *The Formation of the Christian Bible*, transl. J. A. Baker (Philadelphia: Fortress Press, 1972), 182–203.

27. Dockery and Yarnell, *Special Revelation and Scripture*, 190–94.

28. Edmon L. Gallagher and John D. Meade, *The Biblical Canon Lists from Early Christianity: Texts and Analysis* (New York: Oxford University Press, 2019), 118–29.

to recognize the canon. Liberal critics more recently argued the church created the canon and manufactured the doctrine of inspiration. Arguing against such liberal teaching and compelled by the testimony of the Holy Spirit, those of us who are orthodox Christians may only conclude that the Holy Spirit both inspired all of Scripture and led the church to identify the whole biblical canon.[29]

Theological Interpretation of Scripture

The science of biblical interpretation has a deep and difficult history. David Dockery and I studied the diverse disciplines of biblical studies, biblical theology, and biblical hermeneutics, evaluating important movements in each major period of the church.[30] We favor that movement known as the Theological Interpretation of Scripture (TIS).[31] TIS grounds itself in lifelong habits of reading Scripture, honors the ancient rule of faith, and incorporates helpful hermeneutical methods from throughout Christian history. We will now deliberate the Trinity's role in interpretation, the Trinity's rule for interpretation, the church's role in interpretation, and the church's evaluative judgments.

The Trinity's Role in Interpretation

The proper interpretation of the biblical text is a gift of the one God who is the Father, the Son, and the Holy Spirit. The biblical text itself teaches this basic truth as seen in the

---

29. Tridentine Catholicism affirmed two streams of revelation, the church's tradition and the biblical canon. Dockery and Yarnell, *Special Revelation and Scripture*, 194–97.

30. Dockery and Yarnell, *Special Revelation and Scripture*, 263–367.

31. Dockery and Yarnell, *Special Revelation and Scripture*, 323–27.

various texts which emphasize the work of each divine Person in giving us the proper interpretation of Scripture.

Interpretation by the Son of God. After his resurrection and prior to his ascension, Jesus emphasized a particular hermeneutical method. He showed those on the road to Emmaus how to interpret Scripture. The compound *diermaneusin*, "interpreted," derives from the Greek term behind the modern discipline of "hermeneutics." A *hermeneutas*, "interpreter," is "one who helps someone to understand thoughts expressed in words."[32] Jesus interpreted "all the Scriptures" through the lens of his own messianic person and work (Luke 24:27). He repeated the same hermeneutic before a larger and later gathering of his disciples (Luke 24:44–47). Christ's own rule of faith is definitively Christ-centered, and it applies to the entire canon.

Interpretation by the Spirit of God. We previously evaluated the apostle Peter's attribution of biblical inspiration to the Holy Spirit.[33] In that same text, Peter also attributed agency in the reception of prophetic revelation to the Spirit. Just as the Holy Spirit once "carried along" the prophet with original inspiration (2 Pet. 1:21), the Spirit later grants the proper "interpretation" (Greek *epileuseos*) of the prophet's statement (2 Pet. 1:20). *Epilusis*, derived from the terminology for setting something loose, indicates the process of explanation.[34] The Spirit is given to guide the church's interpretation.

Interpretation by God the Father. The church's rule of faith, discussed above, focuses upon the Trinity and the gospel. We just saw how the Son and the Spirit guide proper

---

32. William Arndt, Frederick William Danker, Walter Bauer, and F. W. Gingrich, *A Greek-English Lexicon of the New Testament and Other Early Christian Literature*, 3rd ed. (Chicago: University of Chicago Press, 2000), 393.

33. See chapter 11.

34. Arndt et al., *A Greek-English Lexicon*, 375.

hermeneutics. The Father also set standards for interpretation. First, the Father gave the Shema, in which he called Israel to love him as Lord (Deut. 6:4–5). After affirming the Shema is the "most important" command of God, Jesus identified the other great command as "Love your neighbor as yourself" (Mark 12:28–32). Second, the Father gave the saving confession about Jesus being "the Christ the son of the living God" to Christ's disciples (Matt. 16:16).

Three Theological Rules for Interpretation

Theologians have discerned several major rules which were given by God to lead his church to interpret Scripture properly. Two major theological rules discussed by previous theologians include "the rule of faith" and "the rule of love." We would add a third theological rule for interpretation, "the rule of hope."

The Rule of Faith. As we noted in the previous paragraphs, God the Trinity provided the proper interpretation of his written Word through teaching the rule of faith to the apostles. First, we noted the canon of faith, or rule of faith, was emphasized by God the Son. Second, God the Holy Spirit was given to guide the church's interpretation. Third, God the Father directly revealed the rule of faith to the disciples.

The rule of faith is focused upon Christ as the Son of God who became incarnate, died, and arose from the dead. However, the rule of faith did not stand alone. The Father also gave a rule of love to Israel. And Jesus required love for humanity alongside love for God. The rule of faith included in the Great Commission taught by Jesus Christ should be paired with the Great Commandment which was also taught by our Lord.[35]

---

35. For a deeper study on the integral relationship between the Great Commandment and the work of theology, under the rubric of "Loving

In his hermeneutical guide for proclamation, Augustine of Hippo considers many aspects of proper interpretation, from language to history and beyond. Many of his instructions have made their way into contemporary hermeneutical discourse. Augustine's elevation of the rule of faith (Latin *regula fidei*)[36] has been recovered of late. Less attention has been given to Augustine's other central theological hermeneutic, the rule of love (Latin *regula dilectionis*).

The Rule of Love. Augustine says that when an interpretive method seems to lead away from God and toward evil, it needs to be corrected by the rule of love. "But scripture enjoins nothing but love, and censures nothing but lust, and moulds men's minds accordingly."[37] For Augustine, the interpretation of Scripture certainly begins with hermeneutical method, but it must end in love for God and for other people. Modern hermeneutics is inadequate when it fails to remember its purpose to love God.[38] If the Shema, which contains the rule of love for Israel, and the Greatest Commandment, which augments the rule of love, are emphasized by God, then the rule of love must also be emphasized by his church.

When I am tempted to read inappropriate ideas into Scripture, the Holy Spirit prompts my heart to recall the loving example of my Savior, the Lord Jesus. Christ loved us

---

God with All Your Mind," please see Malcolm B. Yarnell III, "Systematic Theology," in *Theology, Church, and Ministry: A Handbook for Theological Education*, ed. David S. Dockery (Nashville: B&H Academic, 2017), 258–60. "Why do theology? For the love of God! For the purpose of loving God entirely, we must comprehend everything with our minds well." Yarnell, "Systematic Theology," 260.

36. Augustine, *On Christian Doctrine*, transl. R. P. H. Green (New York: Oxford University Press, 1999), 68–69.

37. Augustine, *On Christian Doctrine*, 76.

38. Steven Yong, "Rule of Love and Rule of Faith in Augustine's Hermeneutics: A Complex Dialectic of the Twofold Rule," *Veritas* 20 (2021): 209–10.

when we could not love. He laid down his life for us out of love. God is love, so we should love him and others too (John 3:16; 1 John 4:7–21).

The martyrs of the faith, who shared God's love with their persecutors, are my heroes precisely because of their Christlikeness. The early bishop Polycarp, the female martyrs Perpetua and Felicitas, the medieval missionary Ramon Lull, the Anabaptists Michael and Margaret Sattler, the Bible translator William Tyndale, the English reformer Thomas Cranmer, the Lutheran pastor Dietrich Bonhoeffer—all of these saints interpreted Scripture properly by loving even their enemies (Matt. 5:44).

The Rule of Hope. Following the threefold virtue of 1 Corinthians 13:13, we could also speak of "the rule of hope" as guiding our interpretation of the many eschatological themes of Scripture. The rule of hope, if we may coin such a term, would emphasize the Second Coming of Jesus Christ, his millennial reign, his Final Judgment, and the blessed vision of the eternal God available to all true believers. While eschatology is not the central theme of this volume, all true theology points its hearers not only toward God as "the first" but God as "the last" (Rev. 1:17; 22:13).[39]

The Church's Role in Interpretation

While God gives us the Word, and the Spirit inspires the Word and guides us to recognize and interpret the Word, the church is the interpreter of the Word. We must, therefore, take a few moments to speak about the role of the church in interpretation.

A Universal Christian Responsibility. Whether we are called to become martyrs or not, the role of the church

---

39. Volume 3 of this series will have much to say about *eschatology*, which literally means "the doctrine of the last."

requires it to hear the Word, understand the Word, and proclaim the Word. In the New Testament church, while there was a special limited role for the church elder, proclamation was the responsibility of every Christian.[40] For instance, the term "prophet" in the New Testament was applied to both men and women. Paul defined the role of prophet simply and authoritatively as speaking God's Word to people for "their strengthening, encouragement, and consolation" (1 Cor. 14:3). He envisioned the members of the congregation prophesying "one by one, so that everyone may learn and everyone may be encouraged" (1 Cor. 14:29–33).

In the history of the church, however, bishops, elders, or other officers have sometimes controlled interpretation in inappropriate ways. The authority for interpretation[41] has been consigned to various magisterial offices, from the papacy and councils to universities and scholars to presbyteries and pastors. Before rushing to a conclusion about the virtues or vices of any Christian tradition, however, democratic forms have not necessarily fostered greater participation. On the one hand, a female anchoress in medieval Catholicism like Julian of Norwich could speak with great freedom, even when lay access to Scripture was illegal. On the other hand, nineteenth-century Baptists argued for liberty of conscience and religious freedom, even while African voices were suppressed in American congregations.

Progressive Sanctification in Interpretation. We previously discussed how the Holy Spirit's inspiration of the

---

40. Malcolm B. Yarnell III and Karen Yarnell, "On the Universal and Particular Offices of Proclamation in relation to Women as Teachers in Church and Seminary," *Journal for Baptist Theology and Ministry* 17 (2020): 66–68.

41. For Baptists, the authority to establish an interpretation belongs to the congregation, while the authority to proclaim the church's official interpretation belongs to the elder. Yarnell and Yarnell, "On the Universal and Particular Offices of Proclamation," 68–72.

prophets immediately resulted in the inerrancy of the prophetic writings. Unlike with the immediacy of perfection granted to Scripture, the Holy Spirit's illumination of the church's interpretation of Scripture occurs in the context of the Spirit's progressive sanctification of the people of God. The church and its members, who receive the inspired writings and recognize them as such by virtue of illumination, are never guaranteed the quality of perfection for their hermeneutical conclusions.

The difficult reality is that, before the final consummation, the church must constantly struggle against interpretive error in its ranks. Scripture warns that wolves, false messiahs, and false prophets will damage the church and lead people astray (Mark 13:22; Acts 20:29). Unlike in their perfect writings, the apostles were marred in their persons, as Paul reminded Peter (Gal. 2:11–14). Absolute perfection in theological interpretation, as in life, will be found at the end of the pilgrimage for the church militant. "For we know in part, and we prophesy in part, but when the perfect comes, the partial will come to an end" (1 Cor. 13:9–10). Until the coming of the last day, the church must recognize its need to interpret Scripture wisely.

The Church's Evaluative Judgments

Because of their need to defend the flock against various theological errors, the churches of Jesus Christ must deliver wise evaluative theological judgments. It will be helpful to rehearse the categorical terms which have been used to describe the church's doctrinal judgments. These terms appear periodically in the volumes of Theology for Every Person, especially when discernment is required. Let us consider the terms *dogma*, *orthodoxy*, *heresy*, and *error*. Other evaluative terms include *blasphemy*, an offensive statement which attempts to diminish the glory of God, and *apostasy*, a departure from the Christian faith.

Dogma. In Acts 15, the church of Jerusalem worked through the problem of some Jewish Christians requiring Gentile converts to receive circumcision. The Jerusalem church deliberated, concluded, and issued a declaration regarding the crisis. The Antioch church received their "decisions" with joy. As a result, the churches "were strengthened in the faith" and "grew daily in numbers" (Acts 16:4–5). The Greek term for the church's decisions, *dogmata*, has become the standard term for an official declaration about doctrine. A "dogma" indicates a formally approved ecclesiastical doctrine.

Orthodoxy. Technically, orthodoxy means "right worship," as an Eastern Orthodox priest reminded me during a visit to Russia. However, *orthodoxy* is typically used as a general term to indicate right teaching. I capitalize the word *Orthodox* when speaking of the contributions of the Eastern Orthodox communion of churches. (Kallistos Ware taught me the Jesus Prayer, among other great truths at Oxford, and for his gentle witness I will always remain grateful.)

I use the lowercase "orthodox" when speaking of dogmas widely received as the common core of Christian truth. Universal orthodoxy was at first defined by the rule of faith. But orthodoxy has received more detail in the classic ecumenical creeds, including the Apostles' Creed, the Nicene Creed, the Athanasian Creed, and the Formula of Chalcedon.

Heresy. The English term *heresy* derives from the Greek *hairesis*, which indicated a cognitive choice. According to Paul, a *hairetikos* is "one who stirs up division" (Titus 3:10). Perhaps surprisingly, Scripture says *haireseis*, "factions," are necessary. Heresies allow the genuine teachers to be recognized (1 Cor. 11:19).

In historical terms, a *heretic* was one who willfully refused dogmatic correction by the church and thus faced excommunication. A "heresy" has typically been understood as a form of theological error which is severe enough to disallow a theological movement's teachings and disqualify its teachers.

Advantageously, true dogmas have often received careful definition while correcting error.

Horrifically, some churches have delated heretics to the state for execution.[42] The physical persecution of heretics is itself an error. But the excommunication or removal of heretics from the church community should be expected.

Error. A theological "error" does not rise to the level of a heresy. Errors may be held by a member of a church without requiring discipline. For instance, professional and pastoral theologians may think a colleague is in error without sensing the need for cessation of communion. Heresy is a heavy term, whereas error is less grave.

Please note that the official decision to declare that a certain teaching should be considered a "dogma" or a "heresy" belongs to church communities rather than to individual theologians. "Error" is an evaluative term which can be used with less formality.

Generous Christian Diversity

The existence of diverse interpretations and applications by the various Christian churches often becomes an object of lament. Division among Christians certainly is a fact requiring lament. However, diversity should also be seen as an opportunity for thanksgiving.

The various churches have sometimes adopted offensive interpretations. For instance, the expulsion of the oriental churches during the late classical period, the mutual excommunications between the Eastern and Western churches in the eleventh century, the anathemas hurled by the various Western confessions during the sixteenth century, and the fissiparous

---

42. Malcolm B. Yarnell III, *The Formation of Christian Doctrine* (Nashville: B&H Academic, 2007), 110–11.

even schismatic spirit in modern free churches—these were often preceded by, and certainly succeeded by, radically opposing interpretations of Scripture. One or both parties in such dogmatic divisions were obviously wrong about something.

Despite these difficulties, different communions have much to offer the careful and generous interpreter. During my own theological journey, I have been blessed by Catholic brothers who opened my eyes to the crisp formulations and comprehensive unity of Roman dogmatics. Even more, I remain forever indebted to Lutheran theology for the incredible insights it offers regarding the free offer of salvation by God to those who believe. The Lutheran Law-Gospel dialectic, the humbling doctrine of the theologian of the cross, and Luther's appreciation for paradox are also highly beneficial concepts. Beautiful contributions to the Christian theological conversation come from diverse traditions, many of which I examine elsewhere.[43]

More importantly, however, there is a common core of truth which unites all orthodox theological interpretations of Scripture. Known as the rule of faith, it affirms that God is Trinity, that Jesus is the Christ the Son of God, that the gospel is centered on his death and resurrection, and that God works in creation, redemption, and final consummation. When any theological interpretation of Scripture forsakes this common core of truth, or when it grants its own peculiar understanding primacy over others, or when it makes a variant theology necessary for salvation, that is when that particular theological interpretation becomes an error, perhaps even a heresy.[44]

The common core of truth which unites all orthodox theological interpretations of Scripture should also be

---

43. Yarnell, *The Formation of Christian Doctrine*, 33–72; Yarnell, "Systematic Theology," 278–79.

44. An old Moravian proverb declared, "In the essentials unity; in the non-essentials diversity; in all things charity."

accompanied by a common sense of mission. Called by God, the church must proclaim the gospel of Jesus Christ, the risen God-Man, in the power of the Holy Spirit. If the common core of Christian truth is the rule of faith, then the common mission of the church must be identified with the rule of love.

We love God in Christ by obeying him with Spirit-filled joy and abandon, and we love our fellow human beings by giving them the best news ever. Our mission as the church is to make disciples of everyone by first telling them, "God loves you! Jesus arose from the dead for you! The Spirit wants to bless you! Come and drink freely from the water of life!" (Rev. 22:17).

While divisions may haunt the difficult relationships between different communions of Christian churches, we can nevertheless practice a generous Christian diversity. We can practice a generous Christian diversity even while we seek to maintain a common core of orthodoxy. We can practice generous Christian diversity while maintaining orthodoxy and seeking ways to pursue our common mission to glorify God and fulfill Christ's Great Commission, if we rely entirely upon the grace of his Holy Spirit.

The questions you and I must now face as you enjoy with me this necessary and fulfilling journey of theology are three in number: First, "Will I have true faith in him as I pursue the call of Jesus Christ to follow him and make other disciples?" Second, "Will I love the Lord with all of my mind as well as my heart, soul, and strength, and will I love his people too?" And third, "Will I continue to hope for that day when all Christians shall bow before the one eternal God who is the Trinity, as we together gaze upon his wonderful face and worship him alone?"

> For now we see only a reflection, as in a mirror, but then face to face. Now I know in part, but then I will know fully, as I am fully

known. Now these three remain: faith, hope, and love—but the greatest of these is love. (1 Cor. 13:12–13)

Until the next time we meet as we continue the grand tour of God's truth together, may the Lord keep you and guide you and bless you with every blessing for the sake of his glory.

Study Questions

1. How would you describe the mission of the church in relation to God the Trinity?

2. Who decided which books should be included in the canon? What principles did they use? Who guided them in this choice?

3. Who has authority to decide whether a teaching is a heresy or an error or dogma? Why does God allow heresy to occur?

Suggested Resources

- Everett Ferguson, *The Rule of Faith*

- F. F. Bruce, *The Canon of Scripture*

- David S. Dockery, ed., *Theology, Church, and Ministry*

Acknowledgments

◆

WALTER THOMAS CONNER WAS THE greatest academic theologian of the Southwestern Baptist Theological Seminary during its first half-century. He taught that the best measure for a theology is to ask whether it helps people communicate the gospel.[1] James Leo Garrett Jr., the greatest theologian of the seminary's second half-century, said God and W. T. Conner called him to become a theologian.[2] In turn, Garrett took a personal interest in me as a student, asked me to become his research assistant, and inspired my primary research interest in the universal priesthood. His wise advice resulted in advanced degrees from both Duke University and Oxford University.

God and Leo Garrett then called me to return to our seminary, where I have been teaching systematic theology, biblical theology, and historical theology since before the turn of the seminary's second century. Garrett not only asked me

---

1. W. T. Conner, "Theology, a Practical Discipline," *Review and Expositor* 41 (1944), 360.

2. James Leo Garrett Jr., "Baptist Identity and Christian Unity: Reflections on a Theological Pilgrimage," *American Baptist Quarterly* 24 (2005), 54.

to take his place at Southwestern, but to write more on the priesthood of believers and to popularize his systematic theology. The longer I am here, the more I recognize the great significance of each aspect of this three-part call, not only for me but through me for Southern Baptists and evangelicals around the world.

First, the call to teach in the classroom is for preparing the future leaders of the churches of Jesus Christ. Teaching students personally remains the foundation of my ministry. As a seminary student, God impressed me to become a pastor to pastors, a missionary to missionaries, an evangelist to evangelists, among others. I am doing my best to obey the Lord in that call to minister his profound truth to diverse students with significant needs.

Second, the call to focus on the priesthood of all believers should help remind Southern Baptists of what it means to be Baptist. It is currently necessary to recall the Baptist principles that God alone is Lord of every conscience, that God has called every Christian to sacrificial ministry, and that church democracy, religious liberty, and the separation of church and state are *sine qua non* for true Baptists. These principles are currently waning and must wax bright again, if our churches are to prosper.

Third, however, comes the purpose for this series of volumes. The Spirit of God would not let me forget that call. Garrett and I both recognized the academic complexity of his *Systematic Theology*, so he asked me to help people hear the wisdom he had discerned through great prayer, great effort, and great grace. Therefore, I write these volumes to make Southwestern Seminary's classical empowering theology more accessible to all the people of God. It was Leo's hope and mine that the people of God would be shown how they might grow the church through good doctrine and ethics.

This first volume must also acknowledge the weighty influence of three other people, each of whom was a student of

Leo Garrett. Each person remains quite close to me personally and professionally. Note that I am keeping a long list of the church theologians who have been helping me craft these volumes through conversation, by email, and in evangelistic and other ministry contexts. These fine church theologians will be honored in the next two volumes. For now, however, I must primarily acknowledge three stellar Christian theologians. My brothers and sister in Christ, many good teachings contained in this book came through extensive conversations with you; any errors are entirely my own.

First, Karen Annette Searcy Yarnell is the embodiment of the promise of the proverb, "A man who finds a wife finds a good thing and obtains favor from the LORD" (Prov. 18:22). Honey, God gave you to me for my good. I daily recognize the many ways you bless me. Most important is that we do our theology together. We read and discuss Scripture together. We pray together. We evaluate culture together. We minister in the church together. We proclaim the gospel to the world together. I sometimes chuckle when I tell others you taught me my theology. But there is much truth in the claim. You are a most excellent Bible teacher, and you have taught me to ask, "How does this help a person live for Christ?" I am thankful God granted us a family of curious, careful, and committed theologians. There are twelve of us now, including Truett and Ashlyn and Lucas, Matthew and Victoria and their expected child, Graham and Gracie, Kathryn, and Elizabeth. They are so much like you in personal integrity, love for the lost, and valiance for truth. I cannot wait to see what else God will do through you and through each one of our children and grandchildren.

Second, Mark David Forrest is the embodiment of the promise of the proverb, "One with many friends may be harmed, but there is a friend who stays closer than a brother" (Prov. 18:24). Mark, we met while trying to find Christian community on a secular university campus. We pursued our finance degrees together. We began dating our future wives together and served in each other's weddings. We were called into full-time Christian ministry together, on the same night, in the same church, but in different places, without knowing what the other was doing. We started seminary together. We were ordained to the ministry together. We helped each other survive and thrive on the mission field. Now, we serve together at the Lakeside Baptist Church in Granbury, Texas, where you are my Senior Pastor and I am your Teaching Pastor. Mark, we have learned together the truth about the wolves and hirelings who infest families and denominations, and we have emboldened one another to stand for truth. I have come to see that you are the best pastor I have ever known. May God continue to keep our hearts bound to him and one another, for I am a much better Christian, pastor, and theologian because of you.

Third, David Samuel Dockery is the embodiment of the promise of the proverb, "The mind of the discerning acquires knowledge, and the ear of the wise seeks it" (Prov. 18:15). When I was a student serving the Theological Fellowship at Southwestern Seminary, we needed a speaker for the Day-Higginbotham Lecture series. Leo Garrett recommended your name to me. Although you were busy as a seminary dean, then president at several institutions, you soon became a confidante, a prayer partner, and a coauthor. You have a discerning mind, and I have opened my ears to hear what God says through you. You will recognize the theology in this book, not only because it reflects a foundation in our common mentor, Leo Garrett, but because your teaching permeates mine. When I was granted opportunity to speak to the full board of trustees for the first time, after twenty-three years of faculty service, I reminded them I nominated you twice before to take the leadership of our seminary. They were wise later to invite, and you were gracious to accept the role of being our tenth president. Our colleagues in the Theology Department also deserve mention: Thank you, Jeff Bingham, Madison Grace,

Michael Wilkinson, and Travis Trawick, for helping make Southwestern Seminary the best gathering of systematic theologians anywhere. And thank you to my faithful and brilliant teaching assistants through the years, including Thomas Winborn, Lewis Richerson, John Mann, Sean Wegener, Namkyu Cho, and Wang Yong Lee. You constitute the future of biblical, historical, systematic, and practical theology.

Finally, thank you to Mary Wiley and the fine staff at B&H Publishing for your excellent guidance through this process. It is our hope to make heartwarming practical theological orthodoxy accessible to everyone that drives your publishing and my writing. May the Lord bless our mutual efforts tremendously for his glory.

Scripture Index

Genesis

1   *66*
1:1   *23, 32, 62,*
    64, 72
1:1–3   *55*
1:1–5   *72*
1:2   *62, 72, 106*
1:3   *66, 72*
1:3, 6–7, 9   *207*
1:3, 6, 9   *62*
1–5   *175*
1:25, 28   *123*
1:26   *73, 217*
1:26–27   *56, 96,*
    107
1:28   *129*
1:28–29   *107*
1:31   *57*
2:2   *20*
2:7   *25, 56, 78,*
    168, 193
2:15–17   *57*
2:16   *123, 168*
2:16–17   *129*
2:17   *168*
2:18   *169*
2:19   *123, 168*
3   *25*
3:5   *96*
3:6–7   *57*
3:8   *169*
3:9–19   *129*
3:15   *176*

3:16   *217*
3:17   *217*
3:22   *73*
4:7   *124*
4:15   *121*
6:3   *25*
6–10   *175*
11–35   *175*
11:7   *73*
14:18–20   *104*
16:7–14   *73*
18:2–3   *73*
18:25   *115*
36–50   *175*

Exodus

3:2–4   *73*
3:5   *111*
3:14   *32, 103*
3:15   *33*
19   *175*
19:6   *111*
20:1   *54*
20:1–17   *175*
20:5   *114*
20:7   *98*
20:8, 11   *111*
26:33–34   *111*
33:20   *101*
34:6   *121*

Leviticus

11:44–45   *111*

Numbers

23:20   *104*

Deuteronomy

4:2   *234*
6:1   *17*
6:4   *102*
6:4–5   *17, 72,*
    238
7:7–8   *117*
9:10   *53*
12:32   *234*
26:15   *52*
30:11–14   *215*
32:4, 39–42   *28*
34:10   *175*

1 Samuel

1–16   *175*
16   *113*
16–31   *175*

2 Samuel

1–24   *175*
7:12–16   *176*
23:1–2   *175*
23:2   *191*

1 Kings

1–2   *175*
8:10–13   *176*
22:19   *208*

1 Chronicles

15:16–24 *175*

2 Chronicles

7:14–15 *117*

Ezra

10:1–4 *234*

Nehemiah

7:73–8:18 *234*

Job

1:6–12 *26*
2:1–7 *26*
38:1–7 *102*
42:3–6 *159*

Psalms

3, 4, 5 *175*
8:1–3 *137*
14 *33*
14:1 *45*
14:2–3 *159*
14:3 *46*
14:5 *45*
14:6 *46*
19:1–2 *137*
19:3 *138, 159*
29:1–9 *129*
36:9 *136, 195*
46:6 *129*
51:11 *106*
53 *33*
73 *170*
73:1–16 *170*
73:12 *170*
73:13 *170*
73:16 *170*
73:17 *170*
73:18–23 *170*
82 *194*
82:6 *193*

84:11 *121*
89:1–2, 5, 24,
  33 *121*
90 *70*
90:1 *70*
90:2 *70, 112*
90:16 *70*
101 *67*
101:13, 28 *67*
104:30 *73*
109:28 *104*
110:1–4 *128*
119:105 *215*
119:137–138 *115*
139:5–10 *113*
139:6 *126*
139:7 *106*
147:5 *51*
147:15–18 *73*

Proverbs

3:19–20 *113*
8:1–21 *113*
8:22–31 *73*
8:25 *73, 75*
8:27–30 *128*
18:15 *252*
18:22 *251*
18:24 *251*

Ecclesiastes

3:1 *55*
3:2 *55*
3:2–8 *55*
3:11 *25, 50*

Isaiah

1:4 *111*
4:4 *78*
1:10 *208*
6:3 *28, 111*
6:5–8 *28*
6:8 *73*
6:13 *111*

9:6 *76*
40:6–8 *204*
40:12–14 *113*
44:9–11, 17 *140*
44:17 *137*
44:20 *138*
45:21–22 *115*
52:15 *131*
55:8–9 *95*
55:10–11 *95*
55:11 *207*
57:15 *98*
61:5–6 *131*
62:2 *131*
66:18–23 *131*

Jeremiah

3:20 *117*
8:8–12 *139*
23:16 *139*
23:24 *51, 101*
23:28–30 *139*
23:32 *139*
28:15 *139*
31:3 *120*
31:35–36 *137*

Daniel

9:14 *115*

Hosea

3:1–3 *117*

Micah

6:8 *117*

Malachi

3:6 *112*
4:1–4 *176*

Matthew

3:15 *115*
3:16–17 *107*
3:17 *128*

5:8 *2, 5*
5:17–18 *191*
5:18 *234*
5:48 *37*
6:9 *74, 112*
6:33 *115*
11:9–15 *180*
12:22–32 *210*
13:1–23 *204*
16:13 *209*
16:16 *76, 112,
    178, 205, 238*
22:38–40 *121*
26:39 *107*
28:16–20 *179,
    226*
28:18 *77, 113,
    129, 180, 217*
28:19 *74, 78, 81,
    88, 98, 107, 186*

Mark

1:9–13 *224*
1:14 *224*
1:15 *57, 225*
1:24 *112*
1:41 *122*
3:28–29 *78*
4:1–20 *204*
8:29 *178*
8:34 *2*
9:1–4 *195*
9:7 *195*
10:17–18 *104*
10:19 *104*
10:26–27 *104*
12:28–30 *72*
12:28–32 *238*
12:29 *18*
12:30 *19*
13:22 *242*
14:61–62 *104*
16:15–16 *104,
    179, 226*

Luke

4:17–21 *224*
4:43 *224*
6:46 *217*
8:4–15 *204*
9:20 *178*
10:18 *26*
11:20 *53*
24:25–27 *44,
    177*
24:27 *237*
24:44 *234*
24:44–47 *237*
24:46–48 *226*
24:46–49 *179*
24:49 *226*

John

1:1 *7, 64, 66, 76,
    129, 135, 179,
    208*
1:1 *14, 205*
1:3 *179*
1:9 *8, 135, 137,
    195*
1:14 *7, 114,
    129, 179,
    207–08*
1:16 *79*
1:17 *180*
1:18 *179*
1:33–34 *26*
3:5–6 *26*
3:5–8 *78, 164,
    205*
3:6 *79*
3:8 *5–6, 113*
3:16 *50, 75,
    205, 240*
4:24 *106*
4:34 *224*
4:42 *179*
5:18 *88*
6:46 *180*

6:63 *78*
7:37–39 *179*
8:58 *102*
9:32 *114*
10:30 *179, 181*
10:34–36 *190,
    193*
10:35 *209*
12:27 *225*
12:28 *114, 128*
12:48 *129*
14:6 *161, 180*
14:9 *180*
14:10–11 *90*
14:16–17 *26*
14:16–17 *228*
14:17 *207*
14:17–18 *228*
14:17–18 *90*
14:19 *90*
14:25–26 *228*
14:26 *77, 191*
15:26 *77, 207*
15:26–27 *191,
    228*
16:7–10 *228*
16:7–11 *8*
16:8 *78*
16:8–11 *205*
16:12–13 *228*
16:12–15 *191*
16:13–15 *128*
16:14–15 *78*
16:15 *76, 88*
16:15 *88*
16:32 *207*
17 *107*
17:5 *88, 114*
17:5, 24 *52*
17:5, 25–26 *128*
17:8 *229*
17:17 *207*
17:20 *229*
17:21 *229*

17:26   *229*
19:11   *180, 217*
20:21   *77*
20:21–23   *227*
20:22   *26, 77, 179*
20:28   *76, 181*

Acts

1:8   *227*
1:11   *226*
2   *227*
2:30   *175*
4:12   *188*
4:19–20   *217*
4:24–25   *217*
5:3   *78*
5:3, 5   *210*
5:4   *78*
5:9   *210*
5:29   *217*
8   *227*
9:13, 23   *112*
10   *227*
14:17   *36, 137*
15   *243*
16:4–5   *243*
17:11   *12, 160, 216*
17:25   *57*
17:26   *57, 137*
17:26–27   *41*
17:27   *137*
17:28   *41, 57,*
   95, 101
17:29   *87*
19   *227*
20:29   *242*

Romans

1   *140*
1:1–4, 15–17   *131*
1:2   *131*
1:11   *131*
1:16   *131*

1:16–17   *4, 115,*
   137
1:17   *4, 137*
1:18   *114, 137,*
   138–40
1:18–20   *138*
1:18–2:16   *139*
1:19–20   *97*
1:20   *34, 87, 139*
1:21   *139*
1:21–22   *34*
1:21–25   *96*
1:22   *24, 140*
1:25   *39, 139–40*
1:28   *139*
1:32   *140*
2:2–6   *139*
2:8   *139*
2:12–14   *139*
2:14–15   *40*
2:14–16   *138*
2:15–16   *97, 140*
2:15–16   *40*
2:29   *131*
3:21–26   *115*
3:23   *138*
3:26   *28*
4:17   *129*
4:25   *5, 164, 226*
5:5   *119, 131*
5:8   *119*
5:12   *57, 96*
6:4–7, 22–23   *124*
6:16–21   *124*
8:1–2   *124*
8:2   *79*
8:2, 9, 11, 12–16,*
   23, 26–27   131
8:11, 18–23   *55*
9:7–8   *111*
9:17, 24–26   *131*
10:4   *215*
10:5–8   *215*

10:6–7   *9*
10:8–13   *131*
10:9–10   *5, 99,*
   215
10:12–13   *215*
10:14   *205*
10:14–15   *215*
10:16, 18–21   *217*
10:17   *215, 219*
10:18–20   *131*
11:11–12, 23–*
   24   131
11:25   *174*
12:1   *122*
12:3–11   *131*
13:1   *217*
13:1–7   *217*
15:7–12, 15–16,*
   20–21, 27   131
15:16, 19,*
   30   131
16:22   *229*
16:25–26   *174*
16:25–27   *130*

1 Corinthians

1:1   *229*
1:9   *79*
1:18   *205*
1:18–21   *230*
1:20–21   *141*
1:22   *141*
1:23   *141*
1:24   *113, 141,*
   230
1:27–28   *141*
2:1   *141*
2:1, 7   *174*
2:7–8, 16   *141*
2:10–11   *88, 230*
2:10–14   *141*
2:12   *230*
2:13   *230*

2:14–15 *230*
2:16 *230*
4:1 *174*
5:9 *234*
8:6 *81*
11:19 *81, 243*
12:3 *99*
12:8 *79*
13:9–10 *242*
13:12 *170*
13:12–13 *247*
13:13 *240*
14:3 *241*
14:29–33 *241*
15 *226*
15:3–5 *164*
15:20–28 *23*
15:23–25 *26*
15:25 *24*
15:51 *174*

2 Corinthians

1:1 *229*
3:1–6 *164*
3:5–6 *105, 219*
3:9 *180*
3:17 *88*
5:19 *181*
6:16 *217*
7:8 *234*
10:5 *165*
12:9 *219*
13:13 *78, 81, 88*
13:14 *74*

Galatians

2:11–14 *242*
3:16 *111, 191*
4:4–6 *205*
4:6 *8*
5:1 *123*

Ephesians

1:9 *174*

2:8 *121*
3:3 *174*
3:9 *79, 174*
4:30 *210*
5:3 *112*
5:6 *207*
6:18–19 *174*

Philippians

1:29 *6*
2:1–11 *11*
2:4–11 *181*
2:5–11 *81*
2:6 *76, 87*
2:7–8 *76*
2:10–11 *76, 182*
4:21 *112*

Colossians

1:15–20 *181*
1:19 *76, 87*
1:20 *23*
1:26 *174*
1:27 *174*
2:8 *207*
2:9 *87*
4:16 *234*

1 Thessalonians

2:13 *206–7*
5:24 *121*

2 Thessalonians

1:12 *121*
2:7 *174*

1 Timothy

1:11 *104*
1:16 *121*
2:1–4 *217*
2:5 *x, 92, 186*
3:1–7 *x*
3:16 *81, 174*
5:18 *191*

6:15 *104*
6:15–16 *101*

2 Timothy

2:2 *141*
2:3–5 *142*
2:6–13 *142*
2:8 *11, 15, 142*
2:14 *142*
2:15 *209, 216*
3:7 *142*
3:14–15 *142*
3:14–17 *190*
3:15 *192, 216, 219*
3:15–17 *105, 128, 191*
3:16 *22, 142, 193*
3:16–17 *220*
3:17 *192*
4:13 *234*

Titus

1:2 *207*
1:6–9 *x*
1:10 *207*
3:10 *243*

Hebrews

1:1–4 *173*
1:2 *181*
1:3 *87, 181*
1:3–4 *182*
1:5 *179*
1:5–6 *75*
4:4 *20*
4:9 *20*
4:12 *207, 209–10, 219*
4:14 *180*
7:1 *104*
7:1–10:39 *182*
7:3 *51, 64*

7:11–14 *180*
9:14 *64*
11:1–2 *43*
11:6 *32*
12:1–2 *2*
13:8 *51*

James

1:17 *8, 112, 195*
3:10 *206*

1 Peter

1:15–16 *112*
1:23 *207*
1:23–25 *203–4*
1:25 *204, 209*
2:9 *x*
2:13–17 *217*
3:15 *33*
3:16 *216*
5:3 *x*

2 Peter

1:19 *195*
1:19–21 *190, 194, 203–4, 228*
1:20 *195, 237*
1:20–21 *22, 128*
1:21 *195, 237*
3:8 *65*
3:14–16 *191*
3:15–16 *228*

3:16 *121*

1 John

1:1 *63–64*
1:2 *76*
1:5 *195*
1:9 *121*
2:1 *115*
2:2 *226*
2:19 *11*
3:7 *115*
3:16 *119*
3:20 *113*
4:7–21 *240*
4:8, 16 *27, 119*
4:19 *18, 120*

Jude

19 *11*

Revelation

1:7 *182*
1:8 *112–13*
1:8, 17 *64*
1:17 *240*
1:17–18 *182*
1:19 *23*
1:20 *174*
22:13 *182*
2:1, 7, 8–9,
    11 *234*
4–5 *26*

4:8 *113*
5:6 *78*
5:14 *77*
10:7 *174*
11:17 *113*
13 *217*
13–14 *78*
17:5, 7 *174*
19:13 *129*
19:16 *180*
20:4–6, 12–15 *26*
20:11–15 *50, 55*
20:13 *217*
21:2 *55*
21:3 *55*
21:5–8 *208*
21:5–6 *92*
21:6 *64*
21–22 *2*
22:7, 12–16,
    20 *92, 208*
22:13 *64, 240*
22:17 *184, 208, 246*
22:17 *92*
22:18–19 *191, 234*